Microsoft® PowerPoint 2000

Susan C. Daffron

A Division of Macmillan Computer Publishing, USA
201 W. 103rd Street
Indianapolis, Indiana 46290

SAMS

Visually *in* Full Color

How to Use Microsoft PowerPoint 2000

Copyright © 1999 by Sams Publishing

International Standard Book Number: 0-672-31529-7

Library of Congress Catalog Card Number: 98-88326

Printed in the United States of America

First Printing:

01 00 99   4   3   2   1

This book was produced digitally by Macmillan Computer Publishing and manufactured using computer-to-plate technology (a film-less process) by GAC, Indianapolis, Indiana.

Executive Editor
Jim Minatel

Acquisitions Editor
Jenny Watson

Development Editor
Susan Hobbs

Managing Editor
Thomas F. Hayes

Project Editor
Carol Bowers

Copy Editor
Pat Kinyon

Proofreader
Megan Wade

Indexer
Aamir Burki

Technical Editor
Don Roche

Book Designer
Nathan Clement

Cover Designers
Aren Howell
Nathan Clement

Production
Ayanna Lacey
Heather Hiatt Miller

Contents at a Glance

Contents

About the Author

Susan C. Daffron is the president of Logical Expressions, Inc., a company that offers writing, editing, programming, and layout services. She and her husband operate LEI from a log home located deep in the forests of the Idaho Panhandle and receive moral support from a number of weird and wonderful cats and dogs with whom they share living space.

Acknowledgements

The biggest, most important thanks go to my husband James H. Byrd for moral support above and beyond the call of duty. His contribution to this work includes, but is not limited to, plowing snow so the FedEx man could get here, starting the generator during power outages, assisting with macro and scripting chaos, taking over endless business and home-related duties, and just putting up with me during times of software and writing distress.

I'd also like to thank the folks who helped put this book together. A special thanks goes to my ever-patient Development Editor, Susan Hobbs, for answering my endless questions. Thanks also to my Acquisitions Editor, Jenny Watson, who picked up the pieces and helped get the project back on track.

A big thank you also goes out to the volunteers and staff of the Panhandle Animal Shelter in Sandpoint, Idaho. Their dedication to the welfare of the animals in their care is inspiring. (They inspired the STARS examples in the book, in fact.)

Last but not least, thanks to Leia, Tika, and Cami for reminding me that no book is more important than eating or taking a walk in the woods.

 Dedication

To James, for everything.

How To Use This Book

The Complete Visual Reference

Each chapter of this book is made up of a series of short, instructional tasks, designed to help you understand all the information that you need to get the most out of your computer hardware and software.

 Click: Click the left mouse button once.

 Double-click: Click the left mouse button twice in rapid succession.

 Right-click: Click the right mouse button once.

 Pointer Arrow: Highlights an item on the screen you need to point to or focus on in the step or task.

 Selection: Highlights the area onscreen discussed in the step or task.

 **Click and Type:** Click once where indicated and begin typing to enter your text or data.

Click & Drag
Release
How to Drag: Point to the starting place or object. Hold down the mouse button (right or left per instructions), move the mouse to the new location, and then release the button.

⏎Enter **Key icons:** Clearly indicate which key combinations to use.

Each task includes a series of easy-to-understand steps designed to guide you through the procedure.

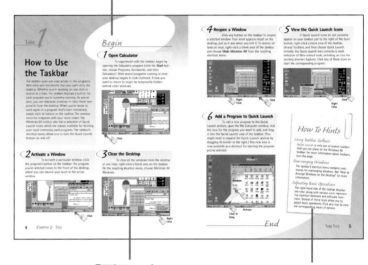

Each step is fully illustrated to show you how it looks onscreen.

Extra hints that tell you how to accomplish a goal are provided in most tasks.

Menus and items you click are shown in **bold**. Words in *italic* are defined in more detail in the glossary. Information you type is in a **special font**.

Continues

If you see this symbol, it means the task you're in continues on the next page.

Introduction

*M*ost people are introduced to presentation software under less than ideal circumstances. For one reason or another, you have to give a presentation. Now, in addition to the stress of having to give the presentation itself, you are faced with the task of learning a new piece of software as well. Not a pretty picture.

Your career could be riding on the professionalism of your presentation, so, of course, you want to create the best possible visuals you can. But what if you aren't a graphic artist and you can't afford to hire one? Not to worry. Microsoft PowerPoint 2000 takes away much of the trauma associated with creating a presentation. Because the program is designed to be used by non-artists, it's extremely intuitive and easy to use. If you've used presentation software before, you will be pleasantly surprised. PowerPoint 2000 is unlike the clunky and complex presentation software of a few years ago. Although PowerPoint 2000 is a feature-rich program, you don't have to be a rocket scientist to figure it out. In fact, with PowerPoint 2000, you might discover that creating your presentation is downright fun.

If you are in the midst of a presentation crisis, you need to learn all you can about PowerPoint as quickly as possible. This book is designed to help you do just that. Because this book uses a visual, task-based approach, you can find the information you need to get the job done quickly and easily.

If you've never used any of the Microsoft Office programs, you may want to go through the book sequentially. By reading the book from cover to cover, you'll find out everything you need to know about using PowerPoint 2000. However, if you already spent some time using PowerPoint, you may prefer to jump right into the middle of the book and read just the tasks in which you are interested. Although the knowledge you gain from learning tasks builds upon itself, each task can stand by itself.

This book shows you how to

- ✓ Create a Simple Presentation. You'll learn how to use all of PowerPoint's wizards, templates, and automated content features to create a professional presentation quickly.

- ✓ Work with Text. Words are at the heart of every presentation, and PowerPoint includes many word-processing features to help keep your text easy to read and error-free.

- ✓ Work with Graphics. The images you add to your presentation are what make it unique. Unlike other "artsy" programs, PowerPoint's drawing tools are easy to use, even for non-artists.

- ✓ Add Effects. Keeping your audience awake in a darkened room is the challenge of every presenter. With PowerPoint 2000, you can add sound effects, movies, and slide transitions to keep your presentation moving and your audience alert.

- ✓ Add Charts and Tables. Sometimes words and pictures aren't the best way to communicate your message. PowerPoint includes built-in features that let you add graphic charts, organizational charts, and tables to your presentation. And if the built-in tools aren't enough, you can add elements such as spreadsheet data from other programs.

- ✓ Put Your Presentation on the Web. In this information age, the Web is an important part of every business. PowerPoint 2000 includes many features that make it easy to put your presentation on the Internet or your company intranet.

The Project section is an added bonus for those people who like to take a peek "behind the scenes." This part of the book shows you how the examples used throughout the book were created. These four projects show typical business uses for PowerPoint. The first project is an onscreen presentation for a Board of Directors annual meeting. The second project is a slide show for a training class that explains company policies to new employees. The third project shows a PowerPoint-generated Web site, and the fourth project is a certificate. Each project shows different PowerPoint features and includes cross-references to the other parts of the book where you can find details on how you can add the same features to your presentation. Links to all of these sample presentations are also available on the Internet at www.logicalexpressions.com.

By the end of this book, you will no longer fear creating presentations. Giving the presentation may still be scary, but at least you can go up there and be confident that your visuals are the best they can be.

Task

1

How to Get Started with PowerPoint 2000

When you learn a new software program, it's always best to start at the beginning. You need to learn the basics before you get to play with the fun stuff. If you've never used a computer or Microsoft Windows before, just figuring out how to get a program to run can be a mystery.

No matter how you plan to use PowerPoint 2000, you need to be able to open, close, and save files. Saving all your hard work is especially important. Until you've experienced it, nothing can match the sinking feeling you get when you realize that the presentation you slaved over for the past two hours just went to the great data dumpster in the sky. If you learn nothing else from this book, learn this: *Save your work often.* Because they contain graphics, PowerPoint files can become large. An unwritten law of computing states that large files are more difficult for your computer to handle than small files. The corollary to this rule is that your computer is more likely to crash while you are working on that enormous incredibly important file than it is while you are working a small file you don't care about. So get into the habit of saving your files frequently.

How to Start and Exit PowerPoint

Starting and exiting PowerPoint 2000 is much like starting and exiting most Windows programs, so if you have used Windows software before, the steps in this task will be familiar. You can start most programs from either the Start menu or from an icon on your desktop. The Exit command on the File menu takes you out of PowerPoint 2000 and returns you to your Windows 95 or Windows 98 desktop.

Begin

1 Click the Start Menu

The Start menu is your gateway to your Windows software. You use the Start button at the bottom-left corner of your display to open the Start menu. If you don't see the Start button, hold your mouse over the bottom of the display until it appears. Click the **Start** button and a menu pops up.

Click

2 Open Programs

Note that certain menu entries have arrows on the right. These arrows indicate another menu level. Use your mouse to highlight **Programs**. Another menu appears with a list of the software on your system.

3 Click PowerPoint

Depending on how PowerPoint 2000 was set up, you may need to make a selection from another menu such as Microsoft Office to find the icon for the program. When you find the PowerPoint icon in the menus, click it to open PowerPoint 2000.

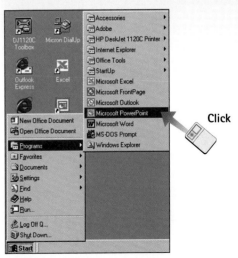

Click

4 Double-Click the PowerPoint Icon

Depending on how PowerPoint was installed, you may be able to run PowerPoint from an icon on your desktop. Double-click this icon to open PowerPoint.

Double Click

5 Exit PowerPoint

Now that you know how to get into PowerPoint, you need to know how to leave as well. From within PowerPoint, choose **File, Exit**. Make sure you save any files you were working on before you leave. Saving files is explained in Task 2, "How to Open, Close, Save, and Print Presentations," step 3.

Click

6 Use the Close Button

Use the **Close** button (**X**) to close either an individual file (which appears as a window within the main PowerPoint window) or to close PowerPoint itself. To close PowerPoint, click the **Close** button on the outermost window at the top right.

Click

End

How to Open, Close, Save, and Print Presentations

Every time you work on an existing presentation, you need to open a file. Every time you finish working, you need to close the file. And if you ever want to see your file again, you need to save the file. PowerPoint files are saved with a .PPT extension, making them easy to find in a directory or folder. By printing your file, you can share your work with others. All these basic file management functions are an integral part of using any piece of software.

Begin

1 Open a Blank Presentation

After you start PowerPoint, the first thing you see is the PowerPoint dialog box. To create a blank presentation, choose **Blank Presentation** and choose **OK**. The New Slide dialog box appears.

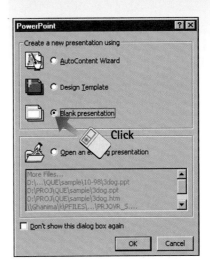

2 Choose an AutoLayout

In the New Slide dialog box, choose an AutoLayout for the first slide of your new presentation. The blue border indicates which layout you have selected. A text description appears to the right of the layouts. After you select a layout, choose **OK**.

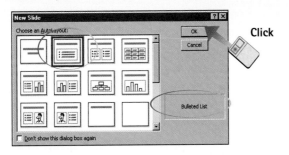

3 Save a Presentation

Choose **File**, **Save As**. The Save As dialog box appears. Choose a folder from the Save In drop-down box and type a filename in the **Filename box**. Click the **Save** button to save the file.

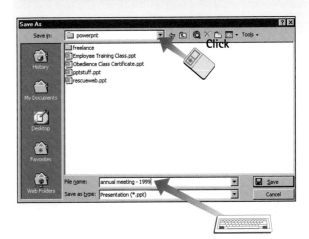

4 Open an Existing Presentation

Once you have created a file, you can go back and work on it anytime you want. To open a PowerPoint file, choose **File**, **Open**. Choose the folder location from the **Look in** drop-down box and click the filename to highlight a file. When you've selected the file, click **Open** to open it.

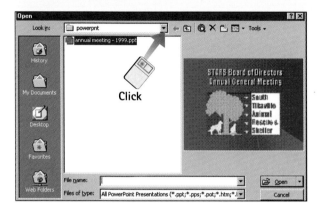

Click

5 Print a Presentation

For many of us, it's easier to proofread on paper. At some point, whether for proofreading purposes or for creating overhead transparencies, handouts, notes, or even just a printout of your outline, you'll want to print. To print any part of your presentation, choose **File**, **Print**. The Print dialog box opens.

Click

6 Choose Print Options

You set print options based on what you want to do. Choose a printer from the **Name** drop-down box. Next choose what to print: **Slides**, **Handouts**, **Notes Pages**, or **Outline View** by using the **Print What** drop-down box. If you are printing to a black and white printer, select the **Grayscale** option. Set other options such as how many copies and choose **OK** to start printing.

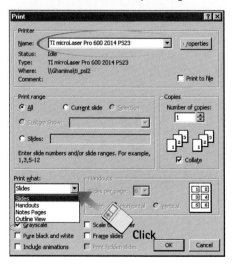

Click

7 Close a Presentation

The last file maintenance task you need to know is how to close a presentation. To close a file, choose **File**, **Close** or click the **Close** button (**X**) on the inner window (remember that clicking the outermost button closes PowerPoint itself).

Click

End

How to Use the PowerPoint Window

Anytime you start using a new software program, you are faced with a new work environment, and PowerPoint is no exception. At first you may find all the icons and information on the screen somewhat disconcerting. However, you'll soon see that the PowerPoint window is an efficient place to work because almost everything you need to do is just a mouse click away.

The main window includes toolbars and menus that run commands and the Status bar and Title bar, which provide information about your presentation.

Begin

1 Use Toolbars

Almost every PowerPoint menu command has an equivalent toolbar button. Many of the most frequently used commands are on the Standard toolbar, which is the toolbar right below the menus. You click a button to run the command.

Click

2 Show Toolbars

PowerPoint also has pop-up toolbars that appear depending on the object on which you're working. If you want to have a toolbar available all the time, choose **View**, **Toolbars**, and click the toolbars you want on the screen. Most toolbars can be docked to the top or side of the window or float so you can move them around the screen.

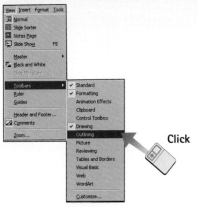

Click

3 Use Menus

If toolbar icons make you squint, you can also access commands the old fashioned way with the menus. Certain menus have cascading submenus with more choices that fly out of other menus. To access any command, all you have to do is highlight your choice with the mouse and click.

Click

4 Show All Menus

PowerPoint includes a new feature of dubious value. By default, the program only shows you the menu commands you have used recently. This feature can be annoying and confusing as you wonder why your menu selections keep disappearing. To keep your sanity and help you follow the instructions in this book, go to **Tools, Customize**. In the Options tab, deselect the option that says **Menus show recently used commands first**.

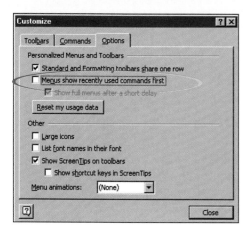

5 Use the Title Bar and Status Bar

The Title bar and the Status bar provide information about your presentation. The Title bar shows the program name (PowerPoint) and the presentation name. In Normal view, the Status bar shows the slide number and the Presentation Design that has been applied to your presentation. If automatic spell checking is turned on, you also see a small book icon, which you can double-click to work with the spell checker.

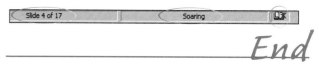

End

How-To Hints

Move a Toolbar

Docked toolbars have a move handle that looks like a vertical embossed line. If you click the move handle and drag the toolbar away from the edge of the screen, a title bar appears indicating that it's now a floating toolbar.

Try a Pop-up

Many commands are accessible from pop-up menus. Right-click an object and a list of commands appears in a small menu.

Turn off Automatic Spell Checking

If you find the automatic spell check distracting, you can turn it off. Choose **Tools, Options** and click the **Spelling and Style** tab. Remove the check mark next to **Check spelling as you type** and choose **OK**.

Don't Use the Print Button

Most toolbar buttons are identical to the menu commands, but the Print button is an exception. If you print by choosing the button, you don't see the Print dialog box so you can't set any options. If you just want to print one slide, print in grayscale, or print something other than slides such as notes pages, you may end up printing out a lot of stuff you don't want.

How to Use Screen Navigation Tools

Sometimes the limitations of your computer monitor make seeing what you've put on the screen a challenge. PowerPoint gives you tools to help make working within the PowerPoint window easier.

Guides help you line up objects on your slides. You can use scrollbars and keyboard commands to move through your presentation. With the Zoom controls, you can magnify your slides so you can see every nuance of every graphic.

Begin

1 Use Guides

Choose **View**, **Guides** to show the guides on your screen. You'll see one horizontal and one vertical guide that cross at the center of the slide.

Click

2 Use the Scrollbar

In Normal view, you scroll through slides by clicking and dragging the slider on the right of the slide pane. By clicking the up or down double arrows, you can move through the presentation one slide at a time.

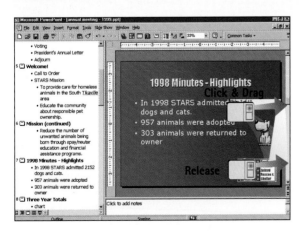

3 Use Zoom Controls

The Zoom controls let you get a better look at your slide so you place items more accurately. In Normal view, click in a pane, choose **View**, **Zoom**, and select a magnification level. Or choose a zoom level from the drop-down box on the Standard toolbar.

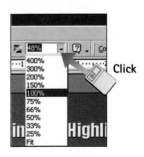

Click

4 Switch Views

You can look at your presentation in a number of ways: Normal view, Outline view, Slide view, Slide Sorter view, and Slide Show view. To switch views, click the icons at the bottom-left corner of the screen. Another view is available on the View menu. Choose **View**, **Notes Page** to get a full-page view of your notes.

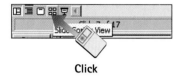

Click

5 Move Through a Presentation

In addition to the scrollbars mentioned in step 2, you can move through your presentation by using the keyboard. In Slide view or the slide pane of Normal view, the Page Up and Page Down keys move you through the presentation one slide at a time. You also can use **Ctrl+Home** to go to the beginning of the presentation and **Ctrl+End** to go to the end (make sure nothing else is selected).

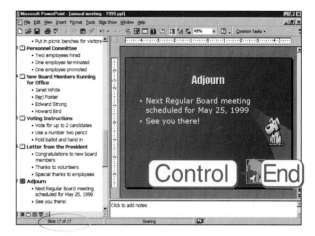

End

How-To Hints

Scroll Horizontally

If you have zoomed in to the point where you can't see the entire slide, the horizontal scrollbar appears. You can use this scrollbar to move across the width of the slide. On any scrollbar, you can click the arrows at either end to move incrementally.

Add and Remove Guides

To add guides, make sure the pointer is an arrow, hold down the **Ctrl** key, and drag a guide to a new location. A new guide appears. To delete a guide, click and drag it off the slide.

Show the Slide Miniature

If you magnify your slide to a high zoom level, it also can be helpful to see what the entire slide looks like while you make changes. Choose **View**, **Slide Miniature** and a small window appears that contains a tiny version of the current slide.

How to Use Views

PowerPoint uses the concept of views to give you the benefits of a number of programs in one. Instead of creating your presentation notes in a different program such as a word processor, you can switch to PowerPoint's Notes view and write your notes at the same time you create your visuals. Slide view gives you a larger look at your slides than Normal view. Slide Sorter view is great for getting the big picture on your presentation and rearranging slides to suit your needs. Outline view is much like the outline feature of most word processors. You can use it to organize your thoughts and easily promote and demote items as you work.

Begin

1 Use Normal View

Normal view is the default view you see when you open PowerPoint for the first time. You can see your outline, slides, and notes all at the same time. You can change the size of the panes by clicking a border and dragging it.

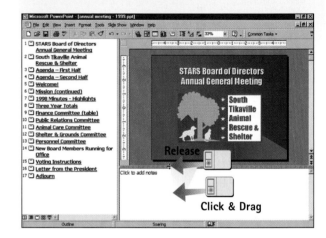

2 Use Slide View

Slide view lets you focus in on just the slides in your presentation. You can switch from one slide to another by clicking the slide icons on the left.

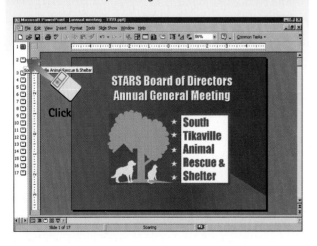

3 Use Outline View

Outline view has a large outline pane, so you can focus on the text of your slides. You can click the **Expand All** button on the Standard toolbar to see just the slide titles or click it again to see all of your slide text.

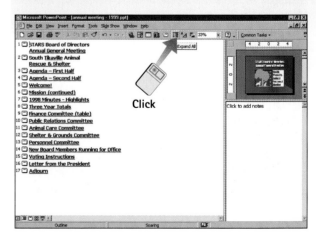

4 Slide Sorter View

Slide Sorter view shows you miniatures of your slides. You can rearrange your slides by clicking and dragging them to a new location. This view is also used for adding transitions and timings. Adding effects is discussed in Chapter 8, "How to Add Multimedia Effects."

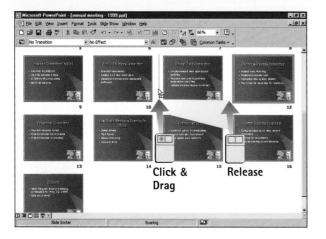

Click & Drag

Release

5 Notes Page View

To switch to Notes Page view, choose **View, Notes Page**. You see a slide and a space below it where you can add speaker notes (click in the box and begin typing). These notes can be used for reference when you give a presentation or as handouts for the audience. You can also add notes in the bottom pane of Normal view. Any notes you add there appear in Notes Page view as well.

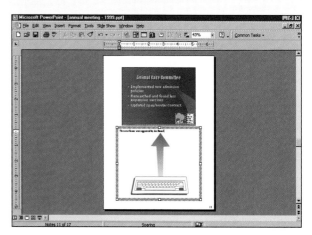

6 Slide Show View

You use Slide Show view to run your presentation. Press the **F5** key to run your presentation from the beginning. Use the **Page Down** key to advance to the next slide or right-click and choose **Next** from the pop-up menu. Press **Esc** to return to the view you were using.

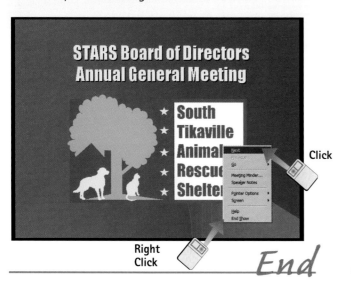

Click

Right Click

End

How-To Hints

Show the Outline Toolbar

When you work in Outline view, it helps to show the Outline toolbar. Choose **View**, **Toolbars** and select **Outlining** from the list. Click the **Promote** or **Demote** buttons to move the text up or down one indention level.

Delete Slides in Slide Sorter View

To delete a slide, click it to select it and press the **Delete** key. You can select more than one slide by holding down the **Ctrl** key and clicking. Then you can either move or delete the slides all at once.

Go to a Specific Slide in a Show

In Slide Show view, you can go to a particular slide in the show by right clicking and choosing **Go, By Title**. Click the Slide title from the list.

How to Work with Placeholders

Placeholders are an integral part of PowerPoint. The placeholder reserves a space for objects such as text, charts, tables, and graphics. On a new slide, a title placeholder contains sample headline text. When you click the text, the cursor changes into an I-beam cursor, so you can enter your own text, which replaces the sample text. A placeholder is also an object on the slide that can be manipulated. You can move placeholders around the slide and change how they look.

Begin

1 Add Text

To add text to a placeholder, click anywhere in the sample text in the placeholder box. When you click, the box changes from dotted lines to slashes to show that the placeholder is selected and the cursor changes to an I-beam. Enter your text.

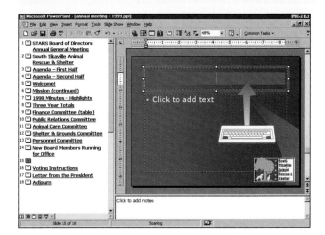

2 Select and Delete Text

To select text, click and drag the mouse over the text. To delete selected text, press the **Delete** key on the keyboard. To delete all the text in a placeholder, press **Esc** and press the **Delete** key.

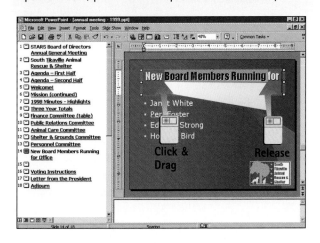

3 Select Placeholder

Click anywhere within the placeholder. The dotted line border changes to slashes. Put your mouse over one of the borders and the cursor changes to a four-headed arrow, and then click.

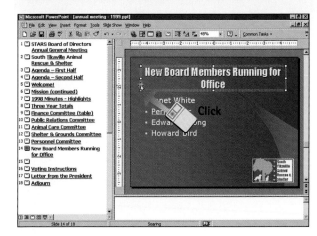

4 Move Placeholder

When the cursor is a four-headed arrow, you can click and drag the placeholder to move it around the slide.

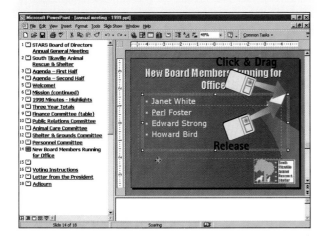

5 Add Placeholder Objects

On certain slide layouts, you see an icon to add an object such as clip art or a chart. Double-click the icon to add the object.

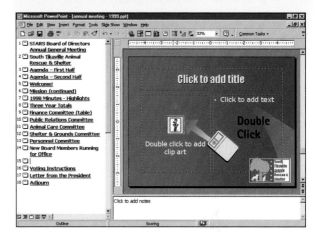

6 Restore Placeholders

If you get overzealous and accidentally delete a placeholder, you can bring it back by choosing **Edit**, **Undo** or pressing the **Undo** button on the toolbar. If you really make a mess, you can restore all the placeholders on a slide by choosing **Format**, **Slide Layout** and clicking **Reapply**.

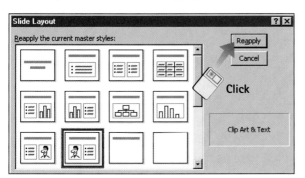

End

How-To Hints

Select Text

You can use a number of shortcuts to select text in a placeholder. To select one word, double-click it. To select an entire paragraph, triple-click it.

Resize Placeholder

You can change the size of the placeholder by selecting it and clicking and dragging one of the eight selection handles. To scale proportionally, click and drag a corner handle. To change the height, click and drag a top or bottom handle. To change the width, click and drag a side handle.

Size Placeholder to Fit Text

If your placeholder is way too large for your text, you can size it automatically. Select the placeholder and choose **Format**, **Placeholder**. Click the **Text Box** tab and click **Resize AutoShape to fit text**.

How to Get Help in PowerPoint

Everybody needs a little help sometimes, and PowerPoint has many ways you can get the help you need to get your job done. For those who like some entertainment with their assistance, Rocky the animated help hound can come to your rescue when you need him; or you change to a different Presentation Assistant character. If cartoon activity annoys you, the standard Windows help screens are also available. And if you can't remember what all the tiny buttons on your screen are supposed to do, ScreenTips are available to take the mystery out of your display.

Begin

1 Use ScreenTips

ScreenTips are little yellow explanatory text snippets that appear when you hold your mouse over a button. If the text doesn't appear, choose **Tools**, **Customize**. In the **Options** tab, make sure a check mark appears next to **Show ScreenTips on toolbars**.

2 Use the Presentation Assistant

The Presentation Assistant is an animated character that sits on your screen waiting for questions. Click the Assistant, type a question in the box that appears, and click **Search**. Click **Options** to turn the Assistant off, change the Assistant character, or modify how he works. Choose **Help**, **Show the Office Assistant** to turn the Assistant on.

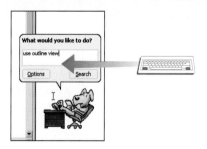

3 Browse Using Contents

For non-animated help, turn off the Assistant as described in step 2. Then choose **Help**, **Microsoft PowerPoint Help**. Click the **Contents** tab to see help topics. Click the plus sign (**+**) next to a topic to see subtopics. Click a topic to view help.

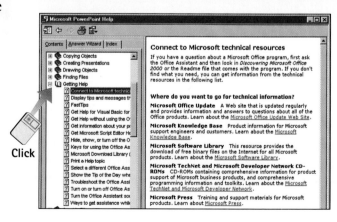

4 Search Using Index

To find a specific term, click the **Index** tab. Type a keyword or choose one from the keyword list and click **Search**. Click a topic from the topic list and the text appears in the right window.

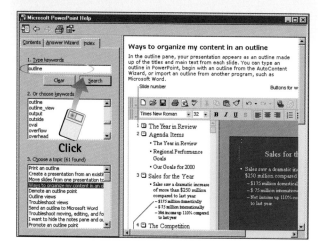

Click

5 Search for Help on the Web

Many help screens have links to search the Web for additional topics. While you are working within PowerPoint, you also can search for help directly from the Microsoft Office Web site by choosing **Help**, **Office on the Web**.

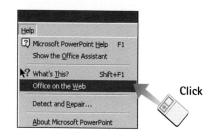

Click

6 Print Help Topics

From within the PowerPoint Help dialog box, you can print a help topic by clicking the print icon on the Help toolbar.

Click

7 Call Microsoft Tech Support

To find the phone numbers for Microsoft Tech Support, choose **Help**, **About Microsoft PowerPoint** and click the **Tech Support** button. A list of phone numbers appears.

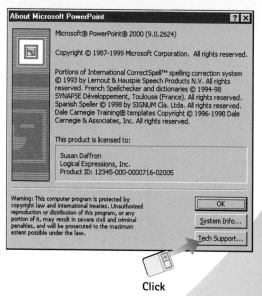

Click

End

Task

2

How to Create a PowerPoint Presentation

Creating a simple presentation is easy in PowerPoint. If you don't have much time, you may want to take advantage of some of the built-in automatic features. The process of creating a presentation can be as automated as you want it to be. If your presentation was due yesterday, you can use the AutoContent Wizard or a Presentation template to create the bulk of the presentation content, so all you have to do is fill in the blanks.

If there isn't an AutoContent Wizard that meets your needs, you still can let PowerPoint take a lot of the work out of presentation design. You can create a presentation based on one of the many Design templates. These templates are especially good for those of us who don't consider ourselves artists. If you don't feel confident about your design skills, starting from a template ensures that you won't create a presentation that will offend anyone's aesthetic sensibilities.

For those who like total control, you can start with a completely blank presentation and build it from the top down. Although this approach can be more time-consuming than the automated techniques, you'll end up with a presentation that is uniquely your own.

Once you get rolling on your presentation, you'll want to add, delete, and rearrange your slides, so the presentation is just the way you want it. PowerPoint also makes it easy to reformat a slide or your entire presentation, in case you change your mind.

How to Use the AutoContent Wizard

If you need a presentation right *now*, you'll love the AutoContent Wizard. This little miracle of modern programming can create an entire presentation for you in mere minutes. All you have to do is follow the steps and answer a few questions. After you finish the Wizard you fill in the sample text with your own content and voilà, your presentation is ready to go. You can get to the AutoContent Wizard in two ways: through the PowerPoint dialog box that appears when you open the program or from within PowerPoint when you create a new presentation.

Begin

1 Use the PowerPoint Dialog Box

When you open PowerPoint, the PowerPoint dialog box appears. To run the AutoContent Wizard, click **AutoContent Wizard** and choose **OK**.

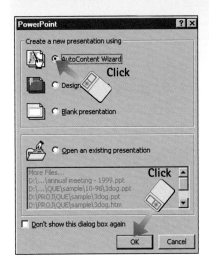

2 Create a New Presentation

If you're already in PowerPoint, you can create a new presentation by using the AutoContent Wizard. Choose **File, New**. In the **General** tab, click **AutoContent Wizard** and choose **OK**.

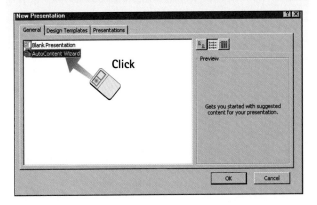

3 Start the Wizard

After you click **OK**, the Wizard runs. You click the **Next** button to move through the Wizard. First, the Wizard asks you to choose a Presentation type. Use the buttons to view presentations by category or select from **All** available presentation types. Click **Next** to go to the next screen or **Back** to go to a previous screen.

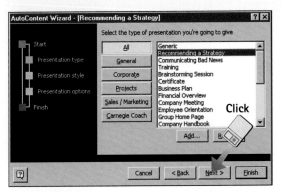

4 Select Options

In the next screens you need to choose the type of presentation (onscreen presentation, Web presentation, slides, or overheads) and add a presentation title and optional items to include on each slide. Click **Finish** to conclude the Wizard.

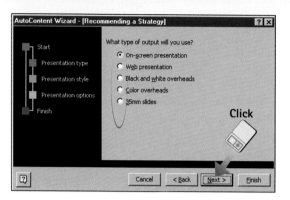

5 Fill in Your Own Content

The presentation appears with text in the placeholders that gives you helpful hints for possible content. Go through the presentation and replace the placeholder text with your own content. Select text in either the outline pane or the slide pane and type in your new text.

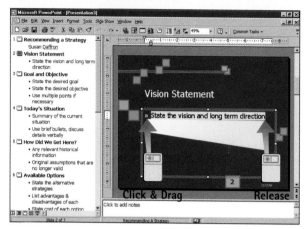

End

How-To Hints

Change the Look

Unless you've selected a certain presentation type before, the design you see at the end of the AutoContent Wizard may come as a surprise. If the design used in the presentation type isn't to your liking, you can change it without affecting the content. Applying a different design template is explained in Task 2, "How to Create a Presentation from a Template," step 4.

Add a Template

You can add templates to the AutoContent Wizard. Choose **File**, **New** and double-click **AutoContent Wizard**. Click **Next**, choose a category, and click **Add**. Find your template and click **OK**.

Don't Show It

If you don't want to see the PowerPoint dialog box when you start the program, click **Don't show this dialog box again**. The next time you open it, the program goes directly into a blank presentation. To restore the PowerPoint dialog box, choose **Tools**, **Options**. In the **View** tab, click **Startup dialog**.

How to Create a Presentation from a Template

If you don't want to create a presentation from scratch, templates can automate the process. PowerPoint has two different types of templates: Design and Presentation templates. With a Design template, you create your own content, but PowerPoint creates the design for you.

If you want more guidance on the content of the presentation, you can use a Presentation template. PowerPoint creates a presentation filled with sample content much like the ones generated by the AutoContent Wizard. Unlike the Wizard, however, the options aren't set automatically. You have to make these changes yourself.

Begin

1 Create a New Presentation

When you open PowerPoint, the PowerPoint dialog box appears. Choose **Design Template** and click **OK**. If you're already in PowerPoint, choose **File**, **New**. The New Presentation dialog box appears. Click the **Design Templates** tab and choose a template from the list. A preview appears to help you select a design. Select a presentation design and click **OK**.

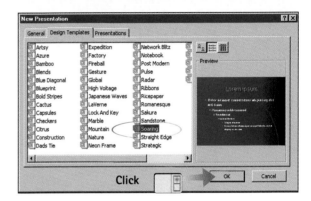

2 Choose a Presentation Type

In the New Presentation dialog box, click the **Presentations** tab. You see a list of presentation types from which you can choose. A preview appears on the right. Choose a presentation and click **OK**.

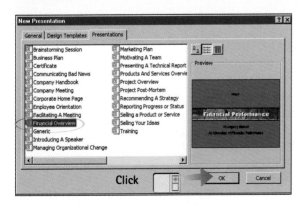

3 Choose an AutoLayout

Because a Design template doesn't include content, after you choose a Design template, you must select an AutoLayout for your first slide. Select a layout and click **OK**.

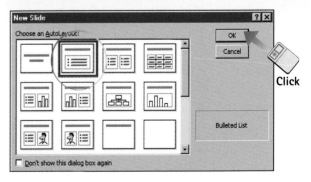

4 Apply a Design Template

You may decide that the Design template you chose wasn't such an attractive idea after all or discover that the Presentation type you selected uses a truly hideous design. To change the design choose **Format**, **Apply Design Template**. Select a new design from the list and click **Apply**.

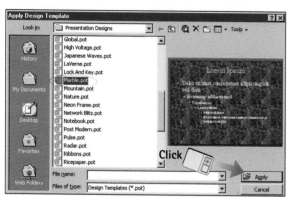

5 Enter Text

After you have used a template to start your presentation, you need to add your own content. Entering text in the Outline pane or Outline view is a quick way to input a lot of text. When you use the Outline feature, if your cursor is on a slide title, pressing **Enter** creates a new slide, **Tab** indents the text one level, and **Shift+Tab** outdents one level.

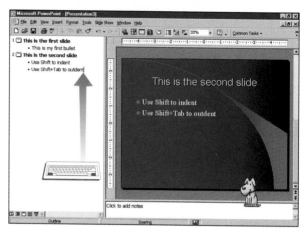

End

How-To Hints

Select a Slide

In the Outline pane or Outline view, you can select the contents of an entire slide by clicking the slide icon. If you start typing, the new text replaces the contents of the slide, starting with the title placeholder. To add lower-level text, you press **Enter** to create a new line, but then you must press **Tab** to demote the text one level.

Get More Templates

In the list of templates, you may see a message instead of a preview for some templates. Templates that aren't loaded on your computer show a message that says **Click OK to install additional templates and create a new file**. To install the template, put the CD-ROM in the drive and click **OK**.

If the templates included in PowerPoint 2000 get tiresome, you can find more on Microsoft's Web site. Point your browser to **http://officeupdate.microsoft.com/ downloadCatalog/dldPowerPoint.htm**.

How to Create a Presentation from Scratch

If you want your presentation to boldly go where no presentation has gone before, you may want to start with a blank slide and build your own masterpiece. However, you should realize that when they say blank presentation, they really mean blank. The single slide that appears has no colors or graphics whatsoever. If you have a problem with writer's block (otherwise known as blank page syndrome), you may want to start with a template instead.

Begin

1 Create a New Presentation

If you are opening PowerPoint, the PowerPoint dialog box appears. Choose **Blank Presentation** and click **OK**. If you're already in PowerPoint, choose **File**, **New**. The New Presentation dialog box appears. In the **General** tab, click **Blank Presentation** and choose **OK**.

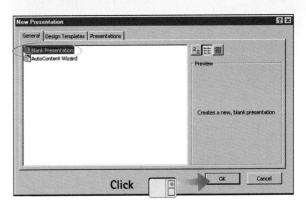

2 Choose an AutoLayout

Next, you need to choose a layout for your first slide. The left pane shows miniatures of the various available slide layouts and a text description appears on the right. Choose a layout and click **OK**.

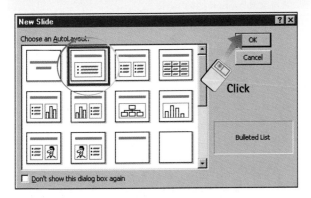

3 Add Background Color

All that bright white is boring, so you should choose a background color for your slide. Choose **Format**, **Background** and click the drop-down arrow to choose a new color. Click a color and click **OK**. Click **Apply** to make the changes to one slide or **Apply to All** to change all of the slides in the presentation.

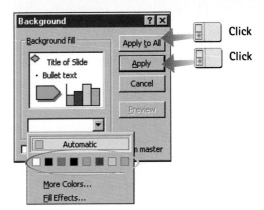

4 Select a Color Scheme

Each template (even the blank presentation) comes with a set of color schemes. Each scheme is composed of eight coordinated colors that are used consistently throughout the presentation. To select a color scheme, choose **Format**, **Slide Color Scheme**, and select a color scheme. Click **Preview** to see what the colors look like on the slide. After you choose a scheme, click **Apply** to apply the colors to the current slide or **Apply to All** to apply the colors to all the slides in the presentation.

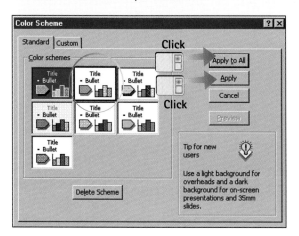

5 Type Text

Once you have the basic colors set up, you need to start adding content. You can type text directly into the text placeholders. Just click the sample placeholder text and start typing. As you type, you also see your text being added in the Outline pane.

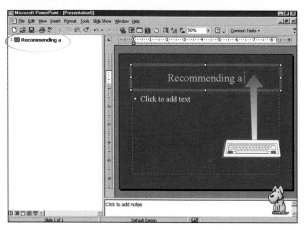

End

How-To Hints

Apply a Custom Color Scheme

To avoid shockingly ugly color clashes, you may want to create a custom color scheme. Choose **Format**, **Slide Color Scheme** and click the **Custom** tab in the dialog box. Under **Scheme Colors** select an item and click **Change Color**. Choose a color and click **OK**. Repeat the process for any other items you want to change. If you come up with a scheme you like, click **Add as Standard Scheme** so you can use it again on another presentations.

Use Other Colors

You aren't restricted to using just the colors in the color scheme. Other colors appear in the color drop-down boxes as well. The colors in the color scheme are the eight colors in the top row of the drop-down box. When you choose **More Colors** and select colors from the Color dialog box, these colors then appear below the row of color scheme colors. The most recently selected colors appear at the left.

How to Add and Delete Slides

No matter how you create your presentation, at some point you'll need to add or delete slides. You can add slides in a number of ways. You can use a menu command or toolbar button to add a new slide or add slides in the Outline pane or Outline view.

If you are going to receive content from someone else, you may need to add a number of slides from another presentation all at once. And as information is never static, at some point you will undoubtedly need to delete slides as well.

Begin

1 Insert a New Slide

With your cursor in the Slide pane of Normal view, click the **New Slide** button to insert a slide after the one on which you're working. Alternatively, choose **Insert**, **New Slide** or press **Ctrl+M**.

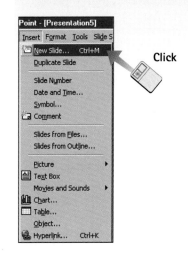

2 Choose Layout

In the New Slide dialog box, choose an AutoLayout for your new slide. Small representations of the layout appear on the left and a text description appears on the right. Choose a layout and click **OK**.

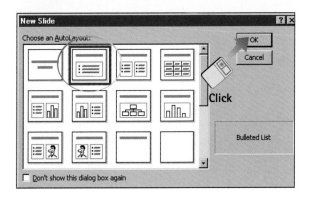

3 Type in the Outline Pane

Another way to add bulleted slides is to type them into the Outline pane or in Outline view. To add a slide, place your cursor in the beginning of the title line of the slide *below* the location of the new slide. Press **Enter**. A new blank slide appears.

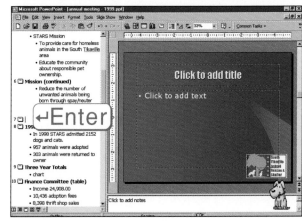

4 Add Many Slides at Once

If you work on a lot of presentations, you may want to insert slides from another PowerPoint presentation rather than recreating them. Slides are inserted after the currently selected slide. Click the desired slide and choose **Insert**, **Slides from Files**.

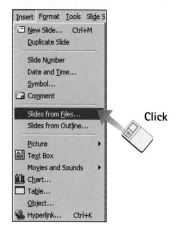

Click

5 Insert the Slides

Click **Browse** to find the file on your hard disk and click **Display** to show miniature slides. Click to select a slide or **Ctrl+click** to select multiple slides. Choose **Insert** to insert the selected slides. Choose **Insert All** if you want to insert all the slides in the presentation. Click **Close** when you are finished. Although inserted slides retain their layout, they take on the design of your presentation.

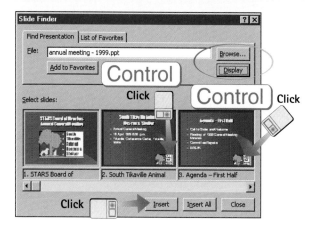

6 Delete Slides

To delete a slide in the Slide pane, make sure your cursor is on the slide you want to delete and choose **Edit**, **Delete Slide**. In the Outline pane, click the slide icon or select the slide text and press the **Delete** key.

Click

End

How-To Hints

Delete Multiple Slides

In Slide Sorter view, hold down **Ctrl** and click to select the slides you want to delete. Press the **Delete** key or choose **Edit**, **Delete Slide**.

Restoring Deleted Slides

If you accidentally delete a slide, choose **Edit**, **Undo** or click the **Undo** button on the Standard toolbar to bring it back.

Insert Slides Versus Copy and Paste

When you use **Insert, Slides from Files**, the slides are inserted with their layout. If you only want to insert the text from a slide into an existing layout, you should use copy and paste commands instead. These steps are described in Task 5, "How to Work with Slides," step 5.

How to Work with Slides

In PowerPoint 2000, you can do a lot more with your slides than just add and delete them. You can copy and paste your slides from one place to another within a presentation or copy and paste the content of one presentation into another. You also can duplicate a slide so you don't have to retype and reformat similar slides. As your presentation evolves, you'll also come to appreciate PowerPoint's Slide Sorter view, which makes it easy to reorganize your slides so that your presentation flows smoothly.

Begin

1 Copy Slides

The easiest way to copy a slide is in the Outline pane. Click the slide icon to select the slide and choose **Edit, Copy.**

Click

2 Paste Slides

In the Outline pane, place your cursor where you want the new slide and choose **Edit, Paste.** The slide is pasted *after* the slide you selected.

Click

3 Duplicate Slides

To create a duplicate slide, display the slide you want to duplicate. Choose **Insert, Duplicate Slide.** The new slide is placed after the original slide.

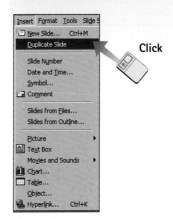

Click

4 Reorder Slides

After you've done a lot of copying, pasting, and duplicating, you should re-examine the organization of the presentation. To rearrange your slides, switch to Slide Sorter view. Click the slide you want to move, drag it to a new location in your presentation, and release the mouse button.

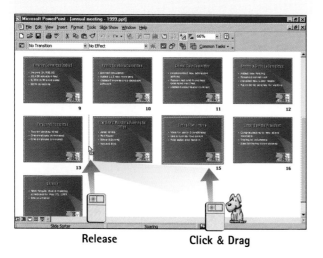

Release   Click & Drag

5 Copy Text Between Presentations

To copy slide text between presentations, open the two presentations. Choose **Window**, **Arrange All**, so you can see both presentations at once. In the Outline pane of the first presentation, click the slide icon and choose **Edit**, **Copy** (or press **Ctrl+C**). Click where you want the slide text in the Outline pane of the second presentation and choose **Edit**, **Paste** (or **Ctrl+V**).

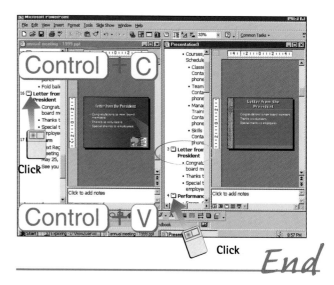

Click

End

How-To Hints

Moving Slides in Outline View

It's easy to move slides when you are in the Outline pane or Outline view. Click the slide icon to select the slide. Drag it up or down to a new location in the outline and release the mouse button.

Selecting Contiguous Slides

In Slide Sorter view, if you want to select a number of slides in a row, say slide numbers 2 though 7, hold down the **Shift** key and click slide number 2 and then click slide number 7. All six slides are selected and you can then cut, copy, move, or delete them.

How to Quickly Change a Slide Layout

One of the things that makes PowerPoint fun to use is that you can completely change the look of a presentation very quickly. If you're one of those people who thinks instant gratification is just a little too slow, you'll appreciate PowerPoint's ability to metamorphosize a presentation from staid and conservative to funky and weird in seconds.

The steps you follow to change a presentation are similar to those you use when you create a presentation in the first place. You can change the layout, background, color scheme, or design template with just a few mouse clicks.

Begin

1 Change the Layout

You can dramatically change the appearance of an individual slide by changing its layout. Choose **Format**, **Slide Layout** and select a new layout. Click **Apply**. If you have modified the slide layout and want to restore it to its original configuration, do not choose a new layout and click **Reapply**.

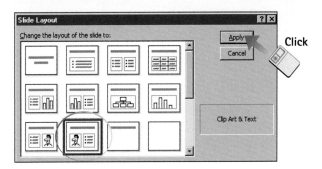

Click

2 Change the Background Color

Color generates an emotional response, so changing the background color of your presentation can have a big impact on how it appears. To change the background, choose **Format**, **Background**. Click the drop-down box and click a color. Or click **More Colors** and choose a color from the Colors dialog box and click **OK**.

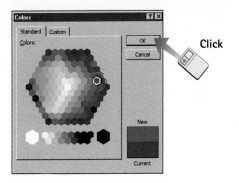

Click

3 Change the Color Scheme

When you change the presentation color scheme, any object that used the old color is automatically changed to the new color. (It's almost like a Find and Replace command for color.) To change the scheme, choose **Format**, **Slide Color Scheme**. Click a new scheme.

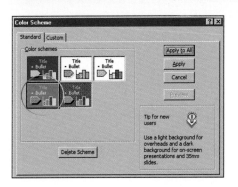

4 Apply or Apply to All

When you make changes to the slide background or color scheme, you can apply your changes to just the current slide or to all the slides in the presentation. To change the current slide, click **Apply**. To change all the slides, click **Apply to All**.

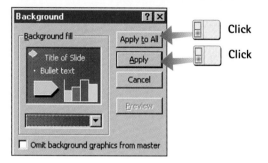

Click

Click

5 Change the Design Template

By changing the presentation's Design template, you can drastically alter the look and feel of your presentation (which can come in handy if you want to present the same presentation to different audiences). To apply a new template, choose **Format**, **Apply Design Template**. Choose a new template and click **Apply**.

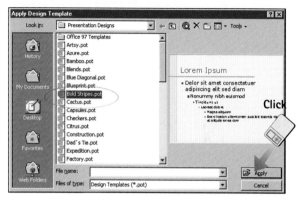

Click

End

How-To Hints

Color Scheme Versus Background

By now, you've probably noticed that you can change the background color in both the Color Scheme dialog box and the Background dialog box. Change the background in the Color Scheme dialog box if you want to use a solid color. For fill effects, use the Background dialog box. Note that the fill you choose in the Background dialog box overrides the background you select in the Color Scheme dialog box. Background fill effects are discussed in Chapter 6, "How to Work with Masters," Task 3, "How to Add a Slide Background," in the context of Master Slides.

Layout Caveats

When you change a slide layout, don't be surprised if the outcome requires some reworking. Not all layouts can be changed seamlessly from one to another. For example, if you change a bulleted list to 2-column text, it will look fine. However, if you change a bulleted list to an organization chart, you end up with the text sitting on top of the organization chart. In these cases, you need to size or scale the placeholders or remove the text to fix the problem.

How to Create Notes

Knowing what you're going to say is an important part of giving a presentation. As you create your presentation, you can simultaneously create the notes you will use as reference when you give the presentation. When you work on a presentation, it's easy to get so involved in creating your visuals that you forget that the most important part of your presentation is *you*. Unless you have a fantastic memory, it's always a good idea to prepare some notes ahead of time. Notes don't have to be just for you, however; you can print out your notes pages and give them to your audience, so they leave the room with something tangible to help them remember what they learned at your presentation.

Begin

1 Use Notes Page View

The easiest way to add notes is to type them into the Notes pane in Normal view. However, if you want to add a lot of text, switch to Notes Page view by choosing **View**, **Notes Page**. In this view, you see the slide and a box for your notes below.

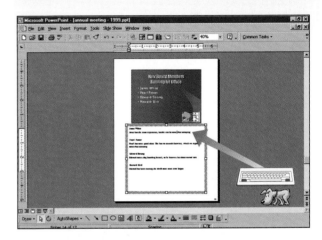

2 Change the Layout

Your notes should be easy to read and comprehend, so change the layout to suit your needs. Choose **Format**, **Notes Layout** and select the items you want to include in your notes.

Click

3 Change the Color Scheme

Just as you can with your slides, you can set a color scheme for your notes pages. If you plan to print to a black and white printer, you may want to select a monochrome scheme. In Notes view, choose **Format**, **Notes Color Scheme**. Choose a new scheme and click **Apply** or **Apply to All**.

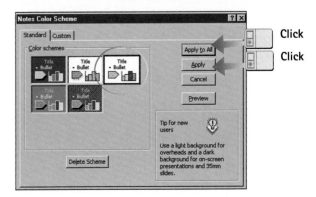

Click

Click

4 Change the Background

You can change the notes background to a different color, which can be useful in certain instances (such as in a Web presentation for example). If you print your notes, however, consider the cost of your printer's color ink cartridges before you change to any color other than white. In Notes view, choose **Format, Notes Background**, choose a color, and click **Apply** or **Apply to All**.

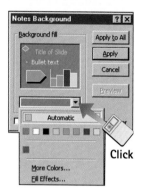

Click

5 Preview in Black and White

If you plan to print your notes to a standard black and white laser printer, it's helpful to see what they will look like when they aren't in living color. Choose **View, Black and White** to see a monochrome version of your notes.

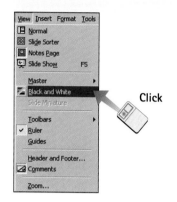

Click

6 Print the Notes

When you print your notes pages, it's important that you *not* use the **Print** button on the toolbar, because that method doesn't let you change any print options. Choose **File, Print**. Change the **Print what** drop-down box to **Notes Pages**. If you are printing to a monochrome printer, be sure to click **Grayscale** or **Pure Black and White**. After you set options, click **OK**.

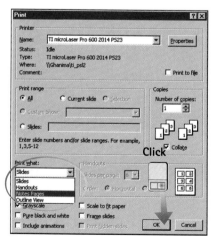

Click

How-To Hints

Zoom In

When you use Notes view, it's much easier to see what you are typing if you zoom in on the text box. Depending on the size and resolution of your monitor, a zoom level of 100% often works well. On the Standard toolbar, click the drop-down arrow next to the Zoom button, highlight the desired zoom level, and click.

Use Notes or Handouts?

Although you can print out your notes pages and use them as audience handouts, PowerPoint also has a handout feature you can use to print your slides as handouts. These handouts show only slides, however; none of your notes are included. Handouts are discussed in Chapter 6, "How to Work with Masters" Task 7, "How to Create a Handout."

End

Task

How to Work with Text

Words are at the heart of your presentation, and in PowerPoint 2000, you can enter and manipulate your words in many ways. The words you use and the way you format them has a big effect on how your presentation is perceived. When you choose a flowery italic typeface, for example, it presents a much different visual impression than a Spartan sans-serif font with no ornamentation.

When you work with type, always keep your audience in mind. You want your presentation to be as clear and readable as possible. The easier and faster your presentation can be read, the happier your audience will be. People struggling to decipher the text on your slides are not going to be paying attention to what you are saying.

PowerPoint gives you many tools you can use to make your presentation text look polished and professional. You can easily edit your text, change fonts and font sizes, adjust spacing, and set tabs and indents. PowerPoint also has options you can set to automatically format your text to fit the slide, correct your spelling errors, or add effects such as bullets and numbering. You can make your words appear twisted and contorted or plain and straightforward. It all depends on what you want to say and how you want to say it. ●

How to Enter and Edit Text

Adding text is a key part of creating your presentation. PowerPoint lets you enter text in a number of ways, so you can work with your words in whatever way feels the most comfortable. If you are one of those people who prefers to type and format your text at the same time, you may want to type your text directly into the slide in Slide view or the Slide pane of Normal view. If you prefer to just type and type and not worry about the formatting until later, you may want to enter your text in the Outline pane or Outline view instead.

Begin

1 Enter Text in Slide View

To edit text in Slide view or the Slide pane of Normal view, click in the sample text in a text placeholder. The arrow cursor changes to an I-beam to indicate that you can start typing.

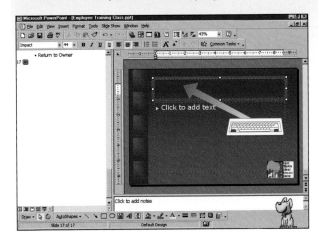

2 Edit Text in Slide View

To edit text, click and drag over the text you want to change to highlight it. When you type over the text, your new text replaces the existing text. Another way to highlight text is to double-click to highlight one word or triple-click to highlight an entire sentence.

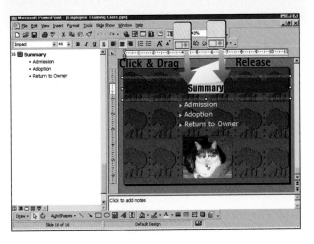

3 Enter Text in Outline View

In Outline view or the Outline pane of Normal view, press the **Enter** key to add a new slide title if your cursor is on a slide title. Press **Tab** to demote an item (move it down one indention level), such as a slide title to a bullet point. Press **Shift+Tab** to promote an item (move it up a level), such as a bullet point to a slide title.

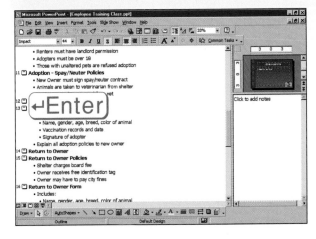

4 Reorganize Text in Outline View

It's easy to reorganize the text in your outline. Click the slide icon to the left of a slide heading. The slide text is highlighted. Click and drag the slide icon and text to a new location in your presentation.

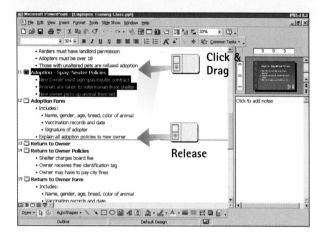

Click & Drag

Release

5 Cut or Copy Text

Click and drag your mouse over text to highlight it. Choose **Edit, Cut** to remove the text or **Edit, Copy** to make a copy of the text. Your text is placed on the *Clipboard*. The Clipboard is the memory area used by PowerPoint and other Windows programs to store a copy of the last item cut or copied into it.

Click

6 Paste text

Click your mouse at the location where you want your text to be placed. Choose **Edit, Paste**. The text you cut or copied to the Clipboard is placed in the new location.

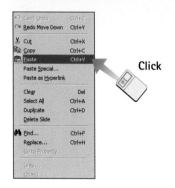

Click

End

How-To Hints

Use the Office Clipboard

When you cut or copy an item in most Windows programs, it stays on the Clipboard until you cut or copy something else, which replaces it. PowerPoint has a special clipboard called the Office Clipboard, where you can store up to 12 items. To show the Clipboard toolbar, choose **View**, **Toolbars**, and click **Clipboard**. The toolbar appears and you can see the 12 most recent items you have cut or copied. Select the one you want and click the **Paste** button.

AutoFit Text

If it seems like your slide text is changing size, that's because it is. PowerPoint, by default, tries to fit text into placeholders by decreasing the line spacing and the font size. You can turn it off by choosing **Tools**, **Options** and click the **Edit** tab. Remove the check mark next to **Auto-fit text to text placeholder**.

How to Add Text Boxes

Most of the text you place on your slides is inserted into placeholders. This text is included in your presentation outline and is reviewed when you run a spell check. However, you also can add what is essentially graphic text. A text box is a graphic that contains text. From a PowerPoint perspective, it's treated as a graphic object, so it is not included in your outline or in a spell check. Although text boxes aren't used as often as the text you add into placeholders, they are useful if you need to add labels or captions to your slides.

Begin

1 Use the Text Box Tool

To create a text box, click the **Text Box** tool on the Drawing toolbar. You can create two types of text boxes: wrapping or non-wrapping.

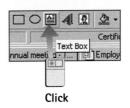

Click

2 Type the Text (no wrapping)

To create a non-wrapping box, click and type. The text appears in a single line.

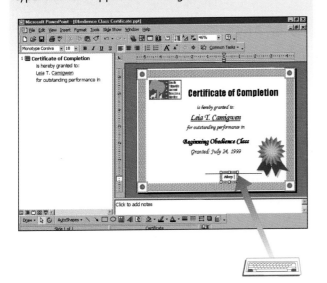

3 Click and Drag

To create a text box in which the text will wrap to the size of the box, click and drag until the box is the size you want. When you release the mouse button, a box appears with an I-beam cursor.

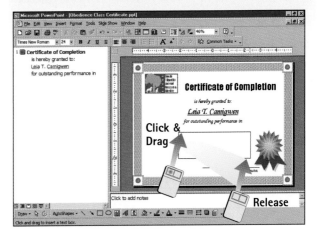

4 Type Text (Text Wraps)

Type the text in the box. The text will wrap at the end of lines so it does not exceed the boundaries of the box.

5 Position Text Box

You can move the text box by clicking one of the borders. The cursor changes to a four-headed arrow. Drag the box to a new location. (If you don't click a border, the cursor is an I-beam and you can't move the box.)

6 Size and Scale

To size the text box, click and drag a selection handle. The cursor changes to a two-headed arrow. Clicking and dragging a corner handle sizes the box proportionally. Clicking and dragging a top or bottom handle changes the height; clicking and dragging a left or right handle changes the width.

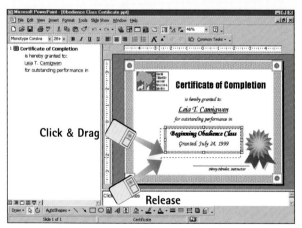

End

How-To Hints

Change the Shape of a Text Box

A text box is a graphic object, so like other objects you can fill it with color, add borders, or change its shape. On the Drawing toolbar, choose **Draw**, **Change AutoShape**, and select a new shape. Your text remains unchanged, although you may have to resize the object to make the text fit better. AutoShapes are discussed in Chapter 4, "How to Work with Graphics," Task 5, "How to use AutoShapes." Formatting objects is discussed in Chapter 5, "How to Format Objects."

How to Change the Font and Font Sizes

Typography is an art unto itself. The fonts you choose have a big effect on your presentation's visual "personality." Selecting a font that is appropriate for your audience is important. The font and font sizes you use for a financial presentation you give to banking executives are probably not the same ones you'd choose for a talk you give to 8-year-olds about *The Wizard of Oz*. Also remember that no one, young or old, likes a typeface that's difficult to read (no matter how cool you may think it looks), so choose type that is as easy for your audience to decipher as possible.

Begin

1 Select the Text

To change a font in the Slide pane of Normal view, first you need to select the text. Click and drag to highlight the text you want to change.

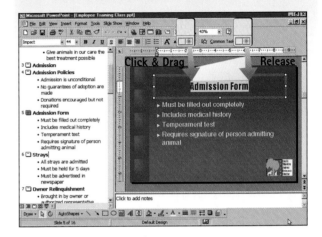

2 Select a Font (Toolbar)

Choose a font from the Font drop-down box on the Formatting toolbar by clicking the down arrow and highlighting a font. If you can't see the box, choose **Tools**, **Customize** and remove the check mark next to **Standard and Formatting toolbars share one row**.

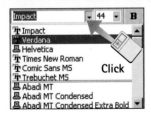

3 Use the Font Dialog Box

Alternatively, you can choose **Format**, **Font**. The Font dialog box appears. Under Font, use the scrollbar to scroll through the list to find the desired font. Click the font and choose **OK**.

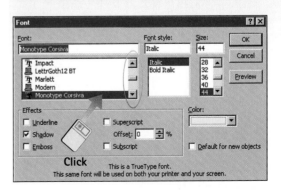

4 Change the Font Size

To change the font size, you can either choose a point size from the Font Size drop-down box on the Formatting toolbar, or select from the Size list in the Font dialog box. You can highlight a point size in the list or click and type a number in the box.

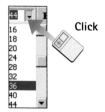

Click

5 Preview the Change

In the Font dialog box, you can click the **Preview** button to see your changes. The selected text appears on the slide with the new settings applied. If you like it, choose **OK**. If you don't, you can keep trying new settings and clicking the **Preview** button until the text looks the way you want.

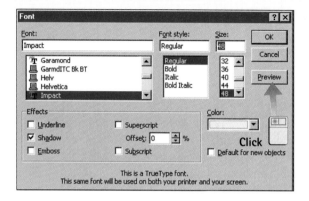

Click

6 Changing the Default Font

For consistency, you may want all the objects you create to use a certain font. In the Font dialog box, choose a font and click **Default for new objects** to change the default font.

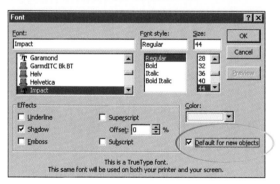

End

How-To Hints

Choose Type Wisely

You can do a couple of simple things to make your type choices work for you instead of against you. First, use fonts consistently. For example, use the same font for headlines in every slide. Don't mix and match unless you have a logical reason for it, such as a special type of slide. Second, keep wordiness to a minimum and don't crowd your slides. If a slide is crammed with text, break it into two slides.

How to Change Formatting

Type is one of the visual elements you use to communicate your presentation's message. Just as you modulate your voice to add emphasis, you can accentuate your type to help drive a point home. By adding formatting such as bold and italic to certain words or phrases, you can emphasize the parts of your message you most want your audience to remember. However, use your formatting tools judiciously. An old graphic design axiom states that if you emphasize everything, you emphasize nothing. Just as people will ignore you if you shout incessantly, they'll ignore the text emphasis if your entire presentation is **ALL UPPERCASE BOLD**.

Begin

1 Select Text

Click and drag to select the text you want to format.

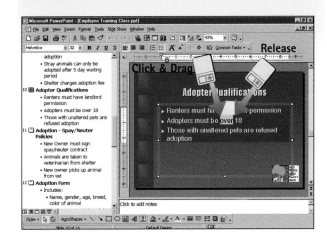

2 Add Text Formatting

Click the **Bold**, **Italic**, **Underline**, or **Text Shadow** button on the Formatting toolbar. You can combine the effects if you want, but keep legibility in mind if you add more than one effect.

Click

3 Add Other Attributes

Alternatively, you can choose **Format**, **Font** to open the Font dialog box. In this dialog box, you can choose other attributes, such as **Emboss**, **Superscript**, and **Subscript** in addition to the Font Style. Click the **Preview** button to see your changes on the slide. Click **OK** when you are content with your selections.

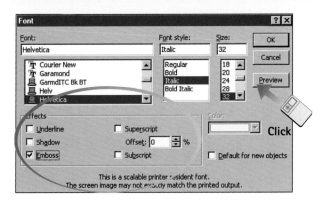

4 Change Alignment

Click the **Align Left**, **Align Center**, or **Align Right** buttons on the Formatting toolbar to change the alignment of the selected text. Or Choose **Format**, **Alignment** and select an alignment. In addition to options for **Left**, **Right**, and **Center** alignment, the menu also includes an option to **Justify** the text.

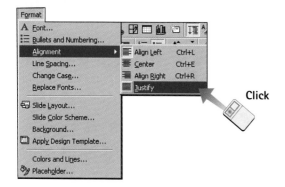

Click

5 Change Case

To change the text case, choose **Format**, **Change Case** to open the Change Case dialog box. You can choose from **Sentence case**, **lowercase**, **UPPERCASE**, **Title Case**, and **tOGGLE cASE**. (The latter is good for those times when you unknowingly press the CapsLock key.)

Click

6 Increase or Decrease Font Size

You can quickly increase or decrease the size of the selected text. Click the **Increase Font Size** or **Decrease Font Size** button, depending on what you want to do.

Click

End

How-To Hints

Use the Keyboard to Change Case

A fast way to change text case is to use the keyboard. Highlight the text you want to change and press **Shift+F3**. The text cycles through lowercase, UPPERCASE, and Title Case. To switch to Sentence case or tOGGLE cASE, you must use the menu command as described in step 5.

Exercise Caution

Today's computer systems generally come with lots of fonts preinstalled. It's easy to go berserk with all those creative choices. But exercise caution when selecting fonts and applying formatting. If you look at the text in printed materials, you'll find that the ones that artistically offend are the ones that are overloaded with fonts and type treatments. Keep it simple, so your audience can focus on the message.

Change Colors

Text color is another option you find in the Font dialog box. You click the Color drop-down box and choose a color to change the color of highlighted text.

How to Change Spacing

The spacing of the text on your slides has more of an impact on your presentation than you might expect. Consider the impression a slide jammed full of text makes on your audience. If you see people squinting or looking away from your visuals, it might be a sign that you've crammed too much text too close together and overwhelmed your audience.

When in doubt, use your common sense. If you were sitting in the audience would the slide you're looking at now seem inviting or threatening?

Begin

1 Select Text

Click and drag to select the paragraphs of text.

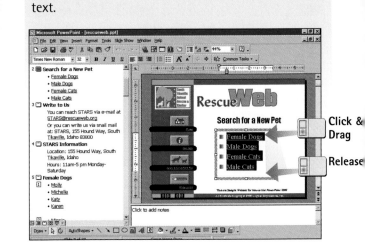

Click & Drag

Release

2 Change Line Spacing

Choose **Format**, **Line Spacing**. The Line Spacing dialog box appears. You can set the line spacing by clicking the up or down spin arrows, or by typing a number directly into the box.

Click

3 Choose Lines or Points

The three drop-down boxes let you choose to measure spacing in either Lines or Points. Lines refers to a line of text and will vary depending on the font size of the text. If you choose Points, you can enter a specific point size that will remain static even if you change the font size.

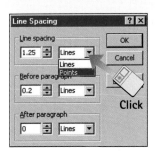

Click

4 Change Space Before and After

You can add space before and after the line of text to give more visual "air" around your paragraphs. Click the spin arrows to change the number, and select **Lines** or **Points** from the drop-down box.

5 Preview Changes

After you make changes, click the **Preview** button to see what impact your changes have on the slide text. Click **OK** when you are done.

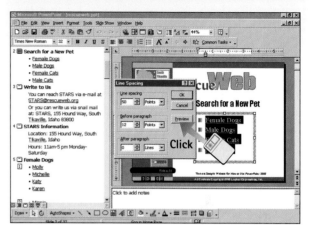

End

How-To Hints

Don't Enter

The Line Spacing dialog box is a much more precise way of adding space than hitting the Enter key extra times. You also can use the **Decrease** or **Increase** buttons on the Standard toolbar to change line spacing. (You can only change space above and below paragraphs in the Line Spacing dialog box, however.)

Add Space

Adding space above and below your paragraphs can improve the readability of your slides, because it visually divides the paragraphs into more unified "chunks" that are easier for the eye to comprehend as a unit.

Change Headline Space

For large type, such as headlines, you may want to decrease the line spacing. Too much space between the lines of a headline diminishes its impact. It's more effective to add more space below to set it off from the rest of the text.

How to Set Tabs and Indents

Tabs and indents are an often misunderstood part of word processing, and they're no less daunting in presentation software. Pressing the spacebar repeatedly is a common workaround to dealing with the nuances of tabs and indents. However, most of the fonts you use in PowerPoint are proportional fonts, and you'll soon discover that the old spacebar trick doesn't work well, especially when your slightly mangled column alignment is projected two feet high. Setting tabs and indents is really easy. Taking three minutes to set a tab can save you large scale embarrassment in the long run.

Begin

1 Show Ruler

To set tabs, you first need to show the PowerPoint ruler. If it's not already shown, choose **View, Ruler**. Make sure there's a check mark next to **Ruler**. If not, highlight it to show it. The ruler above your slide shows you the tab stops for the selected text object.

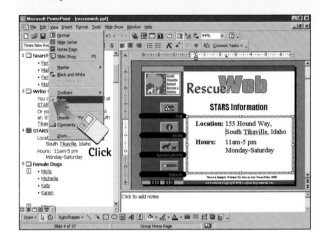

2 Set Tabs

Click the tab button to the left of the ruler to set the type of tab (left, center, right, or decimal). Click in the ruler to set a new tab.

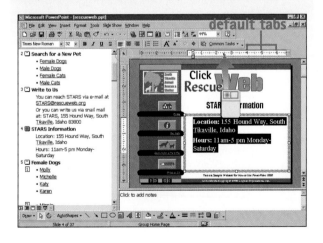

3 Delete Tabs

Tabs you set in front of default tabs replace them. To delete a tab, drag the tab off the ruler.

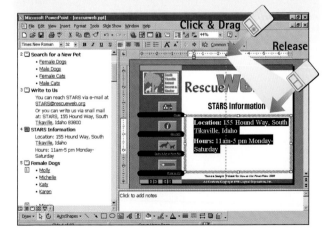

4 Set Indents

The first line indent is indicated by the upside-down triangle at the left of the ruler. The left indent is the right-side up triangle. Highlight the text you want to change. To indent paragraphs, drag the first line indent marker so it is to the right of the left indent marker.

Click & Drag   **Release**

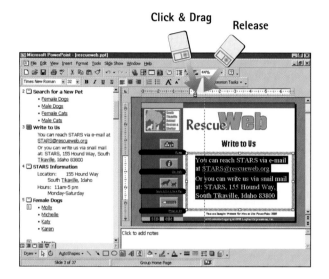

5 Change Default Tab Stops

The default tab stops are the gray tick marks. Click and drag one to move it to a new location. When you move a default tab, the distance between it and the other default tabs changes proportionally (for example, moving a tab to one inch causes the other tabs to be spaced one inch apart).

Click & Drag

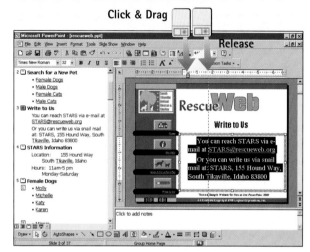

End

How-To Hints

Tab Types

Most people use left-aligned tabs exclusively. But tabs can be used in other ways. For example, if you need to create a table of contents, you can left align your text and use a right tab for the page numbers. You can use decimal tabs to line up a list of dollar amounts or center tabs to quickly create a two-column list of centered text. (Left align the text and set two center tabs. Type a Tab, the first column text, Tab again, and type the second column text.)

Create Hanging Indents

To create a hanging indent, such as for bullets or numbers, drag the left indent marker so it is to the right of the first line indent marker. Bullets and numbering are described in more detail in Task 8, "How to Add Bullets and Numbers."

How to Use the Find and Replace Feature

The Find and Replace feature is probably one of the best ideas programmers ever developed. For example, suppose you have two products that are the same except for their color and model number. The BL500 is blue and the GR500 is green. The text describing the two products would be almost identical. In the dark ages of slides, a designer would have had to re-layout and reshoot all the slides in a presentation that mentioned the color or model number (and accidentally missing a few occurrences of the terms wasn't uncommon). What used to take weeks, now can be done in seconds by using Find and Replace.

Begin

1 Find Text

To search for a term in your presentation, choose **Edit**, **Find**. The Find dialog box appears.

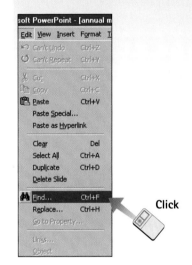

Click

2 Enter What to Find

In the **Find what** box, enter the text you want PowerPoint to find. In our example, you would type **BL500** to find the first occurrence of the model number in the text.

3 Set Options

In the Find dialog box, you can tell PowerPoint to find only text with the same case as your search term (BL500, but not bl500) or to find only text that matches the whole word (BL500, but not BL500A). Click **Match case** or **Find whole words only** to narrow your search criteria. Click **Find Next** to start the search.

Click

4 Replace Text

The Replace command works just like Find except that you can replace the text you find with new text. Chose **Edit**, **Replace** and enter your search term in the **Find what** box. Enter the text you want to insert in place of the found text in the **Replace with** box. Click **Find Next**.

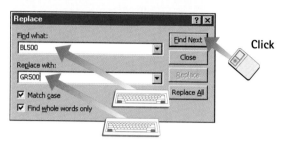

Click

5 Replace or Replace All

When PowerPoint finds a match, click **Replace** to replace text or **Find Next** to leave the text as is and move on to the next match. Click **Replace All** if you want to automatically replace every occurrence of the term in your presentation.

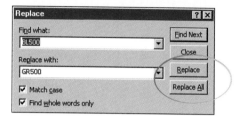

6 Replace Fonts

In addition to replacing text, you also can replace every occurrence of a font. Choose **Format**, **Replace Fonts** to open the Replace Font dialog box. Click the down arrow and choose the font you want to replace from the **Replace** box. Choose a font you want to replace it with from the **With** box. Click **Replace**.

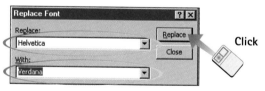

Click

End

How-To Hints

Use Replace All Carefully

Before you click the **Replace All** button, think about what it might do. For example, if you tell PowerPoint to replace "his" with "hers," without specifying the Whole Words Only option "this" would be changed to "thers." It's easy to make a big mess, so be careful.

Remove Extra Spaces

You can search for some surprising things with the Replace function. For example, if you're a little too handy with the spacebar, or you've imported text, you can end up with lots of extra spaces. In the Replace dialog box, type two spaces into the **Find what** box and one space into the **Replace With** box. Click **Replace All**.

Fix Font Failures

If you move a presentation to another computer that has a different complement of fonts loaded, you may find that the font substitution looks awful. You can use the Replace Fonts command to quickly fix the problem.

How to Add Bullets and Numbers

Bullets and numbers play a big role in many presentations. Most of the time, you use visuals to list key points in a topic—bullets and numbers are an ideal method of listing items concisely. In PowerPoint, much of the program is geared around making it easy to add these text features. In virtually all of the slide layouts that include text, the text is automatically formatted as bullets. And the Outline toolbar is optimized to make it easy to promote and demote text to different bullet levels.

Begin

1 Select Text

Place your cursor anywhere in the paragraph of text where you want to add a bullet or number.

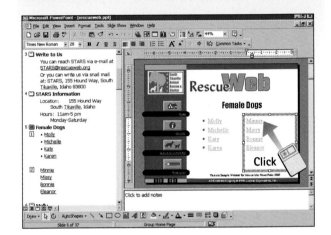

2 Add Bullets

Click the **Bullets** button on the Formatting toolbar. The default bullet (a round dot) is placed at the beginning of the text. For more options, choose **Format**, **Bullets and Numbering** to open the Bullets and Numbering dialog box. Click the **Bulleted** tab, choose a bullet type, and choose **OK**.

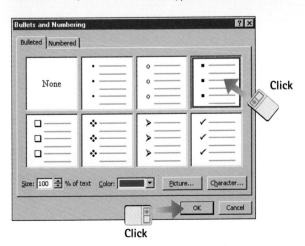

Click

3 Add Numbers

Click the **Numbering** button on the Formatting toolbar and the default number style (1.) appears. For more number formatting options, choose **Format**, **Bullets and Numbering** and click the **Numbered** tab. Click a numbering style and choose **OK**.

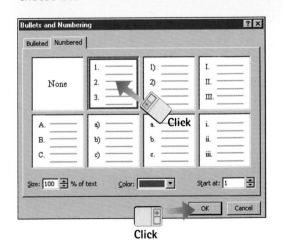

Click

4 Add Numbers Automatically

You can set PowerPoint to automatically format your text when it determines that you are creating a list. Choose **Tools**, **Options** to open the Options dialog box, click the **Edit** tab, and select **AutoFormat as you type**. When you type a number one (1), letter A or a, or Roman numeral one (I or i), and a period or closing parentheses followed by text, PowerPoint formats it and subsequent paragraphs as a numbered list.

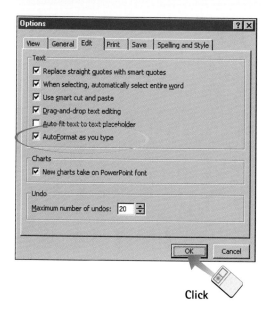

Click

5 Apply Bullet AutoLayout

Anytime you want a typical bulleted list slide, you can apply that slide layout to quickly reformat the slide. Choose **Format**, **Slide Layout** and click **Bulleted List**. Click **Apply**, and your slide is reformatted.

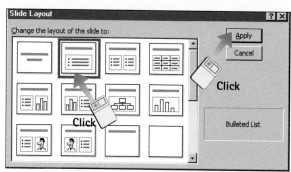

Click

Click

End

How-To Hints

Remove Bullets and Numbers

Press the **Backspace** key to remove a bullet or numbering.

AutoFormat Text

AutoFormatting as you type makes typing numbers faster, but it also affects how other text is formatted as well. PowerPoint recognizes certain symbols such as straight quotes or apostrophes and automatically turns them into their typographic "curly" counterparts. It also automatically converts two hyphens into an em dash and reformats certain commonly used fractions such as 1/2 and 1/4.

Rearrange Lists

A cool side effect of autonumbering your text is that when you add or delete items or rearrange the list, it's renumbered automatically. For example, if you select a paragraph and drag it to a new location in the list, the number changes automatically.

How to Format Bullets and Numbers

Bullets and numbers add interest to your presentation text, but you can make your lists more engaging if you venture beyond the standard default bullets and numbers. Windows comes with a number of fonts filled with bullet characters you can use. For even more options, you can use a clip art picture as a bullet character.

Using the default settings, you can end up with a gigantic bullet nudged right up next to the text, which looks somewhat absurd. However, it's easy to fix these unsightly problems by adjusting the spacing between the bullet and its text and changing the size of the bullet relative to its text.

Begin

1 Select Bullet Text

Place your cursor anywhere in the paragraph you want to format. To format multiple paragraphs simultaneously, click and drag to highlight the text. The changes you make to bullets and numbers affect entire paragraphs, even if you don't select all the text.

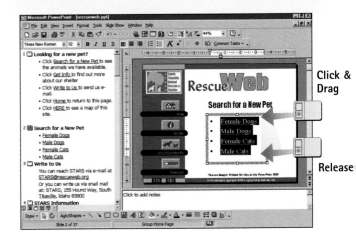

Click & Drag

Release

2 Change Bullet Character

Choose **Format, Bullets and Numbering**. Click the **Bulleted** tab and click **Character**. The Bullet dialog box appears. Choose a character set from the **Bullets from** drop-down box. Click a character and choose **OK**.

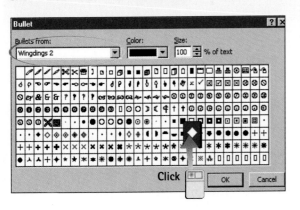

Click

3 Add "Picture" Bullets

In the **Bulleted** tab of the **Bullets and Numbering** dialog box, click **Picture**. The Picture Bullet dialog box appears. Click a bullet to select it, then click **OK**.

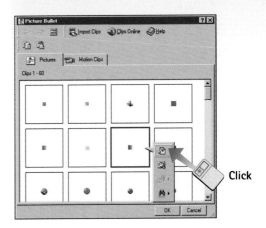

Click

4 Change Spacing Between Bullet

The amount of space between the bullet and the text is controlled by the indents setting. Make sure the ruler is displayed (choose **View**, **Toolbars** and click **Ruler**). Drag the left indent marker (the right-side up triangle) to the right to increase the hanging indent.

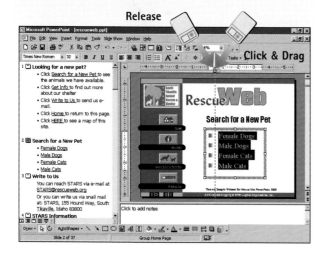

5 Change Relative Size of Bullet

When you add a bullet to a slide, you may be surprised at how very large it is. In the **Bulleted** tab of the **Bullets and Numbering** dialog box, use the spin arrows to change the Size setting. This option sets the bullet size as a percentage of the text size. A setting of 50–60% often looks much better than the default 100%.

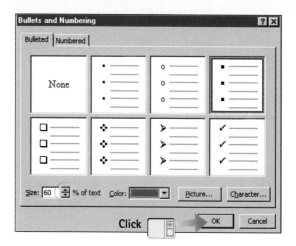

6 Change Starting Number

If you need to continue numbering across slides, you may need to change the starting number of a list. In the **Numbered** tab of the **Bullets and Numbering** dialog box, use the spin arrows to change the number in the Start at box.

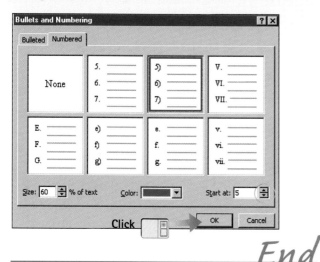

End

How-To Hints

Change the Color

In the Bullets and Numbering dialog box on either the **Bulleted** tab or the **Numbering** tab you can use the **Color** drop-down box to change the color of your bullets or numbers. Click the down arrow and choose a new color. Click **OK**.

Add More Bullets

You can add bullet types to the bullets you see in the Picture Bullet dialog box. Click the **Import Clips** button and find the desired file on your hard disk. Click the filename and choose **Import**. When you create bullets, keep them small. The picture bullets included in PowerPoint are generally around 12×12 pixels to 15×15 pixels.

How to Spell Check Your Presentation

As easy as it is to do, it's inexcusable to *not* run a spelling check on anything and everything you create with your computer. Although mistakes can and do happen to even the best speakers, perfect spelling is a sign of professional presentation. When your audience sees misspelled words, they can assume that you didn't care enough about your presentation to proofread it. Naturally, this impression is not the one you want to impart. If you are in a rush, you don't even have to take the time to run a spelling check per se because PowerPoint has options you can set to check your spelling automatically as you type.

Begin

1 Check Spelling as You Type

When you notice red wavy lines in your text, you are witnessing the automatic spelling checker in action. Right click the word and you see a list of suggestions. Choose a correct spelling from the list or **Ignore All** to tell the spelling checker to ignore this and future instances of the word.

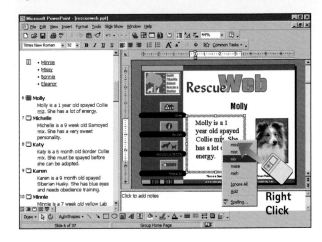

2 Use AutoCorrect

Choose **Tools**, **AutoCorrect** and click **Replace text as you type** to tell AutoCorrect to fix your mistakes automatically. You also can set options to control how AutoCorrect works.

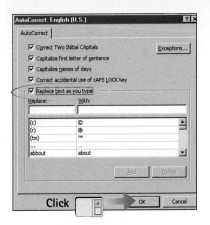

3 Run Spelling Checker

To check the spelling in your presentation, choose **Tools**, **Spelling** or press **F7**. The Spelling dialog box appears with the first word it finds that isn't in its dictionary. You can correct the spelling by typing a word in the **Change to** text box or choosing a word from the list of suggestions and clicking **Change**.

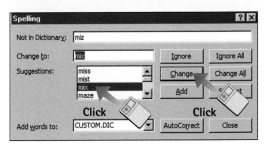

4 Add Items to Dictionary

If the word is correct, click **Ignore** to tell the spelling checker to ignore this instance of the word or click **Ignore All** to ignore it every time it encounters it in the current presentation. Click **Add** to permanently add the word to the dictionary as a correct spelling so PowerPoint never identifies the word as misspelled again.

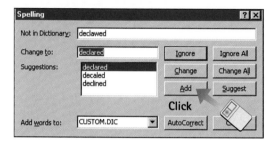

5 Check Foreign Text

If you like to pepper your text with foreign phrases, you can indicate that the text is in a foreign language. The spelling checker will then use a foreign language dictionary to check that text if one is available. Select the text and choose **Tools**, **Language**. Choose a language from the list and click **OK**.

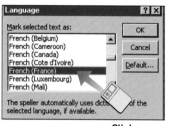

Click

End

How-To Hints

Turn off Automatic Spelling Checks

You may find a whole lot of red wavy lines distracting. If so, you can easily turn off the automatic spelling checker. Choose **Tools**, **Options** and click the **Spelling and Style** tab. Remove the check mark next to **Check spelling as you type**.

Change AutoCorrect Options

If you type text with a lot of abbreviations, you may discover that AutoCorrect is correcting you incorrectly. When AutoCorrect encounters a period, it assumes that you are at the end of a sentence and the next word should be capitalized. To change this option, choose **Tools, AutoCorrect** and click **Capitalize first letter of sentence** to remove the check mark. For more information on customizing AutoCorrect, see Chapter 12, "How to Make PowerPoint Work Your Way," Task 3, "How to Customize AutoCorrect.

Task

CHAPTER 4

How to Work with Graphics

If you don't consider yourself much of an artist, the idea of adding graphics to your presentation may seem intimidating. But the graphics you use in your presentation are a big part of what make it memorable. In fact, studies have shown that including graphics can help your audience understand abstract concepts more easily and retain information longer than just using text alone. Graphics also help keep your presentation interesting. After all, everyone likes to look at pictures.

Considering how important images are to your presentation, you should attempt to use the best graphics you can. Make sure that the images you use are appropriate for your audience. Using cutesy or cartoony clip art may be okay for a very informal presentation, but in most cases you'll want to create or acquire good quality images that enhance your message rather than detract from it. (You don't want your audience marveling at how idiotic your clip art looks.) Also remember that, like words, images are protected by copyright law, so be sure that the images you use are royalty free or that you have paid for the right to use them.

How to Add Clip Art

PowerPoint 2000 comes with a large clip art library filled with images you can use freely. This clip art is easy to add and modify, so even if you don't particularly like the original image, you can change it to suit your needs. Sometimes just breaking the clip art into its component parts and removing elements or changing a few colors can make a marginal image fit better into the overall look of your presentation.

Begin

1 Use a Placeholder

Many slide layouts include a clip art placeholder. Choose **Format**, **Slide Layout** to open the Slide Layout dialog box and choose a layout that includes clip art. Click **Apply**. Double-click the icon to open the Microsoft Clip Gallery to add clip art to your slide.

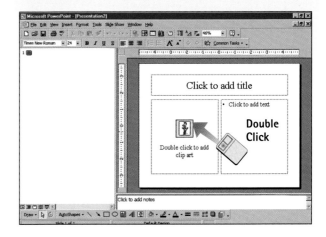

2 Insert Clip Art

You also can insert clip art anywhere on a slide. In Slide view or the Slide pane of Normal view, click and choose **Insert**, **Picture**, **Clip Art**. This opens the Insert ClipArt dialog box, which has tabs for Pictures, Sounds, and Motion Clips.

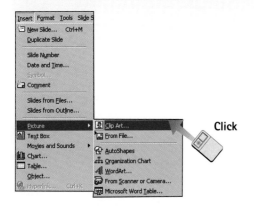

3 View Clip Gallery

Either way you add clip art, you encounter the Clip Gallery. The **Picture** tab shows the categories of clip art. Click a category to see the images. Click the **Back** button to return to the category list.

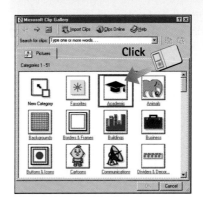

4 Insert Clip

When you click an image, a pop-up tool-bar appears with options to **Insert clip**, **Preview clip**, **Add the clip to another category**, or **Find similar clips**. Click **Insert clip** to add the image to your slide. Minimize or close the Clip Gallery by clicking the **–** or **X** buttons at the top right of the window.

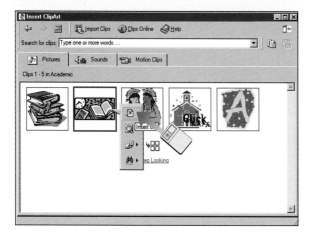

5 Move Graphics

The graphic appears on your slide with eight selection handles. It often overlays any slide text, so you may want to move it. Click the image border to select it. The pointer turns into a four-headed arrow. Click and drag to move the image to a new location.

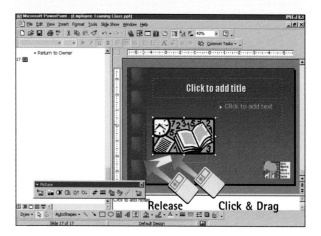

6 Resize Graphics

Clip art often is way too big when you insert it. You can use the selection handles to resize the image to something more manageable. Click and drag a corner handle to resize the image proportionally. Click and drag a top or bottom handle to change the height; click and drag a left or right handle to change the width.

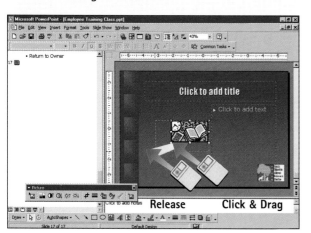

End

How-To Hints

Get More Clip Art

You can find lots of free clip art on the Internet. From within PowerPoint, you can click the **Clips Online** button in the Clip Gallery to get free clip art from Microsoft's Web site. Or you can use your favorite search engine and do a search on the words clip art. Another good source of clip art is the Ultimate Desktop Publishing site at **http://desktoppublishing.com**.

Search for Clips

If you know that you have a clip lurking in the Clip Gallery somewhere, but you can't remember the name or where it's located, you can try doing a search. In the Clip Gallery, type a keyword or phrase to describe the clip in the **Search for clips** text box, and press **Enter**.

How to Add Graphics to the Clip Gallery

It's quite possible that you may find the graphics in the Clip Gallery unsuitable for your presentation or at least monumentally underwhelming. (How many times have you wanted to insert the Microsoft interlocking puzzle piece logo in your presentation, for example?) However, you can add your own clip art into the Clip Gallery and then categorize and recategorize it to your heart's content.

Begin

1 Insert Clip Art

To add new clip art, first you need to choose **Insert**, **Picture**, **Clip Art** to access the Clip Gallery.

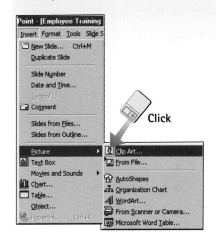

Click

2 Import Clip

In the Clip Gallery, click the **Import Clips** button. If you have clicked a category, PowerPoint will add the clip to that category (unless you specifically change it).

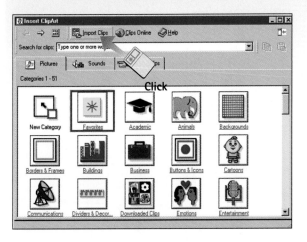

3 Find File

In the Add Clip to Clip Gallery dialog box, find your new clip art on your hard disk. Click the filename and click **Import**. You can have the Clip Gallery make a copy of the clip to insert in the clip gallery, move the file from its current folder into the clip gallery, or leave the file where it is and let the Clip Gallery find the file there.

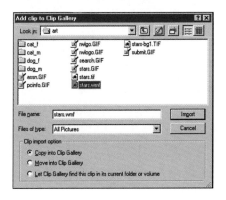

4 Choose or Create Category

In the Description tab, type a description of your clip art. Then click the **Categories** tab. Choose a category in which your clip will appear. You can add a new category by clicking the **New Category** button and typing a name. Click **OK**.

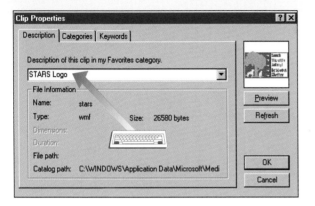

5 Add Keywords

Click the **Keywords** tab to add keywords you can use to help you find the clip art later. Click **New Keyword**, type a new keyword, and choose **OK**. Choose **OK** again to add the clip to the Clip Gallery.

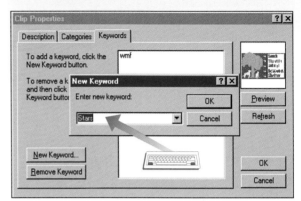

End

How-To Hints

Keep Track of Your Clips

If you use a lot of clip art, it can quickly get out of hand. To keep yourself organized, create new categories and add meaningful keywords and descriptions, so you don't have to spend hours wading through images in the Clip Gallery.

Delete Clips

To remove clips from the Clip Gallery, right-click the clip and choose **Delete** from the pop-up menu. You see a message that asks if it's OK to delete the clip from all Clip Gallery categories. Click **OK** if that's what you want to do. If you want to just remove the clip from a certain category, click **Cancel**. Right-click again and choose **Clip Properties**. In the **Categories** tab, select the categories in which you want the clip to appear.

How to Add Images from a File

When you work with graphics, much of the time you will need to add your own graphic files, such as logos or photographs. You can insert virtually any picture file you have on your hard disk as long as PowerPoint understands the type of file.

When you work with graphics, you should pay attention to the file's extension (in the filename, the extension is the last three letters after the period, such as .WMF, .TIF, .GIF, .JPG, and so on). The extension tells you which graphic format the file is saved as. Some formats are better for certain uses than others. If you are creating a Web presentation, for example, you should use .GIF or .JPG files, which are file types most Internet browsers can understand.

Begin

1 Insert Picture

To insert a picture from a file, choose **Insert**, **Picture**, **From File**. The Insert Picture dialog box appears.

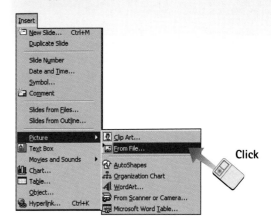

Click

2 Find File

Use the down arrow on the **Look In** drop-down box to find the folder on your hard disk where the file is located. Click to select a filename.

Click

3 Insert

Note that the **Insert** button has a drop-down arrow next to it. To place the graphic into your presentation, click **Insert** or hold down the drop-down arrow and highlight **Insert**. The picture appears on your slide.

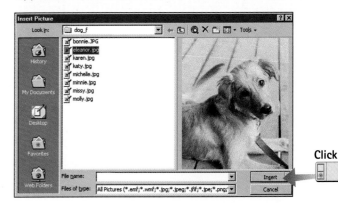

Click

4 Link to File

If you are inserting a large file, you may want to insert a link to the file on your hard disk rather than placing the file within your presentation. Click the drop-down button on the **Insert** button and highlight **Link to File**. The picture appears on the slide.

Click

5 Move, Size, and Scale

After you have inserted a picture, you can select it and move it around on the slide or use the selection handles to size and scale it.

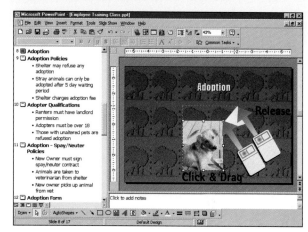

End

How-To Hints

Link That Graphic

Linking a graphic rather than placing it into your presentation can substantially reduce the presentation file size. When you link files, even though you see the graphic, PowerPoint is actually only inserting a "pointer" to the location of the graphic on your hard disk. If you move the graphic file on your computer, PowerPoint may lose track of where it is, so be careful. Linking is discussed in more detail in Chapter 9, "How to Share Information with Other Microsoft Applications," Task 2, "How to Link or Embed Objects."

Vector Versus Bitmap Art

You can insert two basic types of graphics: vector line art and bitmaps. Line art appears the same no matter what size you scale it to because the lines are created using mathematical descriptions rather than by a pattern of dots (pixels) as they are in a bitmap. The number of dots in a bitmap (the resolution) determines how it will look at different sizes. If you scale a low-resolution bitmap, the individual pixels are larger, so you may get an unattractive jagged effect.

How to Recolor Clip Art

Sometimes you find a piece of clip art that would work in your presentation if only the colors matched the color scheme better. PowerPoint makes it easy to systematically find and change the colors in clip art to any colors you choose. The Recolor command works on all of the clip art included with PowerPoint that is saved in the .WMF (Windows metafile) format.

You can also recolor your own inserted graphics, as long as they are .WMF files. Before you recolor your own graphic, however, you must convert it to a PowerPoint Drawing Object.

Begin

1 Recolor Picture

Click a clip art object. If it isn't already visible, choose **View, Toolbars, Picture** to show the Picture toolbar. Click the **Recolor Picture** button. The Recolor Picture dialog box appears with the clip art in the pane on the right and a list of colors on the left.

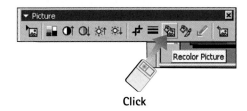

Click

2 Change Colors

Use the scrollbar to scroll through the colors until you find the one you want to change. Click the down arrow next to the color and choose a color, or click **More colors** to see the Colors dialog box. Click a color and choose **OK**. Every occurrence of the color is changed.

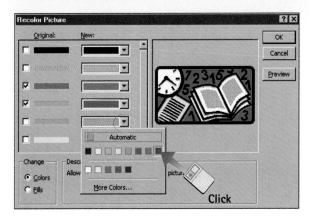

Click

3 Change Fills

If you only want to change the fill colors without changing the line colors, click **Fills**. Then change the colors as described in step 2.

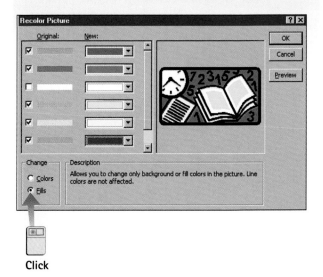

Click

4 Preview Changes

Whether you change all the colors or just the fills, you can preview the changes on your slide before you commit yourself to them. Click the **Preview** button to see your color changes.

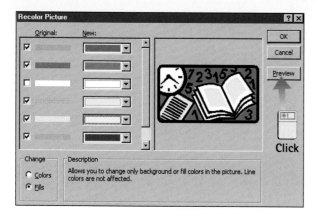

Click

5 Convert to PowerPoint Object

If you import a .WMF graphic that you want to recolor to match your slide, you must first convert it to a PowerPoint object. Double-click the graphic and you see a message box that asks if you want to convert the graphic to a PowerPoint object. Click **Yes**.

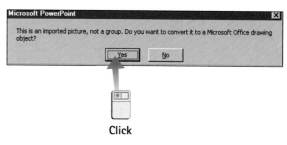

Click

End

How-To Hints

Use Other Tools

Once you have converted your graphic to a PowerPoint object, you can use PowerPoint's other drawing tools to manipulate it as well. The object formatting tools are described in Chapter 5, "How to Format Objects."

Know Your Formats

You can't convert bitmap graphics to PowerPoint objects. Bitmap formats include files with a .JPG, .GIF, .TIF, .BMP, or .PNG file extension. Because .WMF files are vector line art, PowerPoint can manipulate them. To change bitmaps, you need to use a bitmap editing program such as Paint or Microsoft PhotoDraw, which is included with Microsoft Office.

How to Use AutoShapes

AutoShapes are the PowerPoint term for drawing objects. If you draw a circle in the land of PowerPoint, you are drawing an AutoShape. Although it may seem odd to treat a square and a circle as the same thing, the concept is powerful. Because PowerPoint treats all AutoShapes the same way, you can convert one AutoShape into another with just a mouse click. For example, to turn a boring old square box into a multipointed star, you just switch the shape.

Begin

1 Add Lines, Squares, and Circles

To add AutoShapes, the Drawing toolbar must be showing. If it's not, click **View**, **Toolbars**, **Drawing**. Click the **Line**, **Arrow**, **Rectangle**, or **Oval** buttons (depending on what you want to draw). The pointer changes to a cross-hair. Click and drag to draw the shape to the desired size.

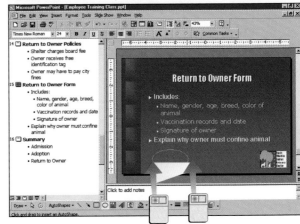

Click & Drag   Release

2 Add an AutoShape

You can add other AutoShapes the same way you add lines, rectangles, and ovals. Click the **AutoShapes** button and a pop-up menu of categories appears. Rest your mouse pointer on the type of shape you want and choose a shape from the menu that appears. Click and drag to draw the shape.

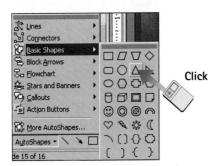

Click

3 Add Shapes from Clip Gallery

More AutoShapes lurk in the Clip Gallery. To access them, click **AutoShapes**, **More AutoShapes**. Click a category and insert clip.

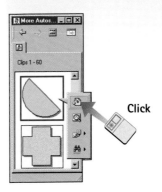

Click

4 Add Text

You can add text to any AutoShape except lines. Click the shape to select it and start typing. By default, the text does not wrap within the confines of the shape (see How-To Hint).

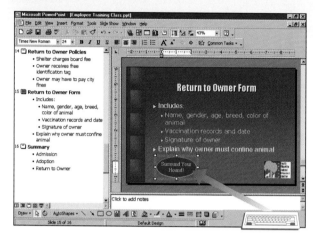

5 Change Shape Type

Choose **Draw**, **Change AutoShape**, click a category and choose a new shape. Note that you can't change a line to another shape or vice versa.

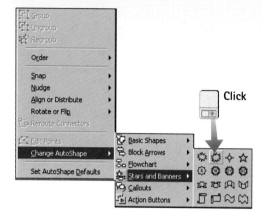

Click

End

How-To Hints

Wrap Text

If you want the text you add to an AutoShape to stay within the shape, right-click and choose **Format**, **AutoShape**. In the Text Box tab, click **Word wrap text in AutoShape** or **Resize AutoShape to fit text**. For more information on formatting AutoShapes, see Chapter 5, "How to Format Objects."

Make a Different Duplicate

If you want two different shapes to be the same size, click the original shape and choose **Edit**, **Duplicate**. Click the duplicate to select it and choose **Draw**, **Change AutoShape** and choose a new shape.

Adjust the Shape

Certain AutoShapes have an extra adjustment handle, which appears as a little yellow diamond. Clicking and dragging the adjustment handle changes the shape in some way, depending on the shape. For example, you can use the adjustment handle to increase or decrease the roundness of corners on a rounded rectangle. Changing other AutoShape attributes is discussed in Chapter 5, "How to Format Objects."

How to Create Complex Drawings

Although the drawing tools in PowerPoint may seem simple, it's somewhat of an illusion largely because they are so easy to use. You can create complex drawings with the PowerPoint drawing tools. Even the most basic drawing program lets you draw squares and circles, but lurking within the PowerPoint AutoShapes are a few drawing tools that are generally only found in high-end drawing programs.

Begin

1 Scribble

For complete drawing abandon, use the Scribble tool. On the Drawing toolbar, click **AutoShapes**, **Lines** and then the **Scribble** button. Click and hold the mouse button and move the mouse at will. Behind your mouse a line appears as if you were using a pencil.

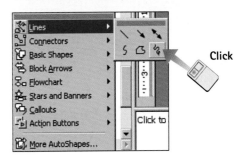

Click

2 Add Freeform Objects

With the Freeform tool, you can draw shapes that combine both straight lines and scribble-type curves. Click **AutoShapes**, **Lines** and then the **Freeform** button. Click and drag to draw curved shapes, or click and move the mouse to draw straight lines. Double-click to stop drawing.

Click & Drag   Release

3 Add Curves

Using the curve tool takes some practice, but with it you can create more precise curves than you can with the Freeform or Scribble tools. Click **AutoShapes**, **Lines** and then the **Curve** button. Click at the beginning of the line, move your mouse, and click where you want the line to curve. Double-click to end the line.

Click   Click   Click

Click   Click   Click

4 Edit Curves

Since drawing well can be tricky, you may want to edit the objects you create. Click the free-form, scribble, or curve object you want to edit and choose **Draw**, **Edit Points**. Small black handles appear. You can click and drag the handles to change the shape of the curve.

Click & Drag

5 Add Connectors

As the name suggests, connectors are lines used to connect two items. When you move the items around, the connector adjusts itself. To add a connector, click **AutoShapes**, **Connectors** and choose a straight, angled, or curved connector. Click the first object to connect, and then click the second.

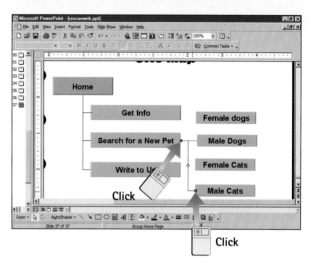

Click

6 Edit Connectors

If an object is connected, the connector handle is red; if it's not really connected, the handle is green. To lock a connection in place, you need to click and drag the handle so it hits the object precisely and turns red. Otherwise the object and line won't stay connected when you move them.

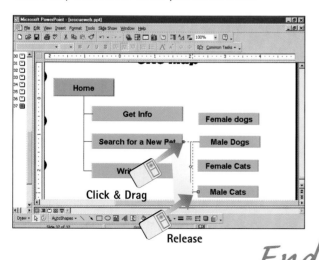

Click & Drag

Release

How-To Hints

Add Points

When editing your freeform, scribble, or curve, you can add or delete editing points. Click the object and choose **Draw**, **Edit Points**. To add a handle, click and drag the line and a new handle appears. To delete a handle, hold the **Ctrl** key and click a handle.

Reroute Connectors

If you move your connectors around a lot, you may want to streamline them. Select one of the connected objects and choose **Draw**, **Reroute Connectors**. The line is modified, so it travels the shortest possible distance between the two objects.

End

How to Add WordArt

Text in a text box or AutoShape is useful, but not necessarily flashy. In some circumstances, you may want a short piece of text to really stand out. To create twisting, turning, slanting, or curving text, you can use WordArt. First you select the way you want the type to look and then you type the text. The text you typed appears on the slide formatted with the WordArt effect you selected. A WordArt object acts like any other graphic you insert: you can size, scale, and manipulate it just like the other graphic objects on your slide.

Begin

1 Add WordArt

To add WordArt, click the **Insert WordArt** button on the **Drawing** toolbar. The WordArt Gallery appears.

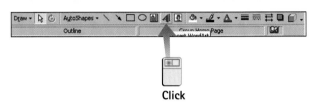

Click

2 Select a Style

Click a WordArt style from the 30 available styles to select it. Choose **OK**. The Edit WordArt Text dialog box appears.

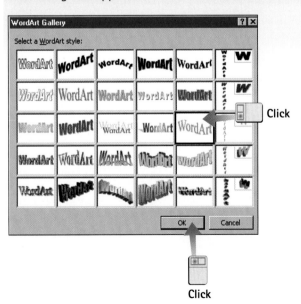

Click

Click

3 Type Text

Type your new text into the Text box. Try to keep the text reasonably short (if it doesn't fit in the box, it's too long). Long text can be difficult to read when it's formatted using the WordArt styles.

4 Change Attributes

You can change the font and font size by clicking the down arrow on the drop-down boxes and making a new selection. You also can add bold and italic by clicking the **Bold** and **Italic** buttons. When you are done, click **OK**.

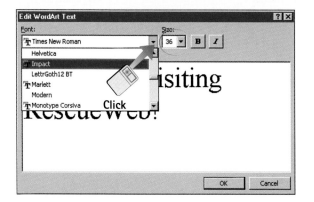

5 Position and Size

Your text appears on the slide in the WordArt style you selected. You can use the selection handles to size it or click and drag it to move it around the slide.

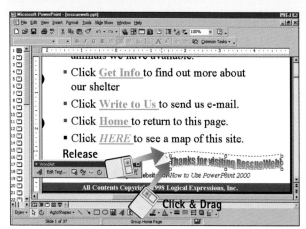

End

How-To Hints

Keep It Simple

WordArt is a tool that should be used with extreme caution. If you aren't careful, you can end up with text that is completely unreadable. Try your text in a few styles before you settle on one. Some text looks fine in one style and illegible in another. Even if you successfully create a readable WordArt object, you may want to refrain from using it in onscreen presentations or slides that will be projected to a large audience. The people in the back of the room may have no idea what the text says. If in doubt, don't use a WordArt object for onscreen presentations.

How to Modify WordArt

After you create a WordArt object, you may be disappointed. When it appears on the slide, its appearance often comes as an unwelcome shock. But you aren't stuck with the choices you made. You can go back and change almost every aspect of your WordArt object by using the tools on the WordArt toolbar. This toolbar appears automatically whenever you insert a WordArt object. By using the tools, you can modify the text and text formatting, change the style you selected, or even change the shape or orientation of the object.

Begin

1 Edit Text

On the WordArt toolbar, click **Edit Text**. The Edit WordArt Text dialog box appears. Type your new text in the Text box. (If the WordArt toolbar isn't available, choose **View**, **Toolbars** and click WordArt.)

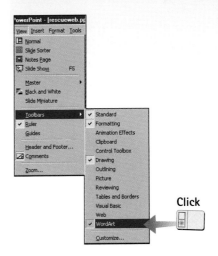

Click

2 Change Style

You can change the font and font size in the Edit WordArt Text dialog box. To change either one, click the down arrow on the drop-down box and highlight a new selection from the list. You also can add or remove bold and italic by clicking the buttons.

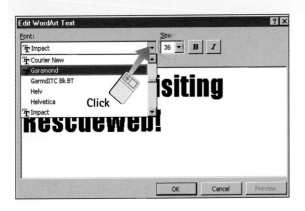

3 Change WordArt Shape

To change the shape of the WordArt object, click the **WordArt Shape** button on the WordArt toolbar. A pop-up menu appears filled with shapes. Click a shape and your WordArt changes.

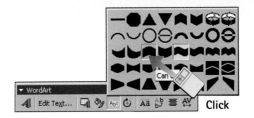

Click

4 Change WordArt Orientation

You can change your text to run vertically, even if you didn't select a vertical style. Click the **WordArt Vertical Text** button to reorient the text. If the WordArt text is vertical, the button appears pressed. Click the button to make the text horizontal.

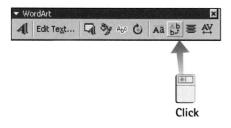

Click

5 Rotate WordArt

You can rotate WordArt using the **Free Rotate** button on the WordArt toolbar. When you click the button, round handles appear. When you place your cursor over a handle, it changes to a rotate icon. Click and drag the handle to rotate.

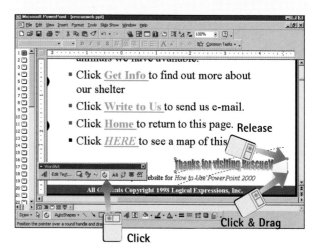

Click & Drag

Click

6 Change Spacing and Alignment

You can change the spacing between the letters of your text. Click the **WordArt Character Spacing** button and choose a setting from the list. Click the **WordArt Alignment** button to change the alignment and justification settings.

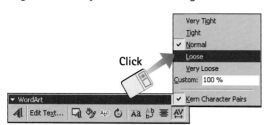

Click

End

How-To Hints

Format WordArt

Click the **Format WordArt** button to change line and fill colors, size, and position, and add alternative text for the Web. Changing these options is discussed in Chapter 5.

Play with the Yellow Diamond

Some WordArt objects have a little yellow diamond that appears when you select the object. This extra handle is an adjustment handle. Generally, if you click and drag it, you can skew the WordArt in some way.

Use the Fiddle Approach

The key to working with graphics in PowerPoint is experimentation, or to put it less eloquently, by using the "fiddle approach." You can learn a lot if you play around with your graphics.

Task

How to Format Objects

When you start using PowerPoint, a big part of learning the program is understanding how it "thinks." Once you begin to grasp the PowerPoint view of the presentation world, it becomes easier to learn how to do new tasks.

The concept of objects is a major element of the PowerPoint world view. Almost everything in your presentation is treated as an object that can be manipulated. Imported graphics (such as clip art and images), placeholders, AutoShapes, WordArt, and lines are all types of objects to PowerPoint. Only a few distinctions exist among the types of objects you can create. For example, text and graphics may seem like two very different items on a slide, but to PowerPoint they're both just objects. You can add borders around text placeholders and text boxes the same way you add borders around imported clip art. In fact, you use the same dialog box and the same commands to color lines and fills for virtually any object you can put on a slide.

You also can manipulate how objects are placed on a slide. You can align them with one another or distribute them evenly across an area, or one object can sit in front or behind another object. For example, you can have your text sit on top of a graphic, or a graphic sit on your text, depending on the look you want to achieve. By placing multiple objects on top of each other in a particular order, you can easily create drawings and layouts that are quite complex.

How to Change Borders

You can add a line around virtually any object you can place on a slide. PowerPoint refers to these lines as *borders*. It's easy to change a border's appearance. You can make thin lines, thick lines, solid lines, double lines, triple lines, dashed lines, or patterned lines appear around any placeholder, AutoShape, or graphic on your slide. Sometimes the most effective border is no border at all, and it's just as easy to remove borders as it is to add them.

Begin

1 Select an Object

In Slide view or the Slide pane of Normal view, click an object to select it. If it's a placeholder, be sure to click the border so you select the placeholder itself and not its contents.

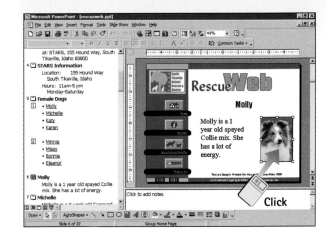

2 Add a Border

Right-click the object and a pop-up menu appears that says **Format <something>**, depending on the type of object you have selected. If you click a placeholder, it says **Format Placeholder**; if you click an AutoShape, it says **Format AutoShape**. Click the appropriate command.

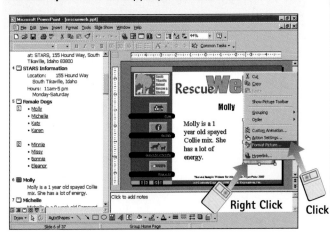

3 Change Line Color

The first tab in the dialog box is **Colors and Lines**. In the **Line** section, click the down arrow in the **Color** drop-down box and choose a color. Click **More Colors** to access the Colors dialog box. Click a color and choose **OK**.

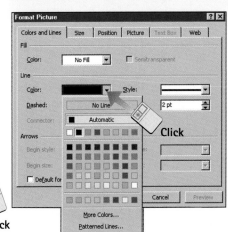

4 Change Line Options

You can change the width of the line by using either the **Style** drop-down box or the spin arrows on the **Weight** box. Using the **Style** drop-down, you also can select double or triple borders.

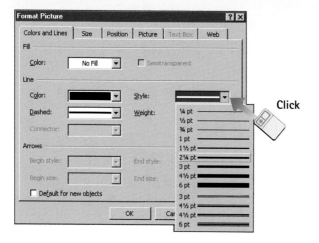

Click

5 Change Line Type

Click the down arrow next to the **Dashed** drop-down box to choose a type of line. You can select dashed or dotted lines in addition to the standard solid line.

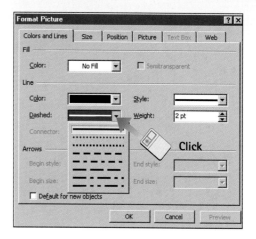

Click

6 Use Patterned Lines

Use the **Color** drop-down list and click **Patterned Lines** to select from 48 line patterns. You can change the foreground and background colors of the pattern. When you have finished setting border options, click **OK** to return to your presentation.

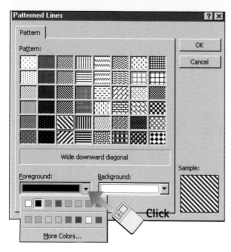

Click

How-To Hints

Use a Menu

If you like to use the menus better than right-clicking, you can format objects by choosing the type of object from the Format menu. For example, to change the borders on a place-holder choose **Format**, **Placeholder**.

Line Options

Obviously you can't add a border around a line, but you can use the same dialog box to change a line's appearance. In addition to the options for changing the appearance, you also can add arrowhead styles at the beginning or ending of a line. Click the drop-down box next to **Begin style** or **End style** and choose a diamond, oval, or standard pointy arrowhead.

End

How to Change Fills

If you want to change the outside of an object, the odds are good that at some point you might want to change the inside, too. Borders and fills go hand in hand and changing them works very similarly. You'll find that you access these commands frequently. In addition to just changing the color of an object, PowerPoint includes some nifty fill effects that can dramatically alter the appearance of your presentation. Adding a gradient screen is an easy way to make a fill more interesting, without obscuring the slide to the point of illegibility.

Begin

1 Select an Object

Click a slide object to select it. Make sure to select the object itself and not the contents.

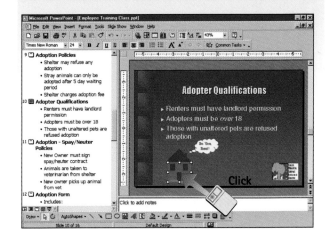

2 Add a Fill

Choose **Format**, **<object>** from the menu (where **<object>** is the type of object you clicked). If you select an AutoShape, for example, you choose **Format**, **AutoShape** to open the Format AutoShape dialog box. Or you can right-click and choose the appropriate Format command from the pop-up menu.

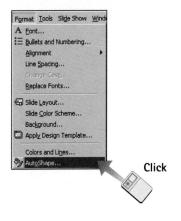

3 Change Color

In the **Colors and Lines** tab of the dialog box, click the down-arrow on the **Color** drop-down box in the Fill section. Choose a color from the list. The top row shows the eight colors in your selected color scheme. The middle section shows recently selected colors, and the bottom area shows any custom colors you have created (see step 4).

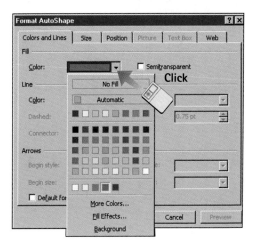

4 Access More Colors

For more color options, click **More Colors**. On the **Standard** tab, click a color from the Color wheel. To make your own colors, click the **Custom** tab; click in the rainbow box; or type values in the Hue, Sat, Lum (hue, saturation, luminescence) or Red, Green, Blue text boxes directly. Click **OK** after you choose a color.

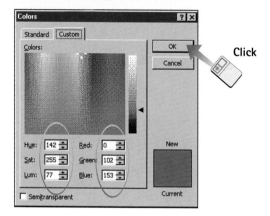

5 Use Fill Effects

In the Fill section of the Colors and Lines dialog box, click the down arrow next to the **Color** drop-down box and click **Fill Effects**. In the Gradient tab you can choose one-color, two-color, or preset gradients and change their shading styles.

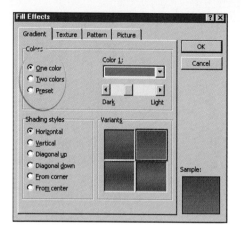

6 Use Textures and Patterns

In the Fill Effects dialog box, click the **Texture** tab and choose a texture, or click the **Pattern** tab and select a pattern. You can change the foreground and background colors used in the pattern. Use the **Picture** tab if you want to load in your own picture to be used as the color. Click **OK** when you're done.

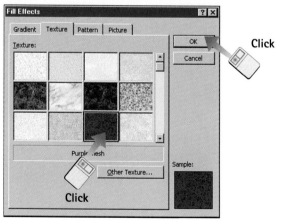

How-To Hints

Make it Transparent

You can choose to make your color semitransparent. When you choose a color, in the color dialog box click **Semitransparent** to allow the background to show through. Click **OK**.

Use Custom Colors

Creating custom colors can be useful if you are trying to match a specific color in a piece of clip art or if you need to make sure that your colors will be viewable on the Internet. To make your object match external clip art, create custom colors by typing in the RGB values directly into the **Custom Color** tab of the More Colors dialog box.

End

How to Add Other Effects

It's a three-dimensional world, but drawing anything that appears three dimensional is tricky unless you are an artist (and a good one at that). Applying the nuances of shadow is another artistic rendering that only the gifted dare to attempt. But with PowerPoint, these effects are available to you with just a click of the mouse. Adding shadow and 3D effects to your objects is just as easy as changing the colors and lines in your slides. To add any effects in this Task, you need to make sure that the Drawing toolbar is displayed. If you don't see the toolbar on the screen, choose **View**, **Toolbars** and click **Drawing**.

Begin

1 Add Shadows

To add a shadow to an object, select it and click the **Shadow** button on the Drawing toolbar and choose a shadow style. A shadow appears behind the object in the style you selected. If you attempt to add a shadow to a text placeholder with no fill, the shadow is applied to the text instead of the placeholder.

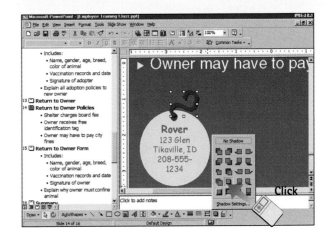

2 Change Shadow Color

To change the shadow color, click the **Shadow** button and choose **Shadow Settings**. The Shadow Settings toolbar appears. Click the down arrow on the **Shadow Color** button. You can choose from the colors in your color scheme and recently used colors or click **More Shadow Colors** to access the Color dialog box. Choose a color and click **OK**.

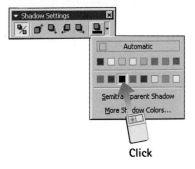

Click

3 Change Shadow Settings

The Shadow Settings toolbar also has buttons that let you turn the shadow on and off or nudge the shadow. Click the appropriate button to move the shadow slightly left, right, up, or down.

4 Add 3D

PowerPoint's 3D effects make it easy to change a square to a cube and a circle to a cylinder. Note that you only can add 3D effects to placeholders if they have been filled with a color. Click an object to select it and then click the **3D** button on the Drawing toolbar.

5 Change 3D Style

When you click the **3D** button, a pop-up list of styles appears. Choose a style from the list. When you release the mouse button, the 3D effect is applied to the object you selected. To change it, click the **3D** button again and choose a new style.

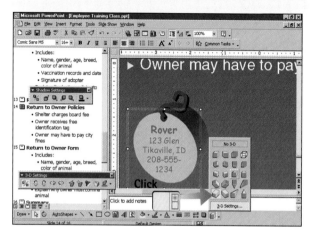

6 Change 3D Settings

To change aspects of the 3D effect, select the object and choose **3-D**, **3-D Settings**. The 3D Settings toolbar appears. Click the buttons to change the color, depth, direction, lighting, or surface used in the 3D effect. You also can click buttons to change the tilt up, down, left, or right.

End

How-To Hints

Copy Attributes

After you have slaved over an effect to get it just right, you might want to copy the effect to another object. Rather than going through the configuration process again, click the object that is set the way you want it. Then click the **Format Painter** button on the Standard toolbar and click the object you want to change. The second object takes on the attributes of the first.

Engrave or Emboss

An engraved or embossed effect can be useful for creating buttons like the ones you often see on Web pages. Choose Shadow style 17 for an embossed effect or Shadow style 18 for an engraved effect.

How to Group and Ungroup

When you were in first grade, you probably learned how to draw a simple picture of a house. Your humble abode was made up of a triangle for the roof, a square for the house and smaller rectangles for the windows and doors. Using PowerPoint's AutoShapes, drawing this house is easy, but moving it around on your slide would be difficult without the ability to *group* the objects. When you group items, they are treated as a single unit. You can size, scale, and move them around as if they were just one object. If you need to edit the elements in your object, you can ungroup it again, make your changes, and regroup it.

Begin

1 Select Objects

To select multiple objects, hold down the **Shift** key while you click.

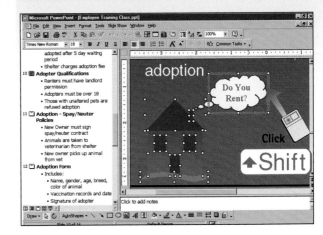

2 Create Marquee

Another way to select many objects at once is to click and drag. A rectangle appears called a *marquee* that indicates the area you have covered. When you release the mouse, all of the objects within the marquee area are selected.

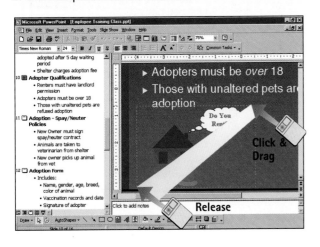

3 Group

Once you have selected more than one object, you can group them. On the Drawing toolbar, choose **Draw**, **Group**.

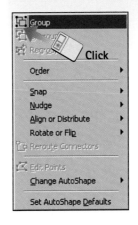

4 Select Grouped Object

After you have grouped a number of objects together, they are treated as one object. Like any other object, you can select your group by clicking it. Click and drag the selection handles to size or scale it.

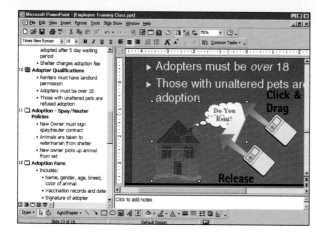

5 Ungroup

To edit the individual elements in a grouped object, you must restore it back into its component parts by ungrouping it. Choose **Draw**, **Ungroup**. Selection handles appear for all the individual objects again.

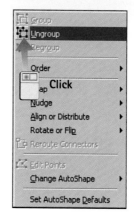

End

How-To Hints

Group and Change Clip Art

You can use grouping and ungrouping to change clip art the same way you modify your own drawings. Double-click a clip art image. A dialog box appears asking if you want to convert the image to a PowerPoint object. Click Yes. Select the image and choose **Draw**, **Ungroup**, so you can change the elements that make up the image. Often deleting extraneous elements in a clip art image can make a marginal image usable. Choose **Draw**, **Group** to regroup it when you've finished making your modifications.

How to Change Order

As you move objects around on a slide, you soon discover that they overlap one another. In fact, you can completely obscure one object with another if you're not careful. Every object you add sits on top of existing objects. This layering system makes it possible to build complex images. By moving the layers around to control the order in which objects appear on a slide, you can generate a particular effect.

Begin

1 Select Object

Click an object to select it. If the item you want to select is difficult to click, try pressing the **Tab** key. Keep pressing **Tab** to select objects in succession. Stop when the item you want is selected.

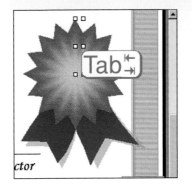

2 Bring to Front

If an object is behind another item, click **Draw**, **Order**, **Bring to Front** to place it in front of all other objects on the slide.

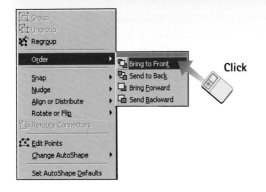

3 Send to Back

If you want an object to be partially or fully obscured by another object, click **Draw**, **Order**, **Send to Back** to place it behind all of the other objects.

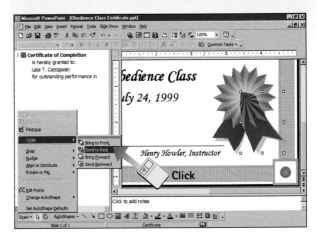

4 Bring Forward

Sometimes you don't want an item at the front or back layer, but somewhere in the middle. To move an object forward one layer, click **Draw, Order, Bring Forward**.

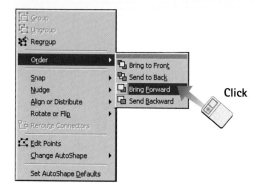

Click

5 Send Backward

Another way to rearrange objects is to move them backward through the layers. Click **Draw, Order, Send Backward** to move an object back one layer. By using a combination of the Send Backward and Bring Forward commands, you can get objects in just the right order.

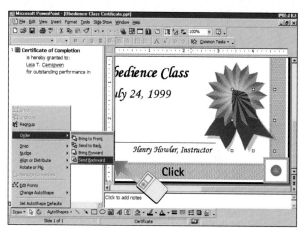

Click

End

How-To Hints

Remove Unwanted Parts of Clip Art

If PowerPoint can convert clip art to an object, you can edit it with PowerPoint's drawing tools. However, PowerPoint can't convert any bitmap images, so you have to use a bitmap editing program to change it. Or you can cheat. If you want to remove part of an image and you don't have (or don't want to learn) a bitmap editing tool, use PowerPoint's drawing tools to just cover up the unwanted area. Use the **Freeform** drawing tool to draw an outline around the area you want to remove. Be sure to close the shape. Then fill the shape with the background color you are using on the slide. Set the line color to **No Line** and make sure your freeform object is in front of the bitmap (click **Draw, Order, Bring to Front**). Finally, group the two objects (**Draw, Group**).

How to Align and Distribute

People have a need for symmetry. Order is comforting, and your audience will be subliminally disturbed if your objects are placed haphazardly on your slide. PowerPoint makes it easy to align objects with one another or relative to the slide itself. It also has tools you can use to arrange objects so that they are all the same distance from one another. To precisely position objects, you can have them snap to a grid or, for really fine adjustments, you can nudge your objects so they are exactly where you want them.

Begin

1 Select Objects

Click an object to select it.

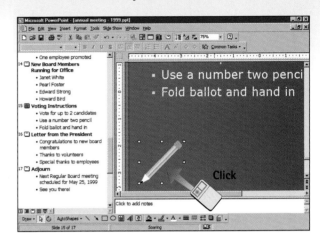

Click

2 Nudge

On the Drawing toolbar, choose **Draw**, **Nudge** and a direction to move an object slightly. You can nudge an object up, down, left, or right. If you prefer using the keyboard, you can use the up, down, left, or right arrow keys to nudge objects as well.

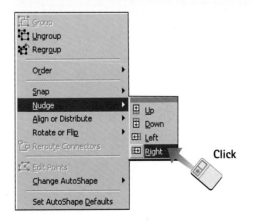

Click

3 Snap

If you need help aligning objects, you can use one of the two snap options. Click **Draw**, **Snap** and choose **To Grid** or **To Shape**. Snapping to the grid makes your objects snap to an invisible underlying grid. Snapping to shape causes objects to align with objects that are already on a slide.

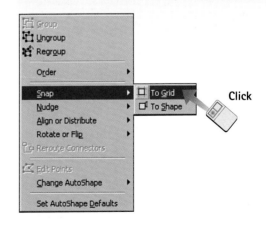

Click

4 Align Vertically or Horizontally

You can easily align your objects with one another. Click a number of objects to select them. Click **Draw**, **Align or Distribute** and choose an alignment (left, center, right, top, middle, or bottom). The objects align relative to the *last* object you selected.

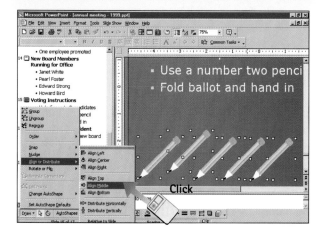

5 Align Relative to Slide

To align objects relative to the slide, instead of other objects, click **Draw**, **Align or Distribute** and click **Relative to Slide**. For example, with the option enabled, choosing **Draw**, **Align or Distribute**, **Align Left** aligns the selected objects to the left edge of the slide instead of to the last object you selected.

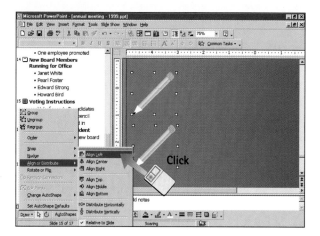

6 Distribute Objects

You use the Distribute command if you need a number of objects to be spaced equally across an area. Click **Draw**, **Align or Distribute** and **Distribute Horizontally** or **Distribute Vertically**.

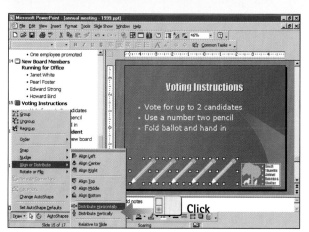

End

How-To Hints

Turn Off the Grid

The Snap to Grid option is turned on by default, which can cause confusion for new PowerPoint users. If you don't know that your objects are snapping to an underlying grid, it can feel like your objects have minds of their own. Choose **Draw**, **Snap** and click **To Grid**. (If Snap to Grid is on, the button will look like it's depressed.)

Snap to Shape

Snap to shape is handy if you want to create a number of objects that are all the same height or width. For example, draw one object, then to the right of it draw another object. As you draw, the height of the second object snaps to the height of the first object.

How to Rotate and Flip

You can use the rotate and flip commands to augment the drawing objects you can create. For example, to draw a picture of a pencil, you would probably use an isosceles triangle AutoShape for the tip. When you draw it, the two even sides face up. But for a pencil, you probably want the point to face down toward the paper. You don't have to try to draw a new triangle free-hand; instead you can flip the triangle, so it points downward. Or you can rotate the triangle, to make the pencil tip appear at an angle. Be inventive—you're limited only by your creativity.

Begin

1 Select Object

Click an object to select it. The object's eight selection handles appear.

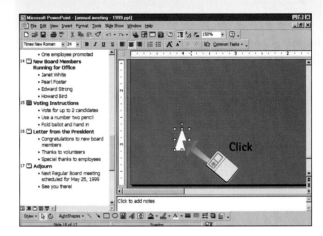

2 Rotate 90 Degrees Left or Right

It's easy to rotate an object 90 degrees. On the Drawing toolbar, choose **Draw**, **Rotate or Flip**, **Rotate Left**, or **Rotate Right**, depending on which direction you want to rotate.

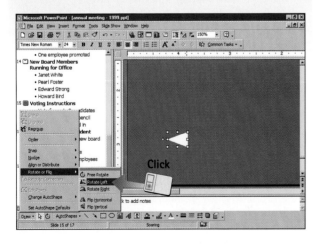

3 Free Rotate

For more flexibility, you can use the free rotate command. Click **Draw**, **Rotate or Flip**, **Free Rotate**. A set of green rotation handles appear. Click and drag a handle to rotate.

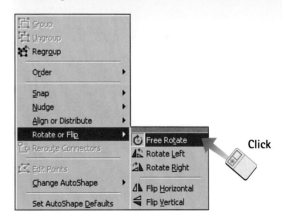

4 Rotate Using Format Dialog Box

For more precise rotation, you can specify rotation in degrees. Right-click an object and choose the **Format** command for the shape (such as **Format, AutoShape**). Click the **Size** tab and enter the number of degrees in the **Rotation** box.

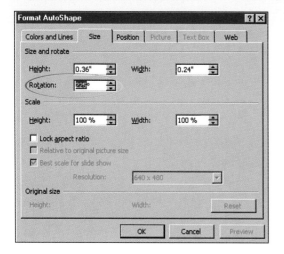

5 Flip Horizontal or Vertical

You use the Flip horizontal or Flip Vertical commands to transform an object to its mirror image. Choose **Draw**, **Rotate or Flip**, **Flip Horizontal**, or **Flip Vertical**, depending on what you want to do. The object flips.

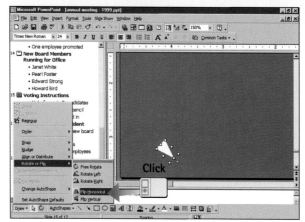

End

How-To Hints

Controlling Free Rotation

Sometimes using the Free Rotate command can be tricky. Hold down the **Shift** key while you drag to constrain the rotation to 15-degree increments.

Rotate This

Depending on the clip art you import, you may not be able to rotate some types of graphics. PowerPoint can't rotate imported bitmaps, for example. If you need the image to be rotated, you need to perform the rotation in another program and reinsert it into your presentation. To modify your bitmaps, you can use a bitmap editing program such as Paint or Microsoft PhotoDraw, which is included with Microsoft Office.

How to Size and Scale Precisely

Sizing and scaling has been discussed throughout this book. And if you've been doing a lot of clicking and dragging, you've probably realized that this interactive approach has a few limitations. For example, suppose you want all your text placeholders to be exactly 1.5 inches wide. Even the best mousers have trouble adjusting boxes with that degree of precision. As usual, however, PowerPoint offers another way: You can enter precise sizing, scaling, and placement coordinates into dialog boxes. And give your long-suffering rodent a rest.

Begin

1 Select an Object

Click an object to select it. Right-click and choose the **Format** command for the type of object to open the specific dialog box (if you select a placeholder, for example, it would be **Format Placeholder**). Or choose the command from the Format menu (**Format, Placeholder**, for example).

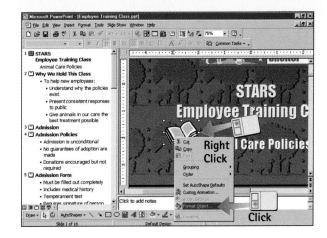

2 Change Size

In the dialog box, click the **Size** tab. In the Size and Rotate section, use the spin arrows to change the **Height** and **Width** or enter a value in the boxes. Enter rotation in degrees. Click **OK** when you are done.

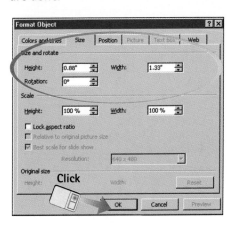

3 Scale Object

In the Scale section, enter the percentage you want to scale the object. Click **Lock Aspect ratio** to scale proportionally.

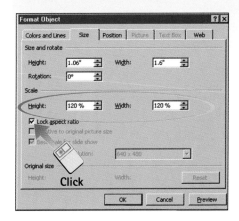

4 Set Position

Click the Position tab to precisely place the object on the slide. Click the down arrow in the **From** drop-down boxes to change whether PowerPoint calculates the distance from the top left corner or the center of the slide.

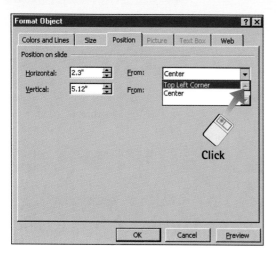

Click

5 Enter Coordinates

Enter a distance in the **Horizontal** and **Vertical** boxes. You can also use the up or down spin arrows to increase or decrease the number. Click **OK**.

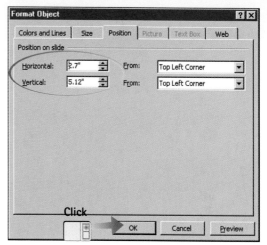

Click

End

How-To Hints

Placing Items

Using the positioning tools can be useful if you want to make two objects in two different slides appear in exactly the same place. Click the object that is positioned the way you like it and write down its horizontal and vertical position. Click the second object and enter the numbers in the **Horizontal** and **Vertical** boxes.

Scaling Pictures

When the object you choose is a picture, you have a couple of other scaling options. **Click Relative to original picture size** to have PowerPoint calculate the scaling based on the size of the original picture. Click **Best scale for slide show** and choose a resolution to have PowerPoint calculate the best scaling percentages based on the type of monitor you plan to use to view the show.

How to Change Text Objects

Although in general all objects are treated the same way in PowerPoint, a few options are available only for text objects or graphic objects. For example, a text object can have margins that determine how far the text is inset inside its placeholder. Text centered in a very large placeholder can create an intriguing look in certain circumstances.

Begin

1 Select Text Object

Click a text placeholder or text box to select it. Choose **Format**, **Placeholder** or **Format**, **Text Box** to open the Format dialog box for the type of object.

Click

2 Change Anchor Point

In the **Text Box** tab, you can change how the text appears within its box. It can be anchored to the top, middle, bottom, top centered, middle centered, or bottom centered. Click the down arrow next to the **Text anchor point** drop-down box to choose an anchor point. Click **Preview** to see the changes. Click **OK** when you're done.

Click

3 Change Margin

You can change how far the text is inset inside the box by altering the margin settings. In the **Text Box** tab, use the spin arrows or enter values in the **Left**, **Right**, **Top**, and **Bottom Internal margin** boxes.

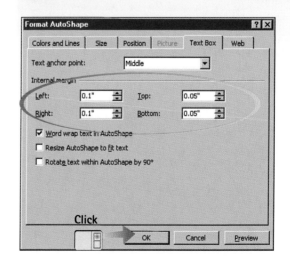

Click

4 Change Wrap Options

It's easy to change the text to fit the shape or force the shape to fit the text. Click **Word wrap text in AutoShape** to make the text line endings wrap within the confines of the box. Click **Resize AutoShape to fit text** to make the shape conform to the size of the text within it.

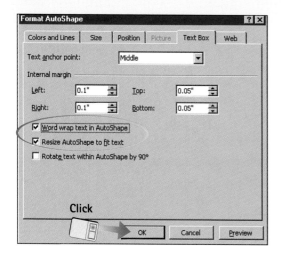

5 Rotate Text 90 Degrees

In addition to the standard rotation tools you use to rotate the object, you can rotate the text within the object as well. **Click Rotate text within AutoShape by 90°** and the text rotates right.

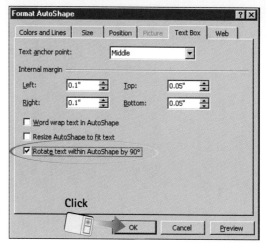

End

How-To Hints

Preview the Consequences

Some of the change you make to text boxes can have unexpected consequences. For example, if you rotate text within a placeholder and the placeholder isn't large enough to hold it in one line, the text wraps within the placeholder. Odd results like these certainly aren't irreparable, but you can experiment more quickly if you press the **Preview** button to see your changes. This way, you don't have to keep entering and exiting the dialog box as you try out changes.

How to Change Picture Objects

Like text, pictures have a number of options that are unique to them. PowerPoint gives you access to a number of features that you generally find in image editing programs. Rather than having to switch to a different program, you can use the tools built into PowerPoint to crop an image, change its type, or adjust its brightness and contrast. If you plan to create a Web presentation, you can also add alternate text that appears when Web surfers hold the mouse over an image or when they visit your site with graphics turned off in their Web browser options.

Begin

1 Set Image Controls

You can change the type of image displayed from color, black and white, grayscale, or watermark. Click **Format**, **Picture** to access the Format Picture dialog box. In the Image control section of the Picture tab, click the drop-down arrow next to **Color** to change the image type. Or click the **Image Control** button on the Picture toolbar to change the type of picture.

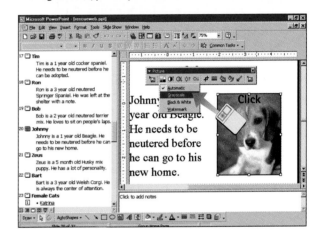

2 Set Brightness

Use the Brightness slider to adjust the brightness of the image or enter a value. Click **Preview** to see your changes. You can also use the **More Brightness** and **Less Brightness** buttons on the Picture toolbar.

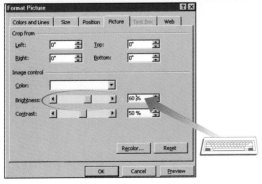

3 Set Contrast

Use the Contrast sliders in the Image control section of the Format Picture dialog box to adjust the image contrast. You also can use the **More Contrast** and **Less Contrast** buttons on the Picture toolbar to change the contrast.

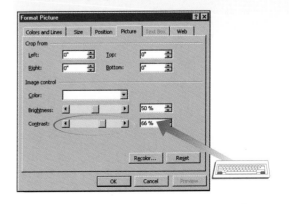

4 Crop Picture

You can crop a picture interactively or by entering values. Click the **Crop** button on the Picture toolbar. Click and drag a handle to crop the image, or enter measurements in the **Crop from** boxes in the **Crop from** section of the Format Picture dialog box.

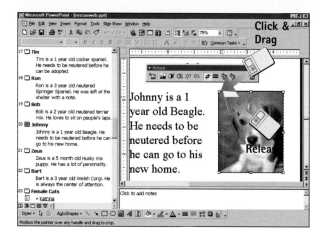

5 Add Alternative Text (for Web)

In the Format Picture dialog box, click the **Web** tab. Enter your text in the **Alternative text** box. Try to use text that describes what the image is so Web surfers have some hint what the browser is downloading. Click **OK**.

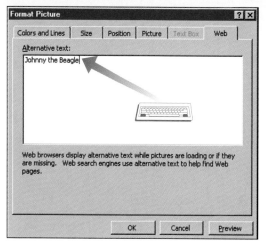

End

How-To Hints

Fix Images

Sometimes when you insert a bitmap, for reasons known only to PowerPoint, it is not scaled proportionally. Click **Format**, **Picture** and click the **Size** tab. Make sure that the **Height** and **Width** values are the same and that **Lock aspect ratio** is checked. Click **Preview** to verify that the distortion is corrected. Click **OK** when you're finished.

Task

6

How to Work with Masters

*I*n general, stress and time are related. The less time you have to do something, the more stress you experience. Time and its sidekick stress frequently play a big role in presentation design. Often you discover that you have to create a presentation by some date in the near future. Next, you experience the onset of stress. This scenario describes the genesis of most presentations.

However, all is not lost. By using PowerPoint's Masters, you can substantially decrease the time it takes to create a presentation. For example, suppose you need to put your company logo on every slide. Rather than inserting a picture on all 42 slides in your presentation, you insert it once on the Master Slide. That power to universally change formatting or layout throughout an entire presentation is what puts the power in PowerPoint. Masters are to PowerPoint what styles are to a word processing program. Just as the changes you make to a style in a word processor ripple throughout a document, the changes you make to a PowerPoint master ripple through to the farthest reaches of your presentation.

PowerPoint has four masters: the Slide Master, the Title Master, the Notes Master, and the Handout Master. Any changes you make on the underlying master are reflected in its corresponding presentation element. For example, if you change the font in the Notes Master, that change affects every Notes page in the presentation. ●

TASK *1*

How to Change Master Slide Text and Bullets

Of all the PowerPoint masters, you'll find you use the Slide Master the most. The Slide Master controls the look of every slide in your presentation. In fact, when you created a presentation from a template, all you were doing was loading a predesigned set of masters, including the Slide Master. (After setting up your own masters, you might want to save them as templates so you can use them again. Saving your own templates is described in Chapter 12, "How to Make PowerPoint Work Your Way," Task 4, "How to Create Your Own Template.")

Begin

1 Switch to Slide Master View

To access the Slide Master, choose **View**, **Master**, **Slide Master**. Or hold down the **Shift** key and click the **Slide View** button. (The ScreenTip changes to say Slide Master View.)

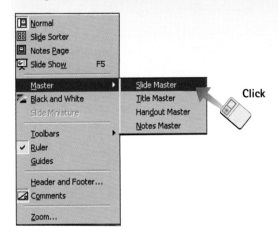

2 Change Text Styles

Slide Master view looks much like Slide view. Highlight the text you want to change and choose **Format**, **Font** to open the Font dialog box. Change the font, font style, size, color, and formatting as described in Chapter 3, "How to Work with Text," Tasks 3, "How to Change the Font and Font Sizes," and 4, "How to Change Formatting." Click **OK**.

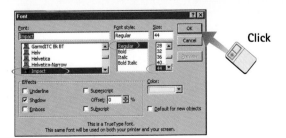

3 Change Color Scheme

Changing the color scheme in the Master Slide affects the colors in all the slides in the presentation. Choose **Format**, **Slide Color Scheme** to open the Color Scheme dialog box and choose a Standard or Custom color scheme. Click **Apply to All**.

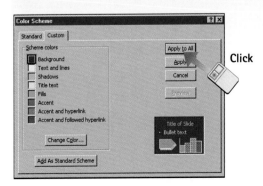

4 Change Bullet Styles

Click in a bullet level and choose **Format**, **Bullets and Numbering**. In the Bullets and Numbering dialog box, you can change the bullet style, color, and size, or remove bullets altogether as described in Chapter 3, "How to Work with Text," Task 8, "How to Add Bullets and Numbers."

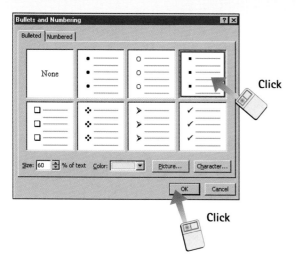

Click

Click

5 Add and Remove Objects

You can delete text or placeholders if you don't want to use them in any of your slides. For example, if you never plan to use the third through fifth level bullets, you can click and drag to highlight them and then press the **Delete** key.

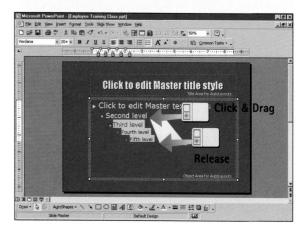

Click & Drag

Release

End

How-To Hints

Minimize Levels

When designing your presentation, it's a good idea to try to avoid going below the second or third bullet level. If your bullet levels get too deep, your slides are likely to be crowded and difficult for your audience to decipher. Remember that your audience sees your outline one slide at a time, rather than the entire outline at once, so deeply indented bullets can be confusing.

How to Set Up Footers and Numbering

Depending on the type of presentation you are creating, you may want text or numbers to appear on every slide. For example, in many cases you may want a copyright notice to appear at the bottom of every slide in your presentation. As in a word processed document, the area for text at the bottom of the slide is called a *footer*. Notes pages and handouts can also include a header as well. As the name suggests, header text appears at the top of every page. (Setting up the Notes Master is described in Task 6, "How to Change the Notes Master Layout.")

Begin

1 Add Date

To edit the date, choose **View**, **Header and Footer** to open the Header and Footer dialog box. Click the **Slide** tab and make sure a check appears next to **Date and Time**. Click **Update automatically** to have the date reflect the current date (which changes whenever you open the presentation). Click **Fixed** and type in a date that doesn't change.

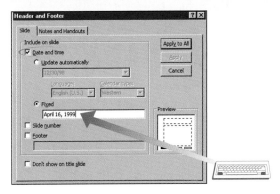

2 Add Automatic Slide Numbering

In the Header and Footer dialog box, click **Slide number** to include the slide number on your slides. Although you don't see a number on the Master Slide itself, every slide in the presentation will be numbered automatically.

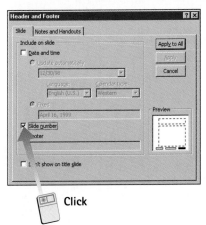

Click

3 Add Footer Text

Click **Footer** to include footer text that will be repeated on all the slides in the presentation. Click and type your footer text into the box. Click **Apply to All** to add your changes to the Master Slide.

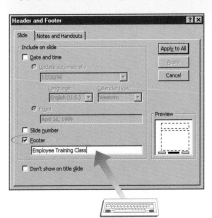

4 Change Text Attributes

You can change the font, font style, size, and attributes in the footer text. Click the text within the angle brackets (such as **<footer>**, for example) to select it and choose **Format**, **Font** to open the Font dialog box. Click **OK** when you've made your text changes.

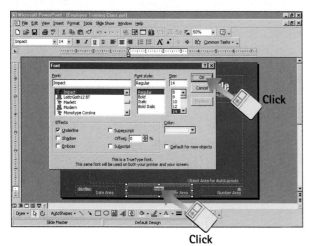

Click

Click

5 Change Placeholders

You can move the placeholders around on the Master Slide or delete them from the slide. For example, to move the slide number to the top of the slide, click and drag the number placeholder to a new location.

Click & Drag

Release

End

How-To Hints

Preview Footer Placeholders

As you add items to the slide footer, watch the Preview area of the Header and Footer dialog box to see where the items will appear on the slide. In the lower part of the Preview area, the position of the item is highlighted.

Restoring Placeholders

After you delete a placeholder, you may decide later that you want it back. To restore missing placeholders, choose **Format**, **Master Layout** to open the Master Layout dialog box. Click to place check marks next to the items you want to restore to the layout. You can only restore items you have deleted. All of the other items are grayed out.

How to Add a Slide Background

When you are working on the Slide Master, it's a good idea to set up your background and color scheme at the same time. In general, when you use PowerPoint, it's easier to make changes that affect the entire presentation first, while you are working in the Slide Master, and then go back and make changes to the individual slides later after you've settled on a few standards. Although backgrounds were introduced in Chapter 2, this task goes beyond basic color choices to describe all the cool effects you can add to make your backgrounds more interesting.

Begin

1 Change Color Scheme

You can access the background colors by changing the slide color scheme. Choose **Format**, **Slide Color Scheme** to open the Color Scheme dialog box and click the **Custom** tab. Click **Background** and click **Change Color**. Choose a color and click **OK**. If desired, you can change other colors in the scheme. Click **Apply to All** to change the colors on all the slides.

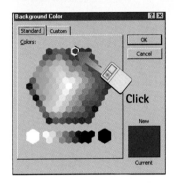

2 Change Background

Another way to change the background color is to choose **Format**, **Background** to open the Background dialog box. Click one of the color scheme colors or click the drop-down box and click **More Colors**. Choose a color and click **OK**. Click **Apply to All** to change all the slides.

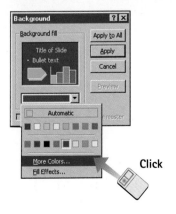

3 Add Gradient Effects

Choose **Fill Effects** in the Background dialog box and click the **Gradient** tab. Click **One color** or **Two colors** and select colors from the drop-down boxes. Click **Preset** to use a predefined gradient. Choose a **Shading Style** to change the gradient direction. Click **OK**, and then **Apply to All** when you are done.

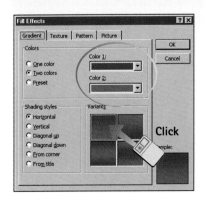

4 Add Texture

The **Texture** tab of the Fill Effects dialog box lets you choose from various textures such as marble or stone. **Click Other texture** if you want to add a texture located on your hard disk. Select a texture and click **OK**. Then click **Apply to All** to add the texture to all the slides.

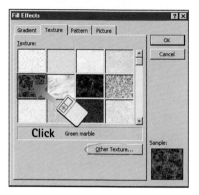

5 Add Pattern

In the **Pattern** tab, you can create a patterned background. Click a Pattern and use the **Foreground** and **Background** drop-down boxes to select the colors for your pattern. Click **OK**, and then **Apply to All** to add the pattern to all the slides in the presentation.

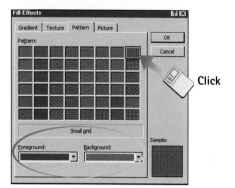

6 Add Picture

You can make any picture act as a slide background. Click the **Picture** tab and click **Select Picture**. Use the **Look in** drop-down box to choose a folder and click a file to select it. Click **Insert** and then **OK**. Then click **Apply to All** to add the background to all the slides.

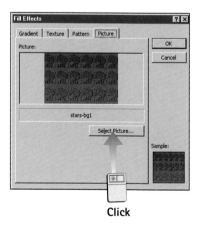

End

How-To Hints

Sizing Background Pictures

When you use a picture or texture for a slide background, make sure that you keep the end result in mind. The page size for a 35mm slide is 11.25×7.5, for an onscreen show it's 10×7.5. Be sure to choose **File**, **Page Setup** and check the size used in your presentation before you create background artwork. In your art program, make sure you set the correct page size, so your picture appears as intended when you add it to your PowerPoint slides.

How to Create a Title Master

The Title Master is intimately associated with the Slide Master. This master is used to format any slide that uses the Title Slide layout. Often this layout is just used for the first slide in the presentation, but you also might want to use it for section title slides to divide your presentation into defined segments. The Title Master is based on the Slide Master, but you can change it any way you want. Creating a title slide or slides that are different from the slides based on the Slide Master lets you add some visual diversity without sacrificing consistency.

Begin

1 Switch to Slide Master View

Before you can work on the Title Master, you must add it to the presentation. Most templates include a Title Master already, but if you start with a blank presentation, you must insert a new Title Master. You add a Title Master from within Slide Master view. Choose **View**, **Master**, **Slide Master**. (You also can hold down the **Shift** key and click the **Slide View** button.)

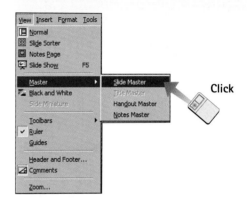

Click

2 Insert Title Master

In Slide Master view, Choose **Insert**, **New Title Master**. The Title Master appears. You'll notice that although the placeholders are different, much of the formatting you applied to the Slide Master is brought into the Title Master.

Click

3 Switch to Title Master View

Once you have inserted a Title Master, it appears as a choice on the View menu. From any view, choose, **View**, **Master**, **Title Master** to switch to the Title Master.

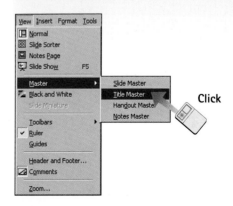

Click

4 Change Text

As with the Slide Master, you can change the fonts or placeholders within the Title Master. Click in a placeholder and choose **Format, Font** to open the Font dialog box and make type changes. To restore any deleted placeholders, choose **Format, Master Layout** to open the Master layout dialog box and click to place a check mark next to the item you want back in the layout.

Click

5 Change Colors

Choose **Format, Slide Color Scheme** or **Format, Background** to open their respective dialog boxes and change the background colors or add one of the background fill effects. You also can change any of the colors used in the fonts or bullets by using the commands on the Format menu.

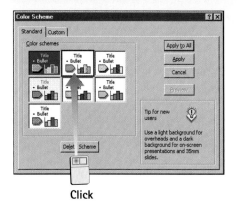

Click

End

How-To Hints

Master Your Changes

Sometimes when you make changes to the Master Slides (either the Slide Master or Title Master) it seems like they aren't reflected in the slides in your presentation. Although it may seem like it didn't work, remember that any changes you make in individual slides override the formatting you put into the Slide Master. To force the changes you make to the Slide Master to appear in a slide, choose **Format, Slide Layout** and click **Reapply**.

Get to the Title Master Quickly

If you set up a Title Master or start with a template that includes a Title Master, you can quickly switch from Slide Master View to Title Master View by clicking the **Next Slide** icon on the scrollbar. From Title Master View, you can switch back to Slide Master View just as easily by clicking the **Previous Slide** icon.

Where's My Master?

In Slide Master view, if the **Insert, Title Master** command is grayed out, you already have a Title Master in the presentation. From any view, choose **View, Master, Title Master** to get to the Title Master.

How to Add a Graphic to a Master

Quite a few companies are madly in love with their logo. If part of your company policy dictates that the company logo should appear anywhere and everywhere, the ability to put a graphic on a master will save you a whole lot of time. Although this task discusses adding a graphic to the slide-related master views, you can add your favorite images to the other master views as well. Any graphic you insert on the master appears in the corresponding part of the presentation. That beloved logo can be added to notes pages and handouts just as easily as it's inserted into slides.

Begin

1 Switch to Slide Master View

To access the Slide Master, choose **View**, **Master**, **Slide Master**. Or hold down the **Shift** key and click the **Slide View** button. (The ScreenTip changes to say Slide Master View.)

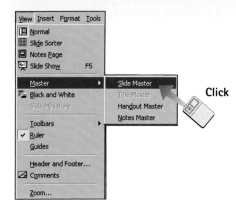

Click

2 Insert Picture

Choose **Insert**, **Picture** and click either **Clip Art** or **From File**, depending on where your graphic is located. (Inserting pictures is described in more detail in Chapter 4, "How to Work with Graphics," Tasks 1, "How to Add Clip Art," and 3, "Add Images from a File.") Select the graphic you want to use from the dialog box and click to insert it into the slide.

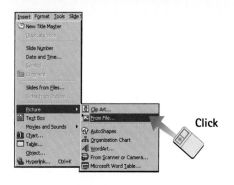

Click

3 Size and Place Picture

Once the graphic is in the Slide Master, you can click and drag the sizing handles to size and scale the graphic, or you can click and drag to move it around just as you would any other graphic. (Working with graphics is discussed in Chapter 4.)

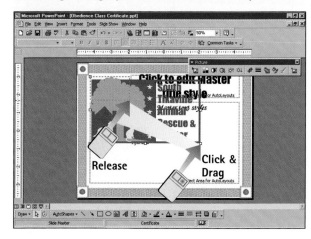

Release

Click & Drag

4 Format Picture

When you insert a graphic, the Picture toolbar appears. You can use the buttons on the toolbar to modify your graphic or right-click the graphic and choose **Format**, **Picture**.

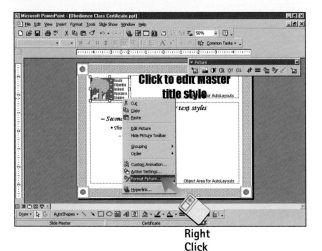

Right
Click

5 Add to Title Master

If you created a Title Master and then inserted a graphic on the Slide Master, you'll have to insert the graphic on the Title Master as described in step 2. The Title Master picks up much of its formatting at the time it's created. Additional formatting you later add to the Slide Master often must be added to the Title Master.

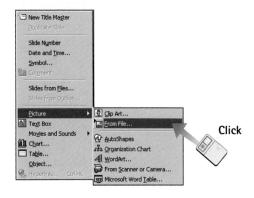

Click

End

How-To Hints

Omit Background Graphics

After you've inserted graphics on the Master slide, they appear on all the slides in the presentation. However, if there are certain slides that would look better without the graphic, you can remove it. Choose **Format**, **Background** and check **Omit background graphics from master**.

How to Change the Notes Master Layout

By using the Notes Master, you can make your notes look as similar or different from the standard layout as you please. Rather than the default large slide with text below, you could change it so you have just a thumbnail view of your slide with lots of room for extra-large–sized text. By sizing and moving the placeholders and changing the elements included in the layout, you can dramatically alter the look of the notes pages to suit your particular needs.

Begin

1 Switch to Notes Master View

To work on the Notes Master, choose **View**, **Master**, **Notes Master**. To work with text, you may need to zoom in to see what you're doing. Click the down arrow on the **Zoom** drop-down box to set the page to a higher magnification, such as 75 percent.

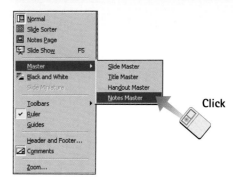

2 Change Master Text Styles

Click in one of the text levels and choose **Format**, **Font** to change the text in the dialog box. Or you can add bullets and numbering by choosing **Format**, **Bullets and Numbering** and choose a bullet or numbering style. Click **Preview** to see your changes on the slide. Click **OK** when you're done.

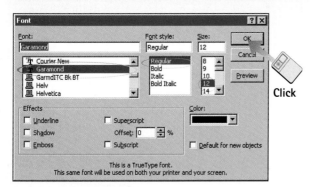

3 Change Color Scheme

To modify the colors used on your notes pages, choose **Format**, **Notes Color Scheme**. The Notes Color Scheme dialog box opens. If you plan to print your notes to a black-and-white laser printer, choose the grayscale scheme. Click **Apply to All**.

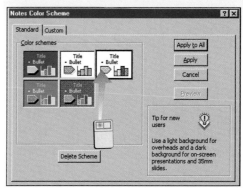

4 Change Header and Footers

Choose **View**, **Header and Footer** to open the Header and Footer dialog box and change the text that appears at the top and bottom of your notes pages. In the **Notes and Handouts** tab, click next to items to include a placeholder and enter text in the boxes as required. Click **Apply to All** when you're done.

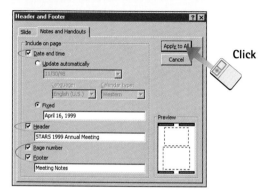

Click

5 Modify Placeholders

All of the placeholders on the Notes Page Master can be sized, scaled, formatted, or removed, just like other PowerPoint objects. (See Chapter 5, "How to Format Objects," for more information on formatting objects.)

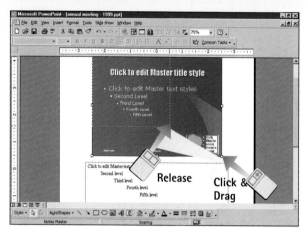

Release

Click & Drag

6 Restore Placeholders

f you delete a placeholder from the Notes Page Master, you can get it back. Choose **Format**, **Notes Master Layout** and click to add a check mark next to the items you want restored to the layout.

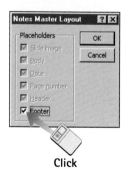

Click

End

How-To Hints

Creating Large Type Notes

Not all of us have 20/20 vision, so the standard speaker notes with itty-bitty 12-point type may be difficult to read, especially if you move around a lot when you speak. To create notes you can see from afar, reduce the size of the slide placeholder and increase the size of the text placeholder. Then change the font size in the Notes Body Area to whatever size seems comfortable to you.

View Notes

You don't see your headers, footers, or other elements you've added to your notes in the Notes pane of Normal view. If you want to see how your notes will look, choose **View**, **Notes Page** to switch to Notes Page view.

7

How to Create a Handout

Handouts are an unusual part of PowerPoint because they don't really exist anywhere except in Handout Master view. Because they are generated on-the-fly, you don't know exactly what they will look like until you make that fateful move and print them out. You aren't completely flying blind, however, because you can change how your handouts appear. Unlike Notes Pages, only your slides are placed in the handouts you set up by using Handout Master view. If you want your audience to see your speaker notes along with the slides, you should set up notes by using the Notes Master Page as described in step 6 and print out your notes as audience handouts instead.

Begin

1 Switch to Handout Master View

Choose **View, Master, Handout Master**. You see the Handout Master Page and the Handout Master toolbar.

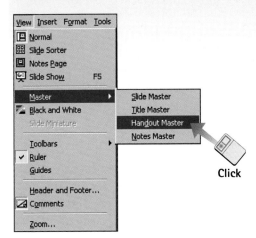

Click

2 Format Layout

Click the buttons on the Handout Master toolbar to change the layout. You can choose from 2, 3, 4, 6, and 9 slides per page or your outline.

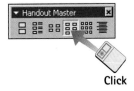

Click

3 Change Color Scheme

To change the colors used in your handouts, choose **Format, Handout Color Scheme**. If you are printing to a black-and-white laser printer, select the grayscale scheme and click **Apply**.

Click

4 Change Placeholders

You can size and scale certain placeholders. Except for the slide placeholders, all the other placeholders on the Handout Master can be manipulated like other PowerPoint objects. (See Chapter 5 for more information on formatting objects.)

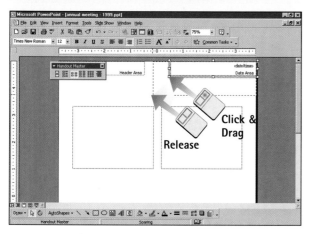

5 Print Handouts

You can only see your handouts by printing them. Choose **File**, **Print** to open the Print dialog box and change the **Print What** drop-down box to Handouts. If you are printing to a black-and-white laser printer, be sure to click **Grayscale** or **Pure black and white**.

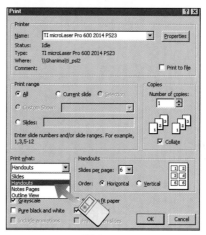

Click

6 Choose Slides Per Page

In the Handouts section, choose the number of slides you want to appear on the page. This setting overrides the setting you chose in the Handout Master. Click **OK** when you are done setting options.

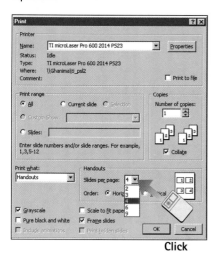

Click

End

How-To Hints

Never Use the Print Button

When you print handouts, don't use the **Print** button on the standard toolbar. You may not get printouts of your handouts; you may get slides (the default) or a printout based on the last print options you happened to set.

Outlines Versus Handouts

To create a handout that contains your outline, you use the Handout Master and choose the outline format on the toolbar. However, instead of choosing **Handout**, choose **Outline** from the **Print What** drop-down list in the Print dialog box.

Task

7

How to Work with Charts and Tables

*I*f you have a lot of data to present, sometimes text and pictures aren't the best means to describe it. The way you organize your information can make the difference between an audience that as a group seems to stare at you quizzically and one that nods appreciatively.

If you have a lot of interrelated words or numbers, a table can organize the data into a more comprehensible format. Adding a chart is a good way to graphically present numeric data because it shows relationships more clearly than a column of numbers. PowerPoint gives you lots of options. You can format your tables and charts so they convey the information as clearly as possible.

Keep your audience's needs in mind every step of the way. If your information would be best presented using a table, take the time to create one. If a chart would explain the information more effectively, you should delve into the thrills and chills of Microsoft Graph. In PowerPoint, the tools are all accessible and easy to use, so you should give them a try. After all, the snore follows the quizzical stare. A snoring audience may be well rested, but they probably won't think much of your presentation.

TASK *1*

How to Create a Chart

Charts are a great way to graphically depict complex data relationships. Plus, a chart is often more interesting for your audience to look at than a long column of numbers. You can add color and enhance a chart so that the information you want emphasized *is* emphasized. When you create a chart, consider what kind of information you are trying to communicate. For example, certain types of charts are better for displaying trends and others are better for showing numeric relationships. PowerPoint gives you lots of choices and lets you preview your options so you can find the best outlet for your charting impulses.

Begin

1 Use Placeholder

The easiest way to add a chart is to use a slide layout that contains a chart placeholder. Choose **Format**, **Slide Layout**, click one of the chart layouts and click **Apply**. Double-click the icon to insert the chart.

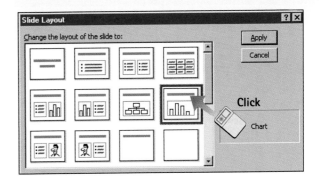

2 Insert Chart

You can insert a chart on any slide by choosing **Insert**, **Chart** or by clicking the **Insert Chart** button on the Standard toolbar. When you insert a chart, you see a datasheet with sample data and behind it a chart on your slide.

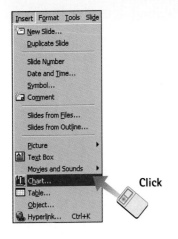

Click

3 Replace Sample Data

In the datasheet, highlight the sample data and press **Delete** to remove it. Type your new data into the datasheet. (If you don't want to remove the data first, you can just start typing to replace the highlighted text.) You see the changes appear on the chart. The first column and row are used for the labels that describe the numbers you enter.

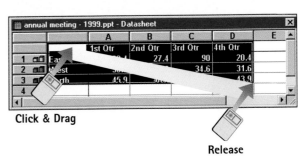

Click & Drag

Release

4 Adjust Placement

If you insert a chart by using the menu or toolbar button, the chart appears in the middle of the slide on top of anything else that might be there. Click on a chart border and drag it to move it to a new location, or click and drag a handle to change the size (use a corner handle to size proportionally).

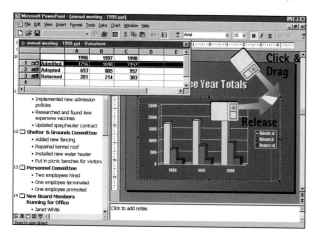

5 Close Datasheet

If the datasheet gets in the way, you can close it by clicking the close box in the upper-right corner. Choose **View**, **Datasheet** to make it reappear.

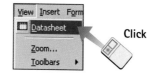

6 Return to PowerPoint

When you are working on the chart, you are using the Microsoft Graph program. The menus switch to Microsoft Graph commands. If you click outside of the graph, you return to PowerPoint and the menus return to normal. Double-clicking in the graph again takes you back into Microsoft Graph.

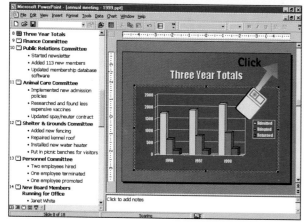

How-To Hints

Find Graph Commands

The first time you insert a chart, you may wonder what happened. It's sort of bizarre to have the menus change. When you insert a chart or double-click a chart, you are basically running a program (Microsoft Graph) within another program (PowerPoint). When you double-click to edit a graph, you enter Microsoft Graph; when you click outside the graph area, you exit Graph and return to PowerPoint. When Microsoft Graph is running, you can access its menus; when it's not, you can't. Also, certain commands are active only when the datasheet is visible.

End

TASK 2

How to Edit Chart Data

Data varies, and not every chart you create will conform to the default rows and columns set up in the datasheet when you create a new graph. If you've used any kind of spreadsheet program such as Microsoft Excel, you'll find that editing the Microsoft Graph datasheet works much the same way. Like Excel, the datasheet is made up of cells. You can edit data within the cells or add or delete columns and rows of cells.

By changing the rows and columns in your data sheet, you alter the way data appears on your chart. Microsoft Graph plots the data in your data sheet in order. For example, to plot monthly data in sequence, make sure you enter the months chronologically.

Begin

1 Select Data

To select the entire datasheet, click the square in the upper-left corner. Clicking the letter at the top of a column selects the entire column and clicking the number at the beginning of a row highlights the entire row.

annual meeting - 1999.ppt - Datasheet					
Click	A	B	C	D	E
	1996	1997	1998		
1 Admitted	1756	1898	2152		
2 Adopted	653	805	957		
3 Returned	201	214	303		
4					

2 Edit Data

After you select an entire row, column, or the datasheet, press **Delete** to remove the data. Anytime you want to change data in a cell, just click in the cell and type in new data. You see your changes reflected in the graph.

annual meeting - 1999.ppt - Datasheet					
	A	B	C	D	E
	1996	1997	1998		
1 Admitted	1756	1898	2152		
2 Adopted	653	805	957		
3 Returned	201	214	303		
4					

3 Insert Cells

To insert cells, place your cursor where you want the new cells. Choose **Insert**, **Cells** to open the Insert dialog box. Click either **Shift cells right** or **Shift cells left**, depending on where you want the new cell. Click **OK**.

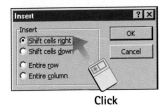

Click

4 Insert Rows

Inserting rows works much the same way as inserting cells. To insert a new row, place your cursor below where you want the row. Choose **Insert**, **Cells**. Click **Entire row** and click **OK**. A new row appears above the existing row.

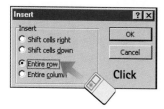

Click

5 Insert Columns

To insert a column, place your cursor to the right of where you want the new column. Choose **Insert**, **Cells**. Click **Entire Column** and click **OK**. A new column appears to the left of the original column.

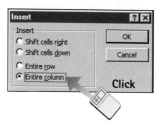

Click

6 Change Column Width

To change the width of the columns in the datasheet, choose **Format**, **Column Width** to display the Column Width dialog box. Enter a number in the column width box (this number is the number of characters that the cell holds). Or you can click the **Best Fit** button to adjust the cell size to the data.

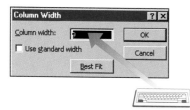

End

How-To Hints

Move Around the Datasheet

If you don't want to use your mouse, you can use the arrow keys to move around in the cells of the datasheet.

Enter Information More Quickly

You can use keyboard shortcuts to enter information into the datasheet more quickly. Click and type in a cell to add data. Press **Tab** to move to the right one cell. Press **Shift+Tab** to move one cell to the left. The selected cell always appears with a thick dark border.

How to Format a Chart

Depending on your data, you may want to change the chart from the default bar chart. For example, you would use a pie chart to show how sections relate to a whole. Sometimes people also use the pieces of the pie to show percentages and how they relate to one another. Bar charts are good for making comparisons between values, whereas line charts are used to show information about trends over a period of time. Before you choose a chart type, think about the data and what information you want it to convey. Once you know what you want to say, it's easy to use the PowerPoint tools to help you communicate it clearly.

Begin

1 Change Chart Type

To change the type of chart, choose **Chart, Chart Type** to open the Chart Type dialog box. In the Standard tab click a chart in the **Chart type** area and then click a chart under **Chart sub-type**. Click the **Press and Hold to View Sample** button to see what it looks like. Or click the **Custom Types** tab and click a chart in the **Chart type** area. A sample appears in the Sample box. Click **OK** when you have selected a chart type.

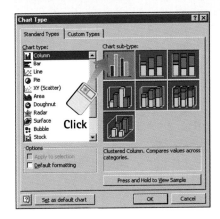

2 Change Chart Titles

Adding titles to your chart helps your audience interpret the data more easily. Choose **Chart, Chart Options** to open the Chart Options dialog box and click the **Titles** tab. Type titles for the chart and the appropriate axes in the boxes and click **OK** when you are finished.

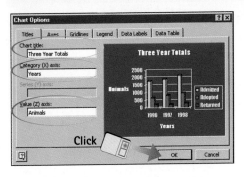

3 Change Axes

In the Chart Options dialog box, click the **Axes** tab. Click next to an axis to display it in the chart. In the Category (X) axis, you can choose from **Automatic**, **Category**, or **Time scale**, depending on how you want data displayed.

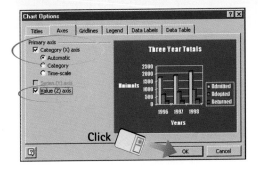

4 Change Legend

Unless the information is obvious, most charts should include a legend. In the Chart Options dialog box, click the **Legend** tab. Click **Show Legend** to include the legend. Click the place where you want it to appear. For more precise positioning, you also can click and drag the legend to a new location.

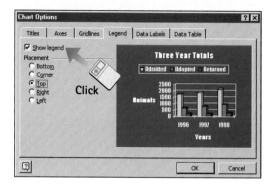

5 Change Labels

You also can add labels that appear within your chart that give the actual values depicted in the chart. In the Chart Options dialog box, click the **Data Labels** tab. Click a type of label or **None** to turn labels off.

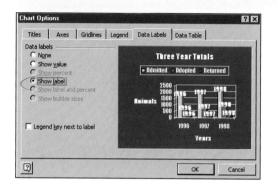

6 Add Data Table

A data table is a table showing the numbers from which the chart is derived. In the Chart Options dialog box, click the **Data Table** tab. Click **Show data table** to include the table below your chart. Click **Show legend keys** to include legend information as well. Choose **OK** when you are done setting options.

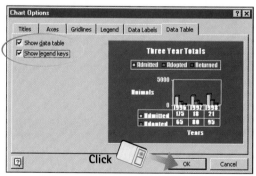

End

How-To Hints

Add Gridlines

In the Chart Options dialog box, click the **Gridlines** tab and click **Options** to display gridlines on the axes in your chart. A preview window shows how the gridlines will appear in the chart.

Know Your X, Y, and Zs

If you've forgotten Cartesian coordinates from 8th grade math class, here's a cheat sheet. The x-axis is generally the horizontal axis. The y-axis is the vertical axis. And the z-axis is the third axis in a three-dimensional chart.

Understand Chart Terms

A *data series* is the data being plotted on the chart. It corresponds to a row or column on the datasheet. In the default chart, East, West, and North are the data series. A chart can have one or more data series, and you'll notice that in the bar chart, each data series has its own color. Unlike a bar chart, a pie chart only has one data series. The *data categories* are the data on the x-axis (the quarters in the default chart).

How to Modify Chart Elements

Almost any aspect of your chart can be changed. Among other items, you can change how the data series, labels, legend, gridlines, background, axes, and numbers appear. In fact, because of the dizzying array of changes you can make, formatting a chart can be very time-consuming. Virtually anything you can select (and even a few things you can't) can be changed. But in general, right-clicking a chart item presents a pop-up menu that lists the commands you can use to modify the item. And if you create something truly hideous, you can always click the Undo button to restore your chart to its former glory.

Begin

1 Format Numbers

You can change how your numbers appear by applying a number format to them. In the datasheet, highlight cells and choose **Format, Number** to open the Format number dialog box. Choose a number format from the **Category** list, or choose **Custom** to create your own number format.

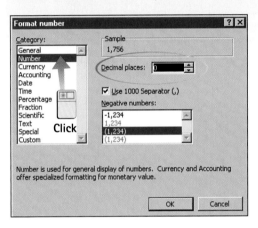

2 Change Data Series

The data series can be plotted from the data that appears in the rows or columns of your datasheet. To plot the data from the rows, click the **By Row** button on the Standard toolbar or choose **Data, Series in Rows**. To plot the data from columns, click the **By Column** button or choose **Data, Series in Columns**.

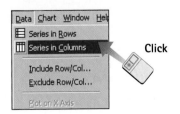

3 Select Chart Items

Click the item in the chart or choose the item from the Chart Objects drop-down box. Choose the appropriate command from the Format menu or right-click the item and choose **Format**.

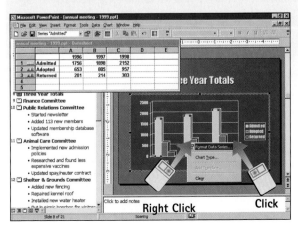

4 Change Chart Items

After you select the Format command for an item, a dialog box appears with the options you can change for that particular chart element. Although the options depend on the item you select, you can change the color of almost all elements and add fill effects. You can change the font, style, and size of text elements as well.

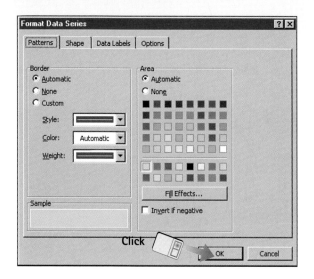

Click OK

5 Change 3D View

If you've selected one of the 3D charts, you can change the appearance of the 3D effect. Choose **Chart**, **3-D View** to open the 3-D View dialog box. You can change values that affect the elevation, rotation, perspective, scaling, and axes of the chart.

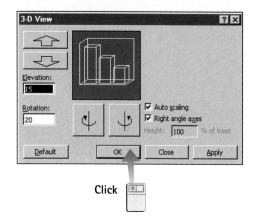

Click

6 Add Trendline

If you are showing trends, you may want to add a trendline to your chart. Select the data series for which you want to show trends and choose **Chart**, **Add Trendline** to open the Add Trendline dialog box. Click the **Type** tab to set the type of trend or the **Options** tab to add trendline and forecast information. Click **OK**.

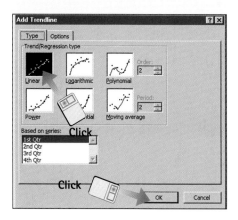

Click

Click

How-To Hints

Fix Chart Font Sizes

The fonts in Microsoft Graph charts scale proportionally with the chart if you change its size. If you want your fonts to remain a fixed size, select the **Chart Area** from the Chart Object drop-down box and choose **Format**, **Selected Chart Area**, click the **Font** tab, and remove the check mark next to **Auto scale**.

Delete a Chart

To delete a chart, make sure that you are in PowerPoint, not Microsoft Graph (if you are in Microsoft Graph, click outside of the chart to return to PowerPoint). Then click to select the chart and press the **Delete** key.

End

How to Create an Organization Chart

Organizational charts, or "org charts," are traditionally used to show the relationships among people in a company. By looking at an org chart, you can determine who reports to whom. However, you can use org charts to describe other relationships as well. For example, most hard disks, help files, or Web sites are set up in some form of tree hierarchy. (Everything branches off the root drive, main screen, or home page.) An org chart can be a good tool to describe these hierarchies. For example, you might use an org chart as a site map to help Web surfers keep track of where they are in a Web presentation.

Begin

1 Use Placeholder

The easiest way to add an org chart is to use the slide layout that includes a placeholder for one. Choose **Format**, **Slide Layout** to open the Slide Layout dialog box, click the **Organization Chart** layout, and click **Apply**. Double-click the icon to insert the org chart.

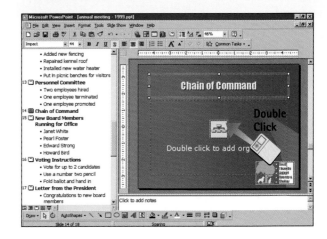

2 Insert Organization Chart

You can insert an org chart on any slide by choosing **Insert**, **Picture**, **Organization Chart**. The Microsoft Organization chart program runs in a new window with a sample org chart in the center of the screen. While you work on the chart, you use the Microsoft Organization chart program. When you exit the program, the chart is placed on your slide.

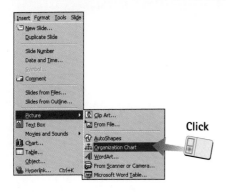

Click

3 Enter Information

Click and type in the boxes to replace the sample text with names or items. By default, each box lets you enter four lines: one for the name, one for the title, and two for comments.

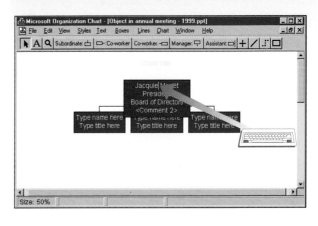

4 Adjust Placement

You can easily change the position of the boxes, but you need to remember that you are working within a hierarchy. You click and drag to move a box. However, because all boxes are related, you must drag the box over another box before you release the mouse button so you change its relationship within the hierarchy.

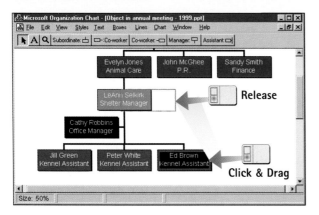

5 Return to PowerPoint

Unlike Microsoft Graph, Microsoft Organization Chart runs outside of PowerPoint, not within it. To return to PowerPoint, you must either close or exit. Choose **File**, **Close and Return to <filename>** or **File**, **Exit and Return to <filename>**, where <filename> is the name of your PowerPoint file. The new org chart appears on your slide.

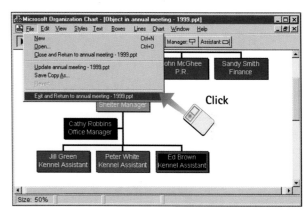

End

How-To Hints

Understand Microsoft Organization Chart

Microsoft Organization Chart has been included with PowerPoint through several versions, and it's starting to show its age. Unlike most PowerPoint components, the Organization Chart program doesn't behave very much like PowerPoint itself, so it's more difficult to guess how to use it. Spend a little time learning its idiosyncrasies and save often. As an elderly program, it can be temperamental at times.

Change Default Options

If you grow weary of the default 4-box org chart, choose **Edit**, **Options**. In the Options dialog box, you can change how the Organization Chart program appears when it starts.

TASK 6

How to Modify Organization Chart Elements

Any org chart you create is basically a bunch of boxes connected together with lines. The way the lines and boxes appear in relation to one another indicates the relationship between the names entered in the boxes. You can create four types of relationships: manager, co-worker, assistant, and subordinate. When you add a box to the org chart, you need to think about how it relates to the box to which you're connecting it. A manager box has subordinates reporting to it. Co-workers share one manager, and assistants report to managers.

Begin

1 Add and Delete Boxes

To add a box, click the button that corresponds to the type of box you want to add. Click the box to which you want the new box to connect. To delete a box, click to select the box and press the **Delete** key.

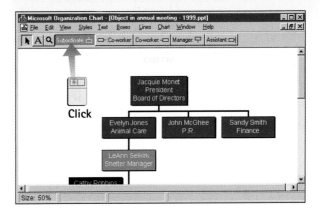

2 Add Multiple Boxes

You can add a number of boxes at the same time by clicking the box button more than once. Click the button the number of times equivalent to the number of boxes you want to add. Click the box to which you want to add the new boxes.

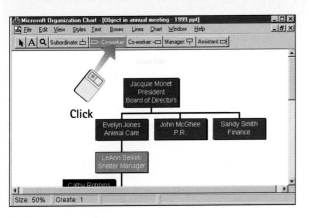

3 Select Elements

You can use selection commands to select all of a particular type of box, which can be handy in a complex org chart. Choose **Edit**, **Select**, and choose a part of the chart to select. You also can select items by level. Choose **Edit**, **Select Levels** to display the Select Levels dialog box and type levels into the boxes.

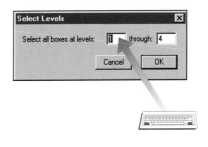

4 Convert Elements

You can change box types by clicking and dragging to move a box or groups of boxes within the hierarchy. The mouse pointer changes to show into what position you're moving a box. An arrow indicates a co-worker; a box with a line indicates a subordinate.

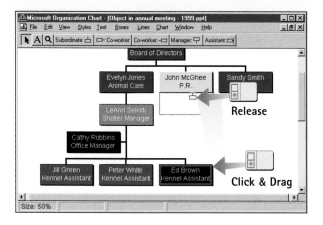

5 Change Styles

You can change how a group of boxes appears. (A group is a set of boxes that all are connected to the same manager.) Hold down the **Shift** key and click to select the boxes in the group. Choose **Styles** and choose a new arrangement.

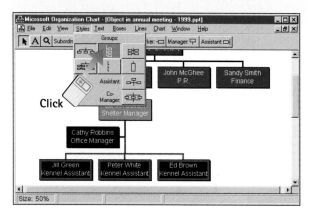

End

How-To Hints

Use Shortcuts

If you have to add a lot of boxes, you can use keyboard shortcuts to speed up matters. Select a box and use the **F2** key to create a subordinate, **F3** to create a co-worker before the selected box, **F4** to create a co-worker after the selected box, **F5** to create a manager, and **F6** to create an assistant.

How to Format an Organization Chart

The default color of the boxes in the Organization Chart program often are a less than attractive addition to most presentations. Fortunately, you can dramatically change the appearance of your org chart by making a few simple changes. You can change how the text, boxes, lines, and fills look and add effects such as shadows and borders to your boxes to make them stand out.

Begin

1 Format Text

You can change the font used in any box. Click and drag to highlight specific text or select the box to select all the text in the box. Choose **Text**, **Font** to open the Font dialog box. Click to select a new font, font style, or size from the lists. Click **OK** to apply the changes.

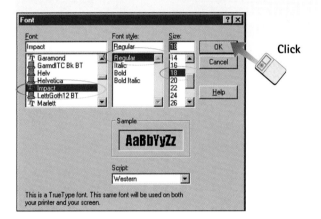

Click

2 Format Boxes

You can change the box border style or add drop shadows to boxes. Click to select a box and choose **Boxes**, **Border Style** or **Boxes**, **Border Line Style** and select a style to change how the border looks. Choose **Boxes**, **Shadow** and choose a shadow type to add a drop shadow to the box.

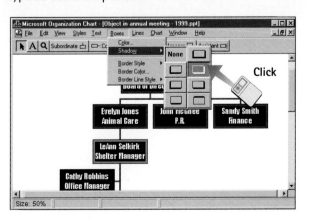

Click

3 Change Lines

To change a line, click to select it. You can select all the lines in the org chart by choosing **Edit**, **Select**, **Connecting Lines**. Choose **Lines**, **Thickness** or **Line**, **Style** and choose a new style to change the appearance of the lines.

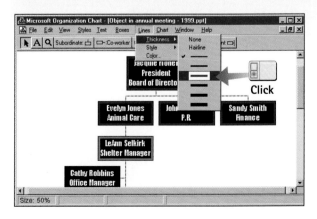

Click

4 Change Colors

You can change the colors of text, boxes, and lines. To change text, select it and choose **Text, Color**. To change a box, select it and choose **Boxes, Color**. To change a line, choose **Lines, Color**. In the Color dialog box that appears, choose a color and click **OK**.

Click

5 Copy Setup

Once you get a box formatted just the way you like it, you can copy its attributes to another box or boxes. Click the box with the attributes you want to copy. Choose **Edit, Copy Setup**. Click to select the box to receive the attributes (or **Shift+click** to select multiple boxes). Click **Edit, Paste Setup**.

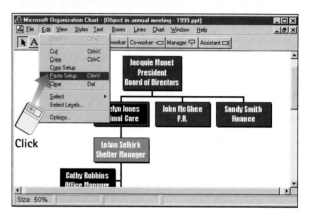

Click

6 Change Background Color

You can change the background color of the entire organization chart as well. Choose **Chart, Background Color**. In the Color dialog box that displays, select a color and click **OK**. (Note that if you don't change the background color, the org chart appears to have no background on the slide.)

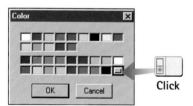

Click

End

How-To Hints

Draw Stuff

The Organization Chart program includes very limited drawing tools. Choose **View, Show Draw Tools**. Buttons for drawing horizontal and vertical lines, diagonal lines, connector lines, and squares appear on the right side of the toolbar. Click a button and then click and drag to draw a new object.

Exit Without Changing

The org chart program takes some getting used to and, unlike PowerPoint itself, you only get one undo level. Sometimes it's better to just cut your losses and start over. In these situations, choose **File, Exit** and click **No** when the program asks if you want to update the object.

How to Create a Table

Tables are a great way to convey a lot of information in a small space. Tables filled with text can say in one small area what would take many sentences (or slides) to explain. Unlike a graph or an organizational chart, tables aren't generally used to show relationships or trends. If you need to present numeric data, you use a table when you want your audience to focus on the numbers themselves as opposed to the relationships among them. With a table, your audience can read down the columns or across the rows to compare specific values. You can use the table formatting tools to help your audience hone in on the most important information.

Begin

1 Use Placeholder

The easiest way to add a table is to use the Table Slide Layout. Choose **Format**, **Slide Layout** to open the Slide Layout dialog box. Then, click **Table** and click **Apply**. Double-click the icon to insert the table. You also can choose **Insert**, **Table** to insert a table on any slide.

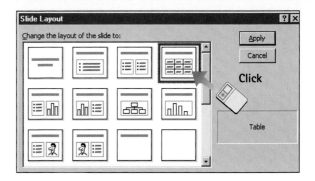

2 Enter Rows and Columns

When you insert a table, the Insert Table dialog box appears. Enter the number of rows and columns you want in the table and click **OK**. The table and the Table and Borders toolbar appear.

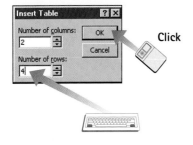

3 Draw Table

Choose **View**, **Toolbars**, **Table and Borders**. Click the **Draw Table** button. Click and drag to create a one-cell table. Click and drag to create horizontal and vertical lines that divide the table into as many rows and columns as you want.

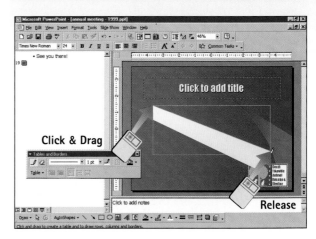

4 Enter Information

If you're using the table drawing tool, press **Esc** to return your cursor to an I-beam. Click in a cell and type your text. Press **Tab** to move to the next cell. Press **Shift+Tab** to move to a previous cell.

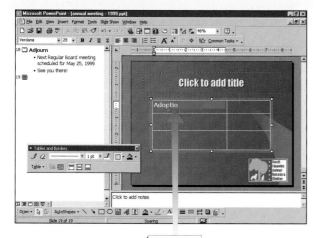

5 Select Items

Click and drag to highlight the text. To delete it, press the **Delete** key. Or you can type in new text that replaces the highlighted text. To select the whole table, rows, or columns, choose the appropriate command from the Table drop-down menu on the Tables and Borders toolbar.

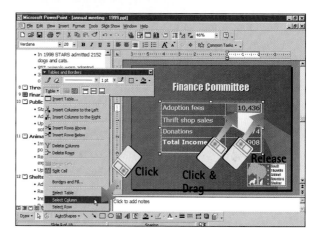

6 Navigate the Table

In addition to Tab and Shift+Tab, you can use other keys to work in tables. The down arrow moves you down a row and the up arrow moves you up a row. The **Enter** key creates a new paragraph within the cell and pressing the **Tab** key at the end of the table inserts a row.

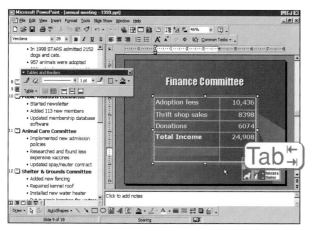

End

How-To Hints

Insert a Tab in a Table

The Tab key is used to move around cells in a table, but what if you actually want to put a Tab in a cell? To add a Tab character within a cell, press **Ctrl+Tab**.

Find That Table

If you look in Outline view, you won't find any indication that you created a table. You may not care, except for the fact that anything that doesn't appear in the outline isn't included in a spell check. So proofread carefully.

9

How to Modify a Table

If you've ever used a table function in a word processor or dealt with formatting cells in a spreadsheet program, you'll find that PowerPoint's table feature is similar. You can easily change the number of rows and columns or change their size. You also can use PowerPoint's formatting tools to change the text and the table itself, so it looks just the way you want. Unlike most of the tables you've probably worked on before, when you create a PowerPoint table, you get to play with color. Bear in mind that adding color can be dangerous, however. Check out the tables in a few 4-color magazines to get ideas on how you can use color effectively in your tables.

Begin

1 Add Rows and Columns

To add columns or rows, place your cursor in a cell next to where you want the new row or column to appear. In the Tables and Borders toolbar, click the **Table** drop-down menu and choose **Insert Columns to the Left**, **Insert Columns to the Right**, **Insert Rows Above**, or **Insert Rows Below**, depending on what you want to do.

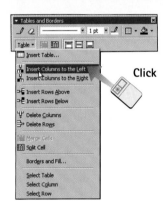

Click

2 Modify Rows and Columns

To delete columns or rows, click in a cell or highlight multiple rows or columns to delete. Click **Table**, **Delete Columns** or **Table**, **Delete Rows**. To change the size of a row or column, click a border and drag it.

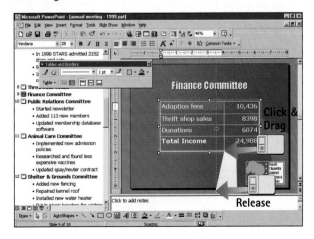

3 Merge and Split Cells

You can join cells together or split one cell into two cells. To merge cells, highlight the cells you want to become one. Choose **Table**, **Merge Cells**. To split cells, put your cursor in the cell to be divided and choose **Table**, **Split Cells**.

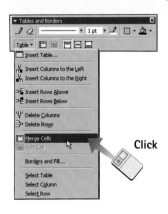

Click

4 Edit Borders and Shading

You can add, remove, or change the formatting of a cell or the entire table. Select the area to be changed and click the **Outside Borders** drop-down menu from the Tables and Borders toolbar to add or remove borders. Click **Border Style** or **Border Width** to change the appearance of the lines. Click **Border Color** to change the line color, and click **Fill Color** to change the fill of the cells in the selected area. Or click **Table**, **Borders and Fill** to make changes all at once.

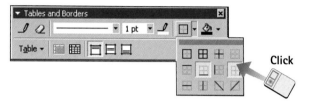

Click

5 Format Table Data

You can change the appearance of the text within the table by highlighting it and choosing commands in the Format menu as described in Chapter 3, "How to Work with Text."

Click

6 Change Vertical Alignment

In addition to formatting text horizontally within the cell by using the standard alignment commands, you can also format it vertically within the cell. Highlight the text and click the **Align Top**, **Center Vertically**, or **Align Bottom** buttons on the Tables and Borders toolbar.

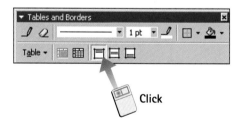

Click

End

How-To Hints

Format a Table Effectively

When you format a table, remember it has to be read by people sitting far, far away. Don't make your tables too tiny and keep them as simple as possible. Be sure to leave enough room around the text in the cells to make them easy to read. Also try making your headings bold to help them stand out from the rest of the table.

Add Color Thrills

All the Fill effects you have for slides are available for tables too. With a little time and creativity you can create a really cool table.

Switch to Word

If you have great tabular ambitions, you may find the built-in PowerPoint table features somewhat lacking. For more table-making power, use Microsoft Word to create your table and then bring it into PowerPoint.

Task

How to Add Multimedia Effects

*I*n life, you get precious few opportunities to make anything fly. Except for those who create model airplanes, parachute, or throw things, on a day-to-day basis most people don't do much to defy gravity. When you create an onscreen presentation in PowerPoint, however, you can make any object or slide fly, zoom, crawl, peek, flash, or dissolve (and more).

These transition and animation effects are cool, but there's more: You can include other types of multimedia in your presentation as well. The term *multimedia* is bandied about a lot, but really all it refers to is the combination of sound, graphics, animation, and video. With PowerPoint, you can add any or all of these elements to create a presentation that dazzles all the senses.

Of course, like most of the PowerPoint tools, you can easily go overboard with PowerPoint's multimedia effects. As with clip art and fonts, more is *not* better. Most people overuse effects in their presentations resulting in a sensory overload that at first bewilders and then annoys your audience. As always, temper your creative fun with a little common sense. The laser noise might be cool once. But only once. Stick to one or two non-distracting transitions and animations. Sound and motion can have almost a visceral effect, so be very sure when you add them that they enhance rather than detract from your message. The most important part of your presentation should be *you*; not the noises being emitted from your laptop.

How to Add Transition Effects

Anyone who has watched television news has seen transition effects. For example, when you see the weather map swish from left to right to switch from the temperature map to the precipitation map, you're seeing a transition in action. These effects, which used to require incredibly costly video equipment, are now common in onscreen presentations. In PowerPoint, you can add transition effects to one or all of the slides in your presentation with just a click of a mouse.

Begin

1 Switch to Slide Sorter View

The easiest way to add transitions is in Slide Sorter view. To switch views, click the **Slide Sorter View** button at the bottom-left corner of the display.

Click

2 Add Slide Transition

Click a slide to select it. To select multiple slides hold down the **Ctrl** key and click. To select contiguous slides hold down **Shift** and click. Click the down arrow on the Slide Transition effects drop-down box. Click to add a transition.

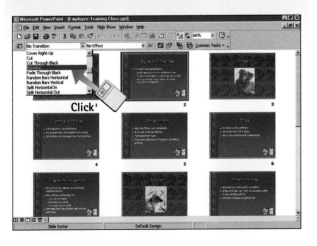

Click

3 Set Sound

For more transition options, choose **Slide Show, Slide Transition** to open the Slide Transition dialog box. In the Sound area, click the drop-down box to choose a sound to accompany the transition. Click **Loop until next sound** if you want the sound to continue until the next sound begins.

Click

4 Set Timings

In the Slide Transition dialog box, you also can set slide timings. Click **On mouse click** to move to the next slide when you click the mouse. Or click **Automatically after** and specify a time the slide remains on the screen before advancing automatically.

5 Rehearse Timings

Another way to set timings is by rehearsing your presentation. PowerPoint records the amount of time you spend on each slide. To rehearse timings, click **Slide Show, Rehearse Timings**. Go through the show and when PowerPoint asks if you want to record the new timings, click **Yes**.

Click

End

How-To Hints

Use Sound Humanely

Although sounds can get an audience's attention, overusing sounds becomes irritating remarkably quickly. The cash register sound that gets a little giggle the first time out (depending on the context) is downright aggravating the third or fourth time. Here's one rule you should never, ever break: Whatever you do, don't annoy your audience.

How to Add Animation

In many ways, PowerPoint's animation effects are similar to its transition effects. When you set transitions, you control how slides move from one another. When you add animation effects, you control how your slide objects move onto the slide. You can animate the text, pictures, and charts to help focus on important points. One way to use animation, for example, is to add bullet points to a slide incrementally as you talk about them and dim the bullet points you've discussed. As with transitions, you have a lot of choices, but you should use animation effects sparingly, judiciously, and only when they will *enhance* the message you are trying to communicate.

Begin

1 Add Preset Animation

The easiest way to add animation is to select an object and choose **Slide Show, Preset Animation**. Highlight an animation type from the submenu and release the mouse button. To see the animation in action, choose **Slide Show, Animation Preview**.

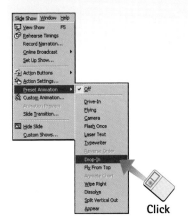

Click

2 Add Custom Animation

For more control over the animation, choose **Slide Show, Custom Animation** to open the Custom Animation dialog box. You see a thumbnail view of your slide and a list of the objects that can be animated. Place a check mark next to the objects you want to animate.

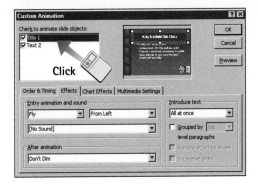

Click

3 Set Order and Timing

In the Custom Animation dialog box, select the **Order & Timing** tab and click the up and down arrows to change the order in which the objects are animated. Click **On mouse click** to have objects move when you click the mouse or click **Automatically** and set the number of seconds you want to elapse between the animations.

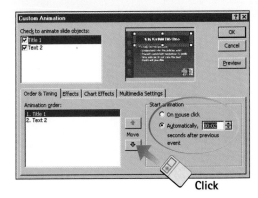

Click

4 Add Animation Effects and Sound

Next, click the **Effects** tab. Click an object in the list and choose an animation and an associated sound (if desired). You also can change how the text is introduced and what happens when the animation is finished.

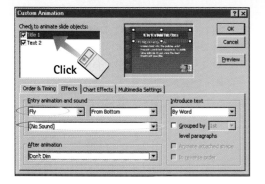

Click

5 Animate Charts

To animate a chart, click the chart to select it and choose **Slide Show, Custom Animation**. In the **Chart Effects** tab, place a check mark next to the elements you want to animate. You can change how chart elements are introduced and their animation settings.

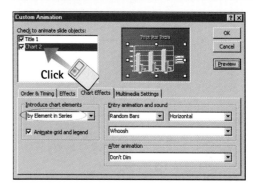

Click

6 Preview Animation

In any of the tabs in the Custom Animation dialog box, you can click **Preview** to see your settings in action. Often you find an effect (most notably sound) that seemed like a good idea, isn't so appealing after all.

Click

End

How-To Hints

Add Effects That Work

As with anything else, there are good uses for animation and not so good uses. One effective way to use animation is to illustrate a process. For example, if you need to show a flow chart, you can animate the AutoShapes that make up the flow chart and bring them in incrementally as you describe the steps in the procedure.

Choose the Right Color

As mentioned earlier, another useful way to use animation is to "build" a bulleted list incrementally and then dim the bullets that have been discussed. However, be careful what color you choose for the dimmed bullets. Try selecting a color that is a few shades lighter than the background, so the bullets appear ghosted. Choosing the wrong color can be confusing if the bullet actually appears emphasized rather than grayed or ghosted out.

How to Insert Sound, Video, and Animations

For a full multimedia experience, you may want to delve into the world of sound, animation, and video. PowerPoint has its own built-in animation, but you also can add animation, video, and sound files just as easily as you can add clip art and other image files. Just right-click an object, choose **Custom Animation** from the pop-up menu, and start experimenting with the options.

Begin

1 Add a Sound from Gallery

Choose **Insert**, **Movies and Sounds**, **Sound from Gallery** to open the Insert Sound dialog box. Click a sound category, choose the sound you want, and then click the **Insert Clip** button.

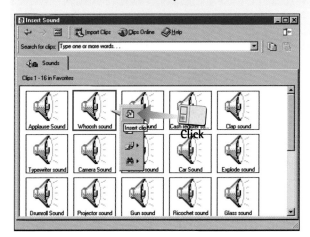

2 Insert from File

PowerPoint can play sound files that have a file type of .WAV, .MID, .RMI, .AU, .AIF, .AIFF, and .AIFC. To insert a sound file, click **Insert**, **Movies and Sounds**, **Sound from File** to open the Insert Sound dialog box. Click the **Look in** drop-down box to choose a folder. Click to select a filename and choose **OK**.

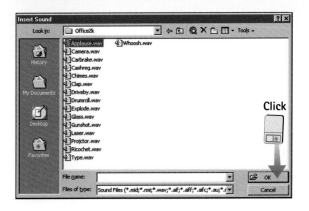

3 Add a Movie

You add a movie the same way you add sounds. Choose **Insert**, **Movies and Sounds** and either **Movie from Gallery** or **Movie from File**. Choose **Yes** or **No** if you want the movie to play automatically.

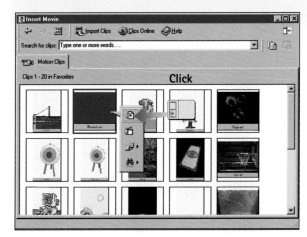

4 Resize Video

You can size the video by dragging the corner handles. Because it is bitmapped artwork, be careful not to size it too large or the image will degrade. For best results, click it and choose **Format**, **Picture** to open the Format Picture dialog box and click the **Size** tab. Click **Best scale for slide show** and choose the destined display resolution.

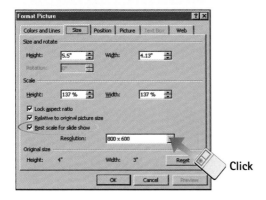

Click

5 Set Options

Right-click a sound or video and choose **Action Settings** in the pop-up menu to change how the file is activated. Click the **Object action** drop-down box on the **Mouse Click** and **Mouse Over** tabs to change how the file reacts to mouse actions.

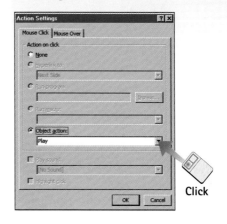

Click

6 Add an Animated GIF File

Another way to add animation is to add an animated GIF file. Choose **Insert**, **Picture**, **Clip Art** and the Insert ClipArt dialog box appears. Click the **Motion Clips** tab and click to select a clip. Click the **Insert Clip** button. The animation plays when you run the slide show.

7 Add a Media Clip

If PowerPoint won't import a certain type of media file, you can insert it as an object and have Window's Media Player run it. Choose **Insert**, **Object** to open the Insert Object dialog box and click **Media Clip** from the Object Type list. Choose **Create from file**, type the pathname, and click **OK**. Click outside the icon to return to PowerPoint. Double-clicking the icon plays the clip.

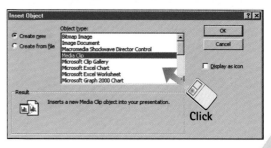

Click

End

How to Add a CD-ROM Audio Track

If you're an audiophile, you've probably noticed that sound files are huge. Even short sounds can occupy many megabytes. If you want to include music in your presentation, you may be disappointed to find that you need to buy a new hard disk just to store your sound file. But there is another way: You can insert sound directly from a CD-ROM track. As long as the CD-ROM is in the CD-ROM drive, PowerPoint can play the file. This feature can be useful if you want to have music playing while people file into the room or during breaks. Who knows—the right music may be able to soothe the savage audience.

Begin

1 Insert Track

Although you don't need to have the CD-ROM in the drive, it must be inserted during the presentation for the sound to play. To insert a track choose **Insert**, **Movies and Sounds**, **Play CD Audio Track** to open the Movie and Sound Options dialog box.

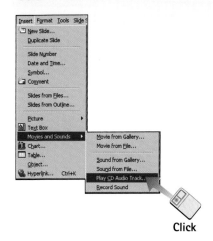

Click

2 Set Track Options

Click **Loop until stopped** if you want the CD-ROM track to play continuously. Use the spin arrows or enter a number in the **Track** boxes to select a starting and ending track to play.

Click

3 Set Timing Options

You can click start and end times, which allows you to do some judicious audio editing. Enter a start and end time into the **At** boxes. Click **OK**.

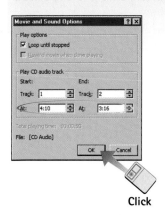

Click

4 Play Automatically

Click **OK** to insert the track. Choose **Yes** or **No** when the message asks if you want the sound to play automatically. A CD-ROM icon appears on your slide.

5 Preview Music

You can double-click the CD-ROM icon to play the sound or right-click the icon and choose **Play Sound** from the pop-up menu.

Right Click

6 Change Settings

If you decide to change the tracks you want to play, right-click the icon and choose **Edit, Sound Object**. The Sound Options dialog box appears again. Change the settings as described in steps 2 and 3. Click **OK**.

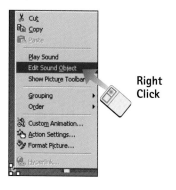

Right Click

How-To Hints

Access More Options

To change how your sound or video files play, right-click the icon and choose **Custom Animation** from the pop-up menu. In the Multimedia Settings tab, you can set options to control when the object plays or click **More Options** for other settings, such as looping a movie or rewinding it when it's done.

End

How to Record Narration and Sound

By using multimedia features such as narration and video, you can create a presentation that presents itself. Self-running presentations like these can be useful for training classes or any situation where people need information, but aren't able to attend a formal meeting or presentation.

To record narration, you need a microphone. You can either record a narrative that runs throughout the show or record short snippets that run in certain slides. Think about your audience, however. If some people who run the presentation aren't using computers with sound cards, you may want to use notes pages to add your commentary instead.

Begin

1 Set Microphone Level

To begin recording narration choose **Slide Show**, **Record Narration**. The Record Narration dialog box opens. Before you dive in however, click **Set Microphone Level** and follow the instructions in the Microphone Check dialog box to set the recording level correctly. Click **OK**.

Click

2 Change Quality

Next, click **Change Quality** to open the Sound Selection dialog box and set the recording quality. Higher quality recordings take up more disk space and vice versa, so consider your situation. Click the **Name** drop-down box to choose a preset quality level. Or click the **Attributes** drop-down box to set your own. Click **OK** when you are finished.

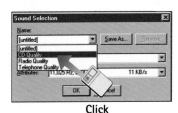

Click

3 Link Narration

Because sound files can be huge, you may want the narration to be a separate file that is linked to the presentation, rather than stored within it. Click **Link narrations in** to link the file. The file is stored in the same folder as your presentation unless you click **Browse** and choose a new folder.

4 Record Narration

When you are done setting options, click **OK**. The show runs. Speak into the microphone and advance through the presentation. When you are finished, a message asks if you want to save the timings along with the narration. Click **Yes** or **No**.

Click

5 Record Sound

You can record a sound or narration for a single slide by clicking **Insert**, **Movies and Sounds**, **Record Sound**. Click the **Record** button in the Record Sound dialog box to begin recording. Click the **Stop** button to stop recording. Type a name for your new sound and choose **OK**.

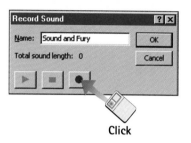

Click

End

How-To Hints

Delete Sound

Every time you insert a sound or narration on a slide, a little icon appears. To remove a sound, click to select it and press the **Delete** key.

Show With or Without Narration

When you run the slide show, the narration automatically plays. If you want to run the show without narration, choose **Slide Show**, **Set Up Show**, and click **Show without Narration**. Running your slide show is described in Chapter 10, "How to Run Your PowerPoint Presentation."

Task

9

How to Share Information with Other Microsoft Applications

*I*nformation rarely exists in a vacuum. The slides you create are likely to be based on information that lurks somewhere else on your computer. You might have created it in another program and are depressed that you'll have to recreate the data in PowerPoint (and everyone knows the only thing more tedious than typing something once, is typing it twice). However, don't despair; in recent years, it has become much easier for programs to "talk" to one another. Thanks to technological magic, you almost never have to retype anything. Not only is the risk of new errors reduced to a minimum, but you can give your poor tired hands a break.

If you installed PowerPoint as a part of the Microsoft Office 2000 suite, you'll be pleasantly surprised to find out how well PowerPoint works and plays with its siblings. To understand the power you can wield, you need to learn a little about object linking and embedding (or OLE for short). OLE is used by Office applications to share data among programs. You create information, such as an Excel spreadsheet for example. In this case, Excel is the *source* program. You then insert the spreadsheet data into PowerPoint, the *destination* program. The way you choose to insert the information depends on how you want to store and edit the data. Using OLE may sound a little convoluted at first, but it's easy and can be a real time-saver, especially if you have information that changes often or rapidly. ●

How to Cut, Copy, and Paste Between Applications

If you've been using Windows for a while, you probably discovered the joys of cutting and pasting long ago. However, with object linking and embedding, there's more than one way to cut and paste. You can paste data into PowerPoint as text or a picture, paste a link to the data that automatically updates when you change the original source file, or embed it so you can double-click the object and edit the data from within PowerPoint. To switch applications, just click on the item in the taskbar.

Begin

1 Cut or Copy Item

In the program that has the information you want to bring into PowerPoint, highlight the information and choose **Edit**, **Cut** or **Edit**, **Copy** (depending on what you want to do).

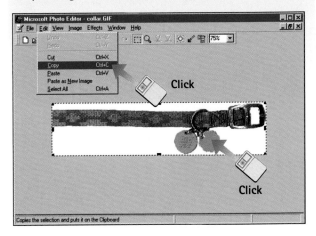

2 Switch Applications

On the taskbar, you see a button for every presentation you have open (you see the PowerPoint filename on the button). Click the button on the taskbar for the presentation into which you want to paste the information.

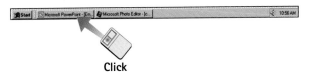

Click

3 Paste

From within your PowerPoint presentation, click where you want to insert the information and choose **Edit**, **Paste**. The data is placed on your slide. If you clicked in a placeholder, text data appears in your outline. If not, it appears as a text box type AutoShape.

Click

4 Paste Special

Using Paste Special instead of Paste maintains the data's association with the source program. Choose **Edit**, **Paste Special** to open the Paste Special dialog box. The source file is listed at the upper-left. Choosing how you want to paste it determines how you can edit it later. For example, if Microsoft PhotoEditor is the source program and you want to be able to edit the picture, choose **Microsoft PhotoEditor 3.0 Picture Object** and choose **OK**.

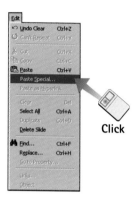

Click

5 Embed Data

In the Paste Special dialog box, you also can choose whether you want a link to be maintained with the source program. Click the **Paste** option button to embed the file. When data changes in the original file, the data you copied into the presentation stays the same. To edit the data, double-click it. Tools and menus from the source program appear within PowerPoint.

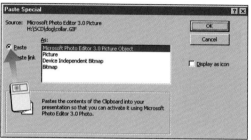

Click

6 Link Data

To maintain a link to the original file, click the **Paste Link** option button. Anytime you change the data in the original file (such as a PhotoEditor picture), the changes are reflected in the data you pasted into your PowerPoint presentation. To edit the data, double-click it. The file is opened in the original program.

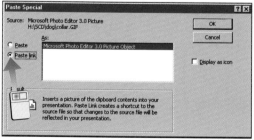

Click

How-To Hints

See the Taskbar

If you are new to Windows, you may wonder where the taskbar is. If you opened an application and you don't see it, don't try opening it again! (Yes, some people keep clicking icons until the system crashes.) Move your cursor to the bottom of the screen and the taskbar pops up. If you want to see the taskbar all the time, right-click it and choose **Properties**. Remove the check mark next to **Auto hide**.

Paste Hyperlink

Another way to create a link to a file is to paste a hyperlink. Copy data from the source program and click **Edit**, **Paste as Hyperlink**. An underlined item appears on screen that points to the original file just as it would in a Web browser. Hyperlinks are explained in more detail in Chapter 11, "How to Put Your Presentation on the Web."

End

How to Link or Embed Objects

Until you get the hang of it, linking and embedding can be confusing. Remember that when you link something, you just get a picture of the original file. When you double-click to edit it, you go directly to the program. If you embed something, the file becomes part of the presentation. It isn't tied to the original file, but if you double-click it, the program tools appear within PowerPoint (a tactic that's referred to as in-place editing). In addition to cutting and pasting pieces, you can access the power of linking and embedding by inserting objects.

Begin

1 Select Slide

Click in a slide to select it.

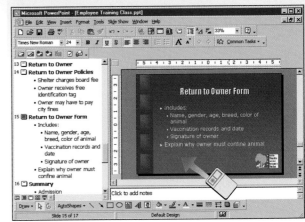

Click

2 Insert Object

Choose **Insert**, **Object** to open the Insert Object dialog box. In the Object type list, click to select the type of file you want to create or insert from a file. You can insert objects from all of the Office programs and other programs that work with PowerPoint, such as Microsoft Organization Chart and Microsoft Graph.

Click

3 Create New or From File

If you want to create a new object, click **Create New**. To insert a file that already exists on your hard drive as an object, click **Create from file**. Then click **Browse** to find the file or type the pathname in the File box. Click **Link** to have PowerPoint create a link to the file instead of embedding it.

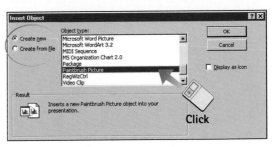

Click

4 Display as Icon

Click the **Display as icon** box if you want the object to appear as an icon rather than showing the contents of the file. When you click it, the **Change Icon** button appears. Click the button to change the icon and caption that PowerPoint displays on the slide.

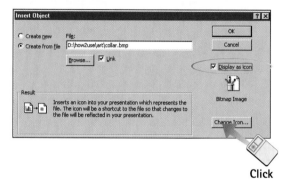

Click

5 Edit Object

Click **OK** to insert the object. If you chose to create a new embedded object, you see a blank window that looks similar to the application you selected. If you embedded an existing file, double-click it and the editing tools appear.

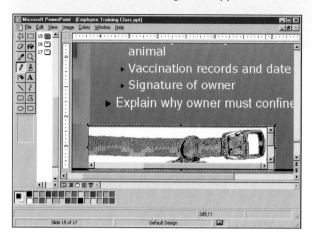

6 Edit Links

If you choose to link to a file, you see a picture of your file. Double-click it to edit it in the original application. To change characteristics of the link, choose **Edit**, **Links** to open the Links dialog box. Because a link only points to the original file, you may need to click **Update Now** to update the links if you change the file.

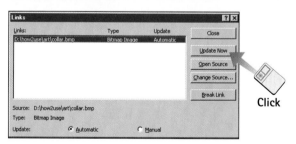

Click

End

How-To Hints

Keep Track of Links

Linking is often used for files that would cause your presentation to become enormous if they were embedded into it. Often it's a good idea to link large graphics, movies, or sound files. If you move your giant file to a new location, PowerPoint can "lose" the link. To fix the problem, choose **Edit**, **Links** and click **Change Source**. Enter the name of the file in its new location.

Use Manual Links

If you link a lot of files in your presentation, it can slow down PowerPoint as it attempts to relink them automatically. In this case you may want to switch your links to manual by choosing **Edit**, **Links**. In the Links dialog box, click **Manual**. However, if you change the linked source file, you must remember to click the **Update Now** button to update your presentation.

How to Add Slides from an Outline

Adding slides from an outline is a good way to get a presentation started quickly. Sometimes its easier to compose your thoughts in your favorite word processing program so you can focus on the content, without the distractions of the layout nagging at you. If you use Microsoft Word, or can import your outline into Word and reformat it in Word's Outline view, you can save even more time. Word's outline levels correspond to PowerPoint's slide hierarchy, so when you import a Word outline the levels transfer seamlessly into PowerPoint slides.

Begin

1 Use Word Outline View

In Microsoft Word, choose **View**, **Outline**. Outline view forces you to format your text by using the heading styles. The styles are important because when you import the text into PowerPoint, a Heading 1 level becomes a slide title, Heading 2 becomes a first level bullet, Heading 3 is a second level bullet, and so on.

2 Save the Outline

In Word, choose **File**, **Save** to save the file. Choose **File**, **Save As** if you want to save your outline with a new filename. Choose a folder on your hard drive to save it into and give it a meaningful file name.

3 Close File

In Word, choose **File**, **Close** to close the file. You can bring the outline into PowerPoint in one of two ways: by either opening the file or importing it. Click the appropriate button on your taskbar to switch to PowerPoint.

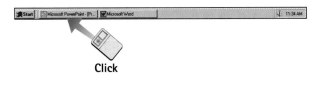

4 Open File

To open the file in PowerPoint, choose **File**, **Open**. The Open dialog box appears. Click the down arrow on the Files of Type drop-down box to **All Outlines**. Click the Look In drop-down box to select the folder where your file resides. Click the filename and choose **Open**.

Click

5 Import Slides

You also can import the outline file. This approach can be useful for bringing slides into an existing presentation. Click in the Outline pane of Normal view at the location you want the text to be inserted. Choose **Insert**, **Slides from Outline** to open the Insert Outline dialog box. Find the file, click it, and choose **Insert**. The new slides appear after the slide you selected.

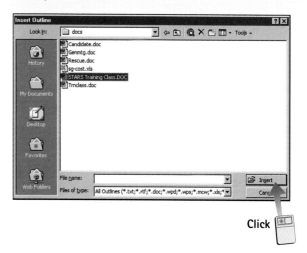

Click

6 Adjust Outline Levels

If you need to change the outline, you can use the buttons on PowerPoint's Outlining toolbar to promote and demote items and move paragraphs up and down in the outline. To view the Outlining toolbar, choose **View**, **Toolbars**, **Outlining**.

Click

How-To Hints

Understand How Outlines Import

Even if you didn't use heading styles in your outline, it will still import into PowerPoint. If PowerPoint doesn't encounter styles, it uses paragraph indentation to figure out the outline levels (the number of tabs determines the structure). If the Word file isn't in any kind of outline format at all, PowerPoint interprets each paragraph as a slide (blank paragraphs are turned into blank slides).

End

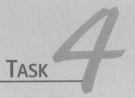

How to Insert Excel Data

If you're a number-crunching wizard, Microsoft Excel is probably your favorite program. And after you've spent hours crafting the perfect worksheet, you certainly don't want to have to recreate it in PowerPoint for your presentation (even if you could, which is debatable). Bringing Excel data into a presentation is a perfect use for the linking and embedding tools. You can paste or insert your Excel data into PowerPoint as a worksheet object. This way, you can create the data by using the best program for the job, and you can make any later edits using your favorite Excel tools as well.

Begin

1 Select Excel Data

Within Microsoft Excel, click and drag to select the worksheet cells you want to bring into PowerPoint. Choose **Edit**, **Copy**.

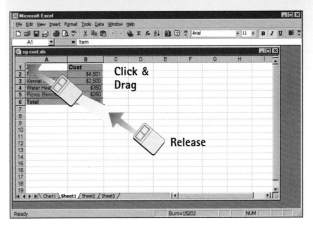

2 Switch to PowerPoint

Click the appropriate button on the taskbar to switch to PowerPoint. Click to select the slide where you want the Excel worksheet data to appear.

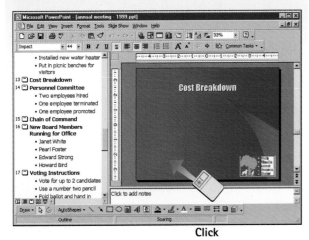

Click

3 Paste Data

Choose **Edit**, **Paste Special**. The Paste Special dialog box opens. Under Object Type, click **Microsoft Excel Worksheet Object**. Click the **Paste** option button to embed the file. (This way, even if the Excel data changes, the data copied into your presentation remains the same.) Choose **OK**.

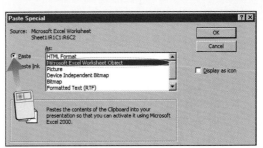

Click

$\mathcal{4}$ Link Data

If you want the Excel data in PowerPoint to reflect changes you make to the original worksheet, click the **Paste Link** option button. Choose **OK**.

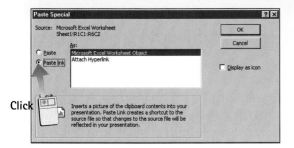

Click

$\mathcal{5}$ Edit Worksheet

Double-click the worksheet to make changes. If you embedded the worksheet, Excel menus and tools appear and you can edit it from within PowerPoint. If you linked the worksheet, Excel opens so you can make your changes.

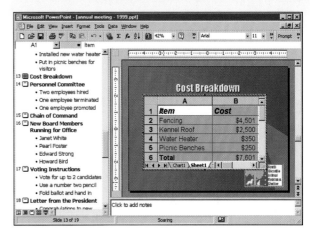

End

How-To Hints

Update PowerPoint from Excel Data

A sneaky way to use OLE is to store data that changes frequently in an external file so it updates automatically. For example, suppose you have to present sales figures every month. Rather than recreating the presentation every time, you just update the monthly numbers in an Excel spreadsheet that you have paste-linked into PowerPoint. Make the changes in Excel, switch to PowerPoint and magically the changes appear on your slide as well.

How to Insert an Excel Chart

Although the charting features built into PowerPoint are powerful and easy to use, if you already charted the data in Excel, why reinvent the wheel? You bring an Excel chart into PowerPoint much the same way as you bring in worksheet data. Instead of pasting or inserting a worksheet object, you insert the chart as a Microsoft Excel Chart object. If you want to maintain a link with the original file, anytime you change the Excel data, you can set it up so the changes are reflected in your presentation as well.

Begin

1 Create Excel Chart

In Excel, use the Chart Wizard or choose **Insert**, **Chart** to create a chart from your data. If it isn't on its own sheet, click the chart to select it and choose **Chart**, **Location** to open the Chart Location dialog box. Click **As new sheet** to move the chart to its own chart sheet. Save the file by choosing **File**, **Save** or **File**, **Save As**.

Click

2 Switch to PowerPoint

Click the appropriate taskbar button to switch to PowerPoint.

Click

3 Insert Object

Choose **Insert**, **Object** to open the Insert Object dialog box. To create a new chart, choose **Microsoft Excel Chart** in the Object Type box. If you want to use the existing Excel chart you created in step 1, click **Create from File**.

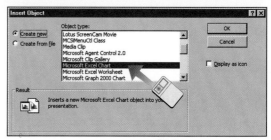

Click

4 Choose File

Type in a pathname for your file or click the **Browse** button to locate it on your hard disk. Use the Look In drop-down box to choose a folder. Double-click the filename. Click **OK** to insert the chart.

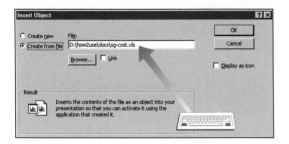

5 Edit Object

If you have multiple sheets in the Excel file, the wrong chart or worksheet page may appear in PowerPoint. Double-click the file and click the sheet tabs to display the correct sheet. Using the Excel tools, make any other changes you want to the chart.

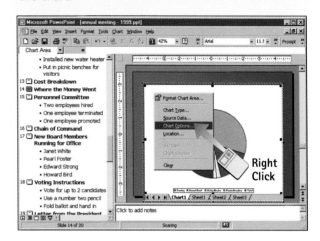

6 Click to Return to PowerPoint

Click outside the chart to return to PowerPoint.

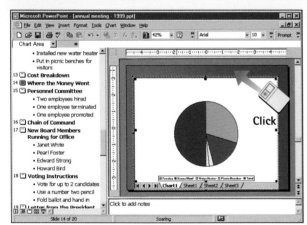

End

How-To Hints

Import Excel Data into a PowerPoint Chart

You can import Excel data into the datasheet used by Microsoft Graph within PowerPoint. From within the Graph Program, switch to the datasheet (choose **View**, **Datasheet** if is not displayed). Choose **Edit**, **Import File**. Use the Look In drop-down box to find the folder in which the Excel file is located. Double-click the file to import it. Click **Entire Worksheet** to bring in the entire worksheet or click **Range** and enter a range of cells. For more about creating charts in PowerPoint, refer to Chapter 7, "How to Work with Charts and Tables," Tasks 1 through 4.

How to Insert a Word Table

Most people spend a lot of time using word processing programs. If you use Microsoft Office, you probably feel right at home in Word. And because tables can be a concise way to express information, you've probably spent a lot of time using Word's table features. With all this time invested in Word tables, the idea of recreating them in PowerPoint probably isn't exactly appealing. However, there is another way. All you have to do is select your Word table or cells within it, switch to PowerPoint, and plunk all that information into your presentation quickly and easily.

Begin

1 Select Cells

In Microsoft Word, click and drag to highlight the cells you want to copy into your presentation.

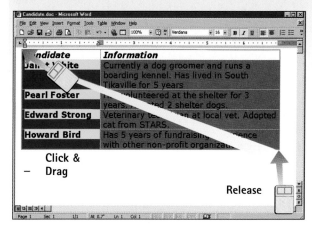

Click & Drag

Release

2 Select Entire Table

Or select the entire table by choosing **Table**, **Select**, **Table**. Once you have selected the desired cells, choose **Edit**, **Copy**.

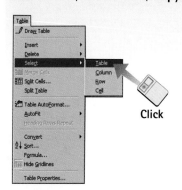

Click

3 Switch to PowerPoint

Click the button on your taskbar to switch to the PowerPoint presentation on which you are working.

Click

4 Paste Table

Choose **Edit, Paste**. The table appears on your slide. It is actually a group of AutoShapes and each cell is a text box. Click within a cell to edit the text. You also can ungroup (**Draw, Ungroup**) the table and format and manipulate each text box individually.

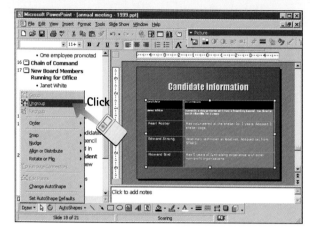

5 Paste Special

If you want the table to maintain its ties to Word, choose **Edit, Paste Special** instead of **Paste** to open the Paste Special dialog box. Under As, click **Microsoft Word Document Object**. Click the **Paste** or **Paste Link** option buttons. Paste embeds the object; Paste Link creates a link to the original Word table.

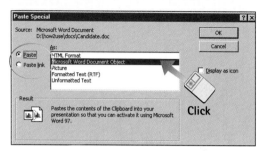

6 Edit Table

Double-click the linked or embedded table to edit it. If you embedded the table, Word menus and tools appear and you can edit it from within PowerPoint. If you linked the table, Word opens so you can make your changes. Click outside the table to return to PowerPoint.

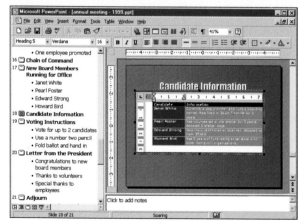

How-To Hints

Update Table Data (or Not)

Sometimes you want your linked data to update automatically and sometimes you don't. To change how PowerPoint updates your linked Word table (or any linked object) choose **Edit, Links**. In the Update section, click either the **Automatic** or **Manual** option button. Automatic updates the data anytime you open the presentation. Manual updates the data only when you click the **Update Now** button in the Links dialog box.

End

How to Add PowerPoint Slides to a Word Document

Using your PowerPoint slides as elements in other Office applications requires just a few simple steps. For example, if you want to use your slides as figures in a manual, you need to get them out of your presentation individually and into their new location. If the topic is one that changes often, you may want to link your slide data to the original presentation in PowerPoint as well.

Begin

1 Switch to Slide Sorter View

In PowerPoint, click the **Slide Sorter** button at the bottom left corner of your display to switch to slide sorter view.

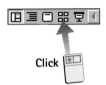

Click

2 Select Slide

In Slide Sorter view, click the slide to select it.

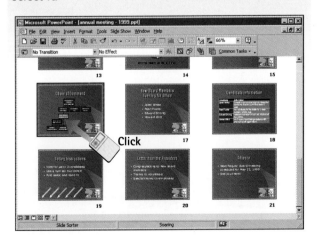

Click

3 Copy Slide

Choose **Edit**, **Copy** to copy the slide to the clipboard. Switch to Word by clicking its button on the taskbar.

Click

4 Paste Slide in Word

In Word, choose **Edit**, **Paste** to paste the slide. Word treats it as an imported graphic that you can manipulate as you would other imported pictures.

Click

5 Paste Special

If you want the slide to retain a tie to the PowerPoint presentation, in Word, choose **Paste Special** instead of **Paste** to open the Paste Special dialog box. Under As, click Microsoft PowerPoint Slide Object and click **Paste** or **Paste Link**, depending on whether you want the slide embedded or linked.

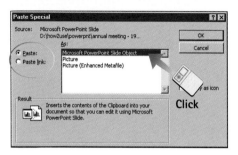

Click

6 Edit Slide

In Word, double-click the linked or embedded slide to edit it. If you embedded the slide, the PowerPoint menus and other tools appear so you can change the slide from within Word. If you linked the slide, PowerPoint opens so you can edit the slide. Click outside the slide to return to your Word document.

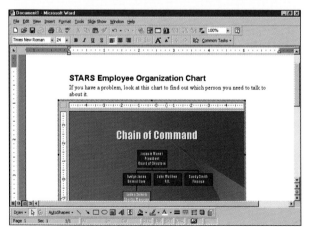

End

How-To Hints

Copy More than One Slide at Once

You can use the Office Clipboard to copy up to 12 slides at a time. In Normal view, be sure the clipboard is visible by choosing **View**, **Toolbars**, **Clipboard**. In Slide Sorter view, click to select one slide. Choose **Edit**, **Copy** to copy it to the Clipboard. Click another slide and copy it and continue until the clipboard is filled. (Note that you can't copy multiple slides at once, you have to copy each one separately for this process to work.) Switch to Word, and choose where you want to put one or all of the slides. In the Office Clipboard, click the picture button to paste the slide. Or click **Paste All** to paste all the slides you copied.

Send to Word

Another way to get your presentation information into Word is to "send" it. You can send notes, handouts, or your outline to Word by choosing **File**, **Send to**, **Microsoft Word**. You can change layout options and choose to link or embed the file.

How to Import Other Presentation Files

With PowerPoint's growing popularity, many people have switched to it from other presentation programs, such as Lotus Freelance. Unfortunately, if you switched, you probably have a lot of old but useful presentation files around. Instead of recreating them in PowerPoint, you can import the old file and let PowerPoint attempt to convert it. If PowerPoint has a converter for the file, it does a pretty good job of retaining much of the formatting as well as the content. If not, you may be able to get a converter from Microsoft or save the old file in a format PowerPoint can convert.

Begin

1 Open File

In PowerPoint, choose **File**, **Open**. The Open dialog box appears.

Click

2 Find File

Use the Look In drop-down box to find the folder where the file is located. If the folder is nested, double-click folders until you find the right one.

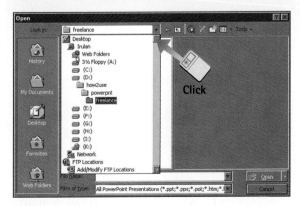

Click

3 Choose Type

Change the Files of Type drop-down box to **All Files (*.*)**. Or to find freelance files, change the drop-down box to **Freelance Windows 1.0–2.1 (*.pre)**. Double-click the file to open it.

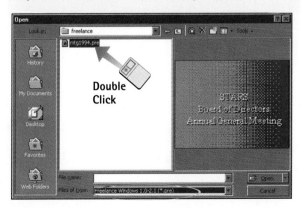

Double Click

4 Save as PowerPoint

After the conversion is complete, choose **File**, **Save As** to save the file as a PowerPoint 2000 file in the Save As dialog box. Choose a folder, enter a filename, and make sure that the Save as type drop-down is set to **Presentation (*.ppt)**.

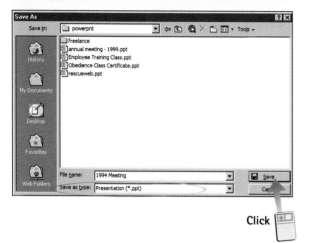

Click

5 Convert Multiple Files

If you want to convert multiple files at once, in the Open dialog box, hold down the **Ctrl** key and click the filenames you want to convert. Click **Open**. After PowerPoint converts them, be sure to save them as PowerPoint 2000 files as described in step 4.

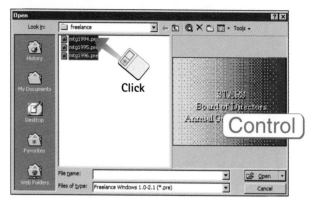

Click

Control

End

How-To Hints

Convert Lotus Freelance or Harvard Graphics Files

PowerPoint has a converter for Lotus Freelance version 4.0 for DOS, Freelance Graphics 1.0-2.1 for Windows, and Harvard Graphics 3.0 charts and shows. To convert later versions, save the file as the older file type. Note that not all of the converters are installed by default so, depending on your installation, you may need to use your Office or PowerPoint CD-ROM to install the converters. Other converters are available in the *Microsoft Office 2000 Resource Kit.*

Convert "Problem" Files

If PowerPoint doesn't have a converter for a particular type of file, in the old program, you usually can export your content into a generic text-based format PowerPoint does support such as Rich Text Format (.RTF) or plain text (.TXT). If the graphics are more important than the content, you might try saving your presentation as a Windows Metafile (.WMF) or Macintosh PICT file. PowerPoint can open these files. If that doesn't work, you can try exporting individual slides as bitmaps in a format PowerPoint can understand such as .BMP or .GIF.

How to Send PowerPoint Slides as an Email Attachment

PowerPoint includes features that make it easy to send your presentation to a friend (or a lot of friends). You can send your presentation to anyone on the Internet or on a company intranet. If your presentation needs to be reviewed by a lot of people in order, you can send it to a list of routing recipients. PowerPoint lets you create a virtual routing slip; each recipient on the list reviews the presentation and passes it on to the next person.

Begin

1 Open Presentation

Open the presentation that contains the slide or presentation you want to send. Choose **File**, **Open**. The Open dialog box appears. Double-click the filename.

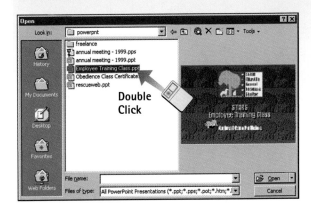

2 Send Presentation

You can send one slide or your entire presentation. Choose **File**, **Send to**, **Mail Recipient** to open the E-mail dialog box and click an option to send one slide embedded in the email or the entire presentation as an attachment.

3 Send as Attachment

Or choose **File**, **Send To**, **Mail Recipient (as Attachment)**. In either case, an email message window appears. Fill in the recipient information and send it the way you normally send email.

4 Send to Routing Recipients

If you want to send your presentation to a group choose **File**, **Send To**, **Routing Recipient**. In the Add Routing Slip dialog box, click **Address** to add names and click options such as whether you want the people to receive the presentation one after the other or all at once. Click **Route** to send it to your Outlook outbox.

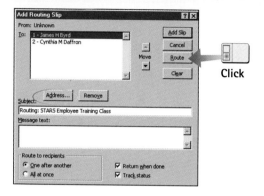

Click

5 Send to Online Recipients

If your system is set up with NetMeeting, you can send the presentation to meeting participants. Choose **File**, **Send To**, **Online Meeting Participant**. All of the participants in the meeting receive a copy of the file.

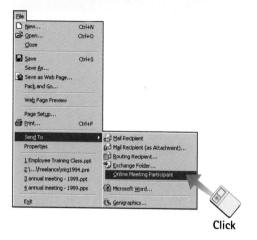

Click

6 Compress Presentation

All PowerPoint's automatic email features are nice, but you may find that sending large presentations can be time-consuming. Large files are more manageable if you first compress them in a program such as PKZip or WinZip. Then you can attach them to your email message from within your email program.

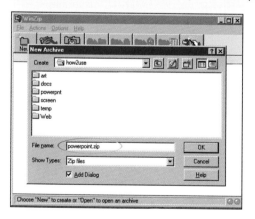

End

How-To Hints

Watch File Sizes

If you are sending an entire presentation over the Internet, consider its size. A presentation with a lot of sound, movies, or graphics can be huge. Some Internet Service Providers (ISPs) are fussy about large attachments. Many of their servers won't permit uploads or downloads of files larger than a certain size, such as 3MB. Even if your provider permits large file uploads, your recipient's may not. Verify with the recipient that there are no restrictions before you waste a lot of time uploading a big file.

Task

CHAPTER 10

How to Run Your PowerPoint Presentation

*I*n an old joke, a New York tourist asks how to get to Carnegie Hall. The elderly musician answers, "Practice, practice, practice." The same is true for your presentation. Creating the presentation visuals is just part of the larger task of getting your message across to the audience. When you give your presentation, you want it to go flawlessly, so like the musician says, you have to practice.

By using PowerPoint's slide show tools, you can rehearse your presentation so it flows smoothly on the big day. When you give a presentation, you don't want the presentation software controls to get in the way. Learn how to use the controls well, so that employing them becomes completely automatic. You'll have enough to think about without trying to remember which key combination advances you to the next slide. And you certainly don't want to find yourself fumbling in front of a crowd.

When you rehearse the presentation, don't just go over your notes. Really *rehearse* it as an actor would—go through every slide and every nuance. If possible, go to the room you will be using and set up your equipment for a dry run. If you plan to use a microphone or laser pointer, try them out, too. New technology can be handy, but you don't want to be frustrated by your lack of experience with tools in front of an audience. If you put in the time to really learn your presentation, you'll be rewarded with a memorable presentation that leaves your audience smiling. ●

How to Set Up the Show

After you've done all the hard work of creating your presentation, you need to set up how you want it to run. Not all presentations require a human to be present when they run. You can set your show to run by itself, which can be useful for trade show booths or other public places. In certain situations, you may want to run only part of the presentation, or run it without narration or animation. You can change all of these options so that the same presentation can be used in a variety of settings.

Begin

1 Set Show Type

To change the slide show options, choose **Slide Show, Set Up Show** to open the Set Up Show dialog box. If you will be presenting the show, make sure **Show Type** is set to **Presented by a speaker**. For self-running shows, you can choose to run it in a window or kiosk.

Click

2 Set Options

Select a range of slides to include in the show or whether you want to run a custom show (custom shows are discussed in step 5). You also can set options to indicate how you want the slides to advance, whether to include narration, and whether it should loop continuously.

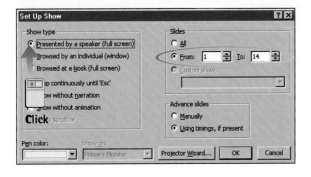

Click

3 Set Pen Color

When you run a show you can add annotations with a pen. In the Set Up Show dialog box, you can change the pen color so it better matches your presentation colors. Click the **Pen color** drop-down box and choose a new color. (Using the pen is discussed in Task 4, "How to Add Annotations with the Pen.")

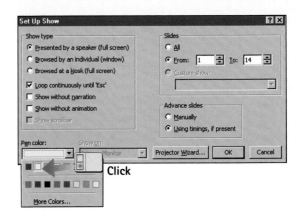

Click

4 Run Projector Wizard

If you will be using a projector with your computer to run the show, click the **Projector Wizard** button to help you set up the connection. When you finish the wizard, choose **OK** to save the changes in the Set Up Show dialog box.

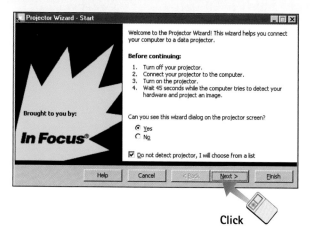

Click

5 Create a Custom Show

If you want to show specific slides or show them in a certain order, you must create a custom show. Choose **Slide Show**, **Custom Shows**. The Custom Shows dialog box opens. Click **New** to open the Define Custom Show dialog box and create a new custom show. Type a name for your show and double-click slide names to add them to the show. To rearrange the list, click a slide in the **Slides in custom show** box and click the arrow keys. Click **OK**, and choose **Close** or **Show** to save the show.

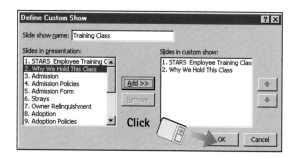

Click

6 Hide Slides

If you just want to hide a particular slide in a show, you don't have to create a custom show. Click the slide and choose **Slide Show**, **Hide Slide**. The selected slide is not included when you show the presentation.

Click

End

How to Add Summary and Agenda Slides

There's an old saying that when you write or present information, you should tell your audience what you're going to say, say it, then tell them what you said. You can use PowerPoint's agenda slide as an introduction, and then use the summary slide to reinforce what you discussed. In PowerPoint, summary and agenda slides are similar. A summary slide simply lists the main topic headings. An agenda slide also lists topics, but includes hyperlinks so you can jump to each topic. At the end, you are automatically returned to the agenda slide so you can jump to the next topic.

Begin

1 Switch to Slide Sorter View

Click the **Slide Sorter View** button at the bottom-left corner of your display.

Click

2 Select Slides

Hold down the **Ctrl** key and click to select the slides you want to include. The summary slide will be composed of the text in the Title placeholders in the slides you select.

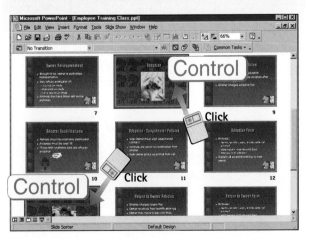

3 Make Summary Slide

Click the **Summary Slide** button on the Slide Sorter toolbar. In front of the first slide you selected, you see a new slide with bullet points corresponding to the titles on the slides you selected. Click and drag to move the summary slide to the end of the presentation.

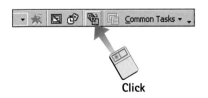
Click

4 Create Agenda Slide

To create an agenda slide, create a custom show for each section of the presentation as described in Task 1, step 5. Create a summary slide as described in steps 1 through 3. Double-click the summary slide to show it in Normal view.

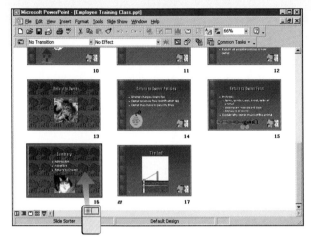

Double Click

5 Add Hyperlinks

Click and drag to highlight the bullet point, right-click, and choose **Action Settings**. Change **Action on click** to **Hyperlink to** and choose **Custom Show** from the drop-down box. This opens the Link to Custom Show dialog box. Click a custom show in the list. If you want to return to the agenda slide automatically, check **Show and return**. Follow the same process for the rest of the bullets. (Hyperlinks are discussed in more detail in Chapter 11, "How to Put Your Presentation on the Web.")

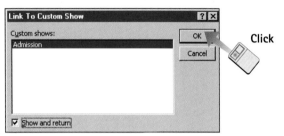

Click

End

How-To Hints

Keep it Short

When you create an agenda or summary slide, make sure you don't end up with too many bullet points. If your summary slide ends up with ten (or more) topics, you may want to rethink the organization of your presentation. Try to divide your presentation into less than five or six major topic headings. Not only will they fit better on the agenda and summary slides, but your audience has a much better chance of remembering them.

Update Summary Slides

If you change the titles of the slides you used to create a summary slide, the summary slide isn't updated automatically. For the titles to match the summary slide, you must recreate the summary slide as described in step 3.

How to Run Your Presentation

Once you have your slides completed, your charts drawn, your custom shows set up, and your agenda and summary slides in place, it's time to try it all out and see how it works. When faced with a deadline, often the tendency is to procrastinate; however, when you have to do a presentation, you really want to leave enough time for plenty of practice. A very talented improvisational actor might be able to get away with "winging it," but, for the rest of us, lots of rehearsal is what makes the difference between a presentation that is an enjoyable experience and one that replays itself endlessly in your darkest nightmares.

Begin

1 Show Presentation

You can show your presentation in a number of ways. To start the show at the current slide, click the **Slide Show** button at the lower-left corner of the display. To start at the first slide, choose **Slide Show**, **View Show**. Or choose **View**, **Slide Show**, or press **F5**.

2 Play Manually

If you haven't set slide timings, you can run through your show manually. Use keyboard shortcuts to move through your show. Right-click and choose **Help** to view navigation shortcuts.

3 Rehearse Timings

You can have PowerPoint record the amount of time you spend on each slide if you want slides to advance automatically. To rehearse timings, click **Slide Show**, **Rehearse Timings**. Go through the show. When PowerPoint asks if you want to record the new timings, click **Yes**.

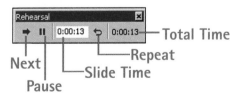

4 Use the Slide Navigator

During the show, if you want to go to a specific slide in the presentation, right-click and choose **Go, Slide Navigator** from the pop-up menu. The Slide Navigator dialog box appears. Double-click the slide name and PowerPoint takes you to that slide.

Click

5 Play Continuously

You also can set up your show to play continuously. This option is useful if the presentation will be shown at a kiosk or other area where the audience is transitory. Setting up the show and setting options in the Set Up Show dialog box is described in Task 1.

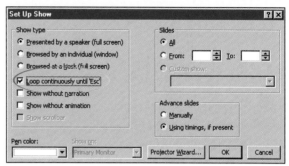

End

How-To Hints

Pick Your Favorite Shortcut

PowerPoint provides many keyboard shortcuts you can use to move through your presentation. Some of the most common ones include **F5** to start the show, **Esc** to end the show, **Page Down** to go to the next slide, and **Page Up** to go to the previous slide. If you can't remember a particular shortcut, you can always right-click with the mouse and access the navigation controls on the pop-up menu.

How to Add Annotations with the Pen

Even in this digital age, old-fashioned ugly whiteboards are popular because sometimes the only way to describe something is to draw it. When you give a presentation, you don't need to have access to a blackboard, whiteboard, or easel to draw explanatory pictures. You can add temporary text or drawings right on your slides from within PowerPoint using the pen. Although it can be difficult to write with, the pen is great for drawing arrows, circles, and other quick highlights to help reinforce a point and keep the audience focused. The annotations are not saved; they disappear when the show ends.

Begin

1 Activate Pen

During the show, you can change the pointer to a pen by right-clicking and choosing **Pointer Options**, **Pen**. Or press **Ctrl+P** to change the arrow to a pen.

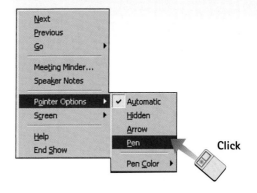

2 Draw Annotations

Click and drag to add annotations. Using the pen is much like using the Scribble drawing tool that was described in Chapter 4, "How to Work with Graphics," Task 6, "How to Create Complex Drawings."

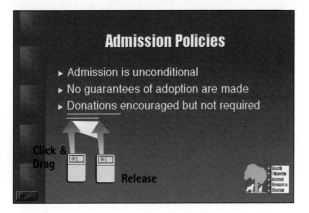

3 Erase Annotations

To erase annotations, press **E**. The annotations disappear.

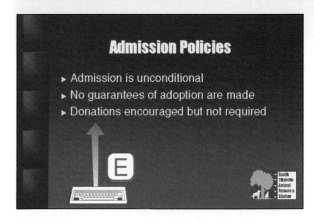

4 Deactivate Pen

You can change the pointer back to an arrow by right-clicking and choosing **Pointer Options**, **Arrow**. Or choose **Automatic** if you want the arrow to disappear after 15 seconds. Anytime you move the mouse, the arrow reappears. If you prefer keyboard shortcuts, press **Ctrl+A** to switch the pointer to an arrow or press **Ctrl+U** to switch to automatic.

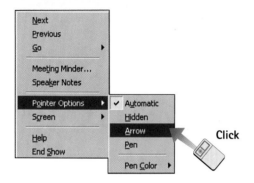

Click

5 Change Annotation Color

You can change the pen color during the presentation by right-clicking and choosing **Pointer Options**, **Pen Color**. Choose a color from the sub-menu list.

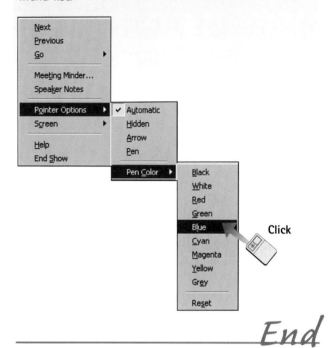

Click

End

How-To Hints

Control that Pen

The pen can be difficult to use unless you are an extremely steady mouser. If you want to draw straight horizontal or vertical lines on your slides with the pen, hold down the **Shift** key while you click and drag.

How to Add Comments to Slides

Virtually every office or cubicle has one of those ubiquitous colored sticky notes affixed to something (monitor, desk, papers, you name it). If sticky notes are a way of life for you, you'll like PowerPoint's comment features. You can insert the computer equivalent of a little yellow sticky on any slide in your presentation. These comments can be handy for you, but are especially useful if your slides need to be reviewed by committee. Rather than having a long, tedious review meeting, you can use a routing slip, email the presentation to the reviewers and get everyone's feedback right inside the presentation. All without leaving your desk.

Begin

1 Select Slide

Click in a slide to select it.

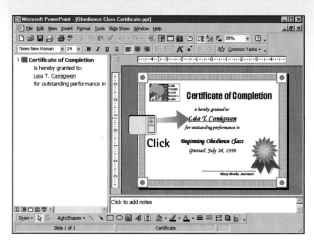

2 Insert Comment

Choose **Insert**, **Comment**. The Reviewing toolbar displays and a yellow box appears at the top-left of the slide with your name in it. Type your comment. If you add more than one comment, you may need to click and drag the second one to a new location so you can see the first one.

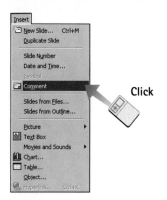

Click

3 Move Through Comments

On the Reviewing toolbar, click the **Previous Comment** and **Next Comment** buttons to scroll through the comments in the presentation. (If the Reviewing toolbar isn't visible choose **View**, **Toolbars**, **Reviewing**.)

Click

4 Reformat Comments

Comments are just another AutoShape, so if you want to be creative you can change the shape as described in Chapter 4, Task 5, "How to Use AutoShapes." (You can change any number of the object's other attributes, such as text formatting as described in Chapters 3, "How to Work with Text," and 5, "How to Format Objects," as well.)

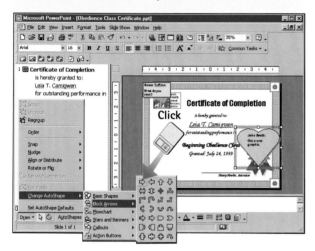

5 Hide or Show Comments

On the Reviewing toolbar, click the **Show/Hide** button to hide all the comments in the presentation. Click the button again to show them. To delete a comment, click on a border to select it and press the **Delete** key. Or click the **Delete Comment** button on the Reviewing toolbar.

Click

End

How-To Hints

Create Task

If you use Outlook to schedule your day, you might find it handy to create a task from within PowerPoint that reminds you to make changes in your presentation. Be sure that the presentation is open and the Reviewing toolbar is visible. On the Reviewing toolbar, click **Create Microsoft Outlook Task**. The task appears with a shortcut to your presentation. For more information on Outlook tasks, please refer to the online help within Outlook.

How to Save Your Presentation as a Show

After your presentation is finalized, you can save it as a show that runs without the need for you to go into PowerPoint. This way, you don't have to open PowerPoint and choose **View**, **Slide Show** to run your presentation. Instead, the show runs automatically when you open the file. Slide show files are saved with a different file extension (.PPS) than regular PowerPoint files (.PPT) and they have a different icon, so they are easy to spot in Windows Explorer.

Begin

1 Open Presentation

Choose **File**, **Open** and click the **Look in** drop-down box in the Open dialog box to find the folder where your presentation is located. Double-click the filename to open the presentation.

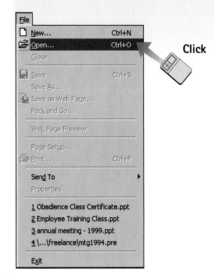

2 Save As

Choose **File**, **Save As**. The Save As dialog box appears.

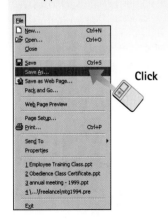

3 Change Type

Change the Save as Type in the drop-down box to **PowerPoint Show**. Leave the default file name (your presentation filename with a .PPS extension) or type a new one.

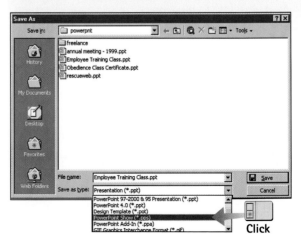

4 Save Presentation

Click **Save**. The file is saved to your hard drive with the filename you specified. If you look at the file in Windows Explorer, you see that it has a "show" icon instead of the regular PowerPoint file icon.

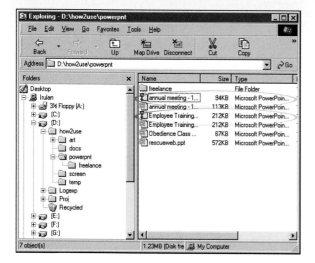

5 Add Desktop Icon

If you want to run your show from your desktop, open Windows Explorer. Find your new PowerPoint show on your hard disk. Right-click and choose **Create Shortcut**. Then drag the shortcut to your desktop. Right-click the icon and choose **Rename** to give the shortcut a more user-friendly name. Double-click the icon to run the show.

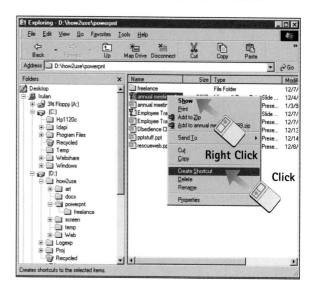

End

How-To Hints

Do it Over

If you decide to change your presentation later, you need to save it as a slide show again to run it from the slide show file. Follow steps 1 and 2, and then in step 3 be sure to save the new .PPS file with the same name as the old one. When PowerPoint asks if you want to replace the existing file, click **Yes**.

How to Broadcast Presentations

You and your coworkers may be located in different offices, different buildings, or on different continents. You may need to work with other people in remote locations by using such technologies as email, fax, telephone, and the Internet. Using PowerPoint's broadcast features in conjunction with Microsoft NetMeeting, you can broadcast your total presentation audio and exchange information with people in multiple locations as if you were all in the same room. All the meeting attendees need is a Web browser to participate in the online meeting.

Begin

1 Set Up a Broadcast

Before you can broadcast your presentation, you need to set it up. To set up a broadcast, choose **Slide Show**, **Online Broadcast**, **Set Up and Schedule** to open the Broadcast Schedule dialog box. Click an option button to indicate whether you are setting up a new broadcast or rescheduling an existing one. Click **OK**.

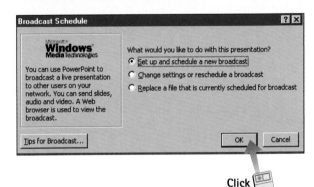

Click

2 Change Settings

In the **Description** tab, type a description of your presentation and change the speaker or contact information, if necessary. Click the **Broadcast Settings** tab and select options. Click the **Server Options button** and specify a shared location on a server for the broadcast (for more than 15 viewers, you must have a NetShow server).

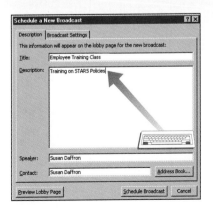

3 Preview Lobby Page

On either tab, click the **Preview Lobby Page** button to see how the lobby page will look to the participants. The lobby page is an informational page people see in their browser when they join a broadcast.

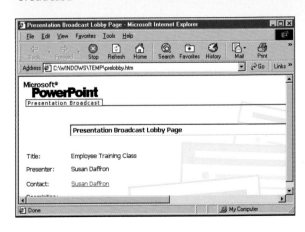

4 Schedule Broadcast

Click **Schedule Broadcast** and the presentation is copied to the server. If you are using Outlook, a window appears and you schedule the broadcast as you would other meetings. In other email programs the message includes a URL, which people click to join the broadcast.

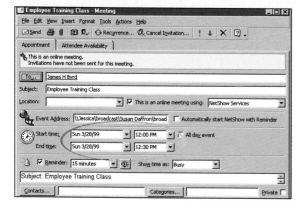

5 Start Broadcast

Meeting participants need to be using Internet Explorer 4.0 or later to view a broadcast. After you have scheduled a broadcast, choose **Slide Show**, **Online Broadcast**, **Begin Broadcast**. Click the **Audience Message** button in the Broadcast Presentation dialog box if you want to send out last minute information. Click **Start** when you are ready to begin.

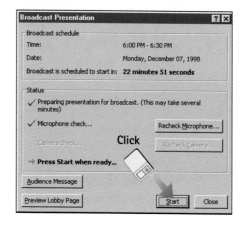

6 Join Broadcast

If you are using Outlook when a reminder message appears, click **View NetShow**. In other email programs, click the URL included in the message. You will see the lobby page. If you come into a broadcast in the middle, you can click **View previous slides** to see the slides you missed.

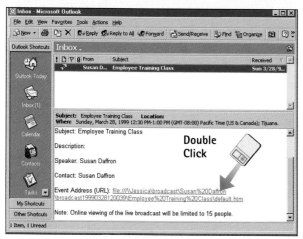

How-To Hints

Record a Broadcast

If some people won't be able to attend the broadcast, you can save it for viewing later. In the Broadcast Settings tab of the Schedule a New Broadcast dialog box, click **Record the broadcast and save it in this location**. Click the **Browse** button to choose a location on a server to which everyone has access.

End

How to Use Online Collaboration

Many times it can be difficult to get a lot of people in one room. If your presentation is a hot topic around the company and you have an intranet, you can use PowerPoint's online collaboration features to talk it over. You can use Microsoft NetMeeting to hold online meetings or have a Web discussion. Web discussions are *threaded* and work much like Internet newsgroups. One person sends a comment and then people reply creating a long chain or "thread" of messages. To use NetMeeting, it must be installed on your system and all the participants' systems as well. PowerPoint's Web discussion features require your system administrator to set up Microsoft Office Server Extensions on a Web server in your intranet.

Begin

1 Schedule a Meeting

You can schedule a Microsoft Outlook online meeting from within PowerPoint. Choose **Tools, Online Collaboration, Schedule Meeting**. You see a Meeting dialog box where you can set options for the meeting.

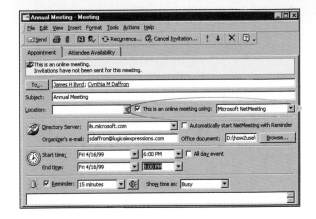

2 Meet Now

If you are more spontaneous, you can choose **Tools, Online Collaboration, Meet Now** to invite people to a unscheduled meeting. For more about NetMeeting, refer to the Outlook and NetMeeting online help.

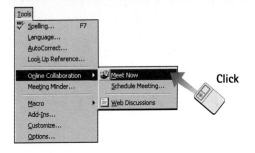

3 Add Minutes in the Meeting

During the meeting, you can add minutes to the Meeting Minder. Click **Tools, Meeting Minder**. The Meeting Minder dialog box appears. In the **Meeting Minutes** tab, click and type to add minutes.

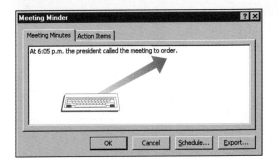

4 Add Action Items in the Meeting

Click the **Action Items** tab and type a description of items that must be acted on after the meeting. Type in the person's name who must perform the action and the day it's due. After you have entered all the information, click **Add**. If you need to change an item, click **Edit** to modify the text. Click **Delete** to delete an action item.

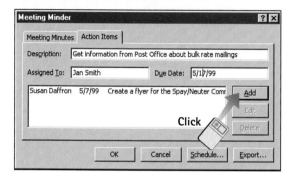

5 Export Meeting Minder

Click the **Export** button to export the information you've entered into the Meeting Minder. The Meeting Minder Export dialog box opens. Click **Post Action items to Microsoft Outlook** or **Send meeting minutes and action items to Microsoft Word**, depending on how and where you plan to use the information.

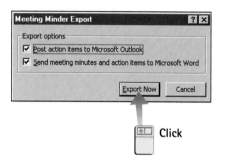

Click

6 Engage in Web Discussion

Another way to confer about a presentation is to have a Web discussion. Choose **Tools, Online Collaboration, Web Discussions**. You need to choose a discussion server in the Add or Edit Discussion Server dialog box. Follow your system administrator's instructions for selecting and working with discussion servers.

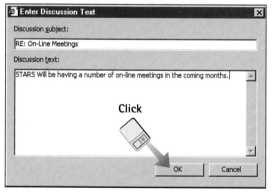

End

How-To Hints

Control that Meeting

In NetMeeting, as the presenter you have control of what goes on. If you want a collaborative environment, you can let other people control the presentation by clicking **Allow others to edit** on the **Online Meeting** toolbar (click it again to turn it off). NetMeeting also has Chat and Whiteboard features that participants can use to communicate with one another. (Collaboration must be turned off for these features to work, however.) For more information about online collaboration, refer to the NetMeeting online help.

How to Transfer Presentations to Other Computers

At some point, you may need to copy or move your presentation to another computer. However, because a presentation may contain a number of linked files and use fonts that aren't available on another computer, it's not a good idea to just copy the PowerPoint .PPT file. Making sure everything gets to the destination location correctly would take you a lot of time if it weren't for PowerPoint's Pack and Go Wizard. With the Wizard, all you have to do is follow the steps and your presentation should run just as well on the new computer as it did on the old. And if you are relocating the presentation to a computer that doesn't have PowerPoint installed, you can include the PowerPoint Viewer, which lets you run a presentation without PowerPoint itself.

Begin

1 Use the Pack and Go Wizard

To use the Pack and Go Wizard, choose **File, Pack and Go**.

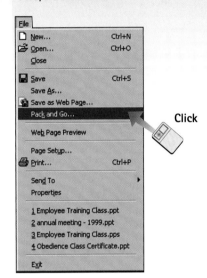

Click

2 Select File

You can choose to pack the presentation you have open at the moment or select another presentation by clicking the **Browse** button. You are asked to choose a destination location, which can be the A drive or another location you select.

3 Select Presentation Options

If the presentation has linked files and uses True Type fonts, you can choose to include them. You also can choose to include the PowerPoint Viewer. When the Wizard finishes, it compresses the presentation into the location you selected.

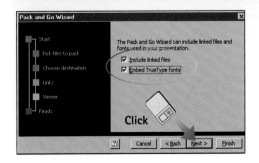

4 Unpack a Presentation

To unpack a presentation that has been compressed with the Pack and Go Wizard, go into Windows Explorer and find the location where you told the Wizard to place the file. Double-click the filed named pngsetup.exe. When the program runs, provide a destination where you want the presentation to be unpacked.

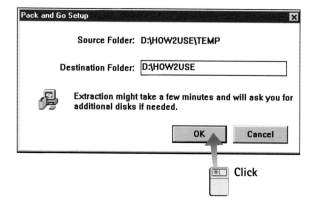

Click

5 Show Presentation with Viewer

To show the presentation by using the viewer, double-click the file called **Ppview32.exe**. Select the presentation you want to show and click **Show**.

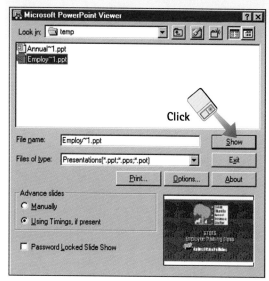

Click

End

How-To Hints

Find Out if it Works

You can tell if the PowerPoint Viewer or PowerPoint is installed without attempting to run the presentation. In Windows Explorer, right-click the presentation file. If the Viewer or PowerPoint is not installed, the **Show** command will be grayed out on the pop-up menu. In that case, you should repack the presentation by using the Pack and Go Wizard and make sure you include the PowerPoint Viewer as described in step 3.

How to Transfer Slides to Service Bureaus

Although PowerPoint has lots of features that are geared toward giving computer-based presentations, sometimes at the presentation site you don't have access to the equipment to use it. Or disaster may strike—for example, your laptop could get smashed on the plane getting there (a true story!). In these situations, you may need to resort to good old fashioned slides. Getting slides made is extremely easy with the help of the folks at your friendly neighborhood service bureau. Service bureaus have lots of extremely expensive equipment, such as film recorders, that allow you to output slides, overheads, color prints, or large format printouts. Most slide service bureaus charge anywhere from $2-$5/slide, depending on the quality and how quickly you need them.

Begin

1 Call Service Bureau

The first thing you should do before even thinking about sending your slides to a service bureau is *call* or communicate with them somehow. Talk to the experts before you create your slides. Tell them you are using PowerPoint 2000, what you want to do, and when you need it done. They will tell you how you need to set up your presentation to work with their equipment.

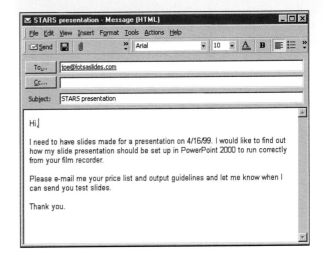

2 Set Up Slides

If you are sending slides to a film recorder, the first thing most service bureaus will tell you is to make sure that your page size is set for slides. Choose **File**, **Page Setup** to open the Page Setup dialog box and under Slides Sized For, choose **35mm Slides**.

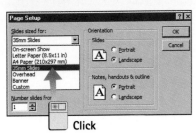

Click

3 Use Pack and Go

Some service bureaus may ask you to use the Pack and Go Wizard to package up your entire presentation, as described in Task 9. Often, you can send files via email or FTP. At the service bureau, they then unpack your presentation on their system, print the slides to their film recorder, and send slides to you.

Click

4 Create PostScript File

Some service bureaus may ask you to create a PostScript file instead. (Note that it is not the same as an Encapsulated PostScript or EPS file.) You should receive detailed instructions, but basically you add a PostScript printer in Windows that is attached to FILE. You print to that printer and send the resulting file to the service bureau.

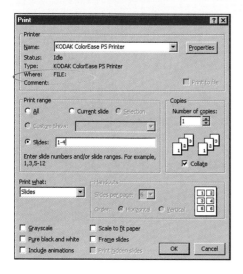

5 Send to Genigraphics

If you can't find a service bureau you like, PowerPoint comes with a wizard that makes it easy to send files to a very large service bureau called Genigraphics. Choose **File**, **Send to**, **Genigraphics** to run the Genigraphics Wizard.

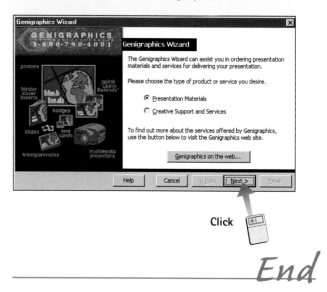

Click

End

How-To Hints

Test a Few Slides First

Before you send an large presentation, the folks at the service bureau may ask you to send a few test slides. This is good advice because colors can vary widely among film recorders. You also can see how the colors you selected in the presentation appear on film, which is often much darker than you might expect. It's better to make changes and troubleshoot problems during the test phase than when you are in a deadline crunch.

Ask Questions

Ask a lot of questions when you talk to the service bureau. They are the experts and they've seen a LOT of slides. Ask if there are any fonts that you should use or avoid. And if you've used some particular font that's not widely available, be sure to tell them. Or if you've used complex patterns or fills, make sure the film recorder can handle it. Like any other technology, sometimes things don't work as planned. A good service bureau will tell you about anything "questionable" for which you should watch out.

Task

How to Put Your Presentation on the Web

A few years ago, the folks at Microsoft woke up to the fact that the Internet was the NBT (next big thing). Even if you don't buy into Microsoft's new-found, all-consuming Internet vision, almost everyone appreciates how easy it is to communicate now that we have access to email and the World Wide Web.

Every Web page on the Internet is written in Hypertext Markup Language (HTML). As part of Microsoft's move toward a more "Web-centric" world, they have made HTML a *native* file format in all Office programs. In other words, PowerPoint can read an HTML file as easily as it can read a .PPT file. The corollary is that you can use PowerPoint to create HTML files as easily as you create PPT files. So, you can use the PowerPoint knowledge you've gained creating presentations to create Web pages as well.

Of course, like any new technology, PowerPoint's HTML features have a few limitations. The trouble with the Web is that you never know who will visit your site or what hardware or software they will use. Some of PowerPoint's HTML features only work if Web surfers use Internet Explorer 5. Although you can save your file so it works with earlier versions of Internet Explorer, your presentation may not work well for visitors using other browsers. (Of course, on an intranet where everyone in the company has standardized on one version of Internet Explorer, you don't have to worry about these issues.)

If you want to see the sample PowerPoint Web site shown in this chapter, point your browser to **www.rescueweb.org**.

How to Use Web Templates

Creating a Web presentation is similar to creating other PowerPoint presentations, and the easiest way to get started is to use the AutoContent Wizard or a template. For your first Web presentation, you should start with one of the built-in Web templates. These templates have all the options set up properly, so you know that the presentation will run correctly when it's viewed in Internet Explorer. As with other presentations, create Web presentations with your audience in mind. On the Internet, users may be using a low-speed modem over a dial-up connection, so keep graphics small, use browser-safe colors, and don't include effects, such as video and sound that require special add-on programs or take a long time to download.

Begin

1 Create a New File

If you just opened PowerPoint, the PowerPoint dialog box appears. If you are already in PowerPoint, choose **File**, **New** to open the New Presentation dialog box.

2 Use the AutoContent Wizard

From the PowerPoint dialog box, click **AutoContent Wizard** and choose **OK**. Or from within the General tab of the New Presentation dialog box, click **AutoContent Wizard** and choose **OK**.

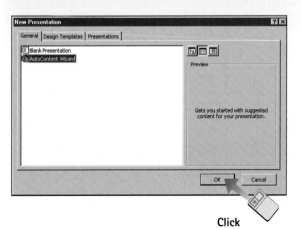

Click

3 Choose Template

The first Wizard panel is the introduction. Click **Next** and in the second panel, click **All**. Look through the list and find a home page template, such as **Group Home Page**. Click it and click **Next**. On the next panel, click the **Web presentation** selection button and click **Next**. Go through the rest of the Wizard and click **Finish**.

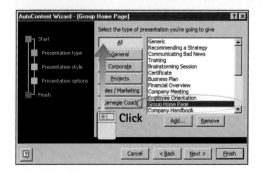

Click

4 Add Content

Type the text you want to include in the Web presentation just as you would for a slide presentation. (Working with text is explained in Chapter 3, "How to Work with Text"). Keep in mind that most browsers show text in one serif font (Times New Roman) and one sans-serif font (Arial), so keep fonts to a minimum.

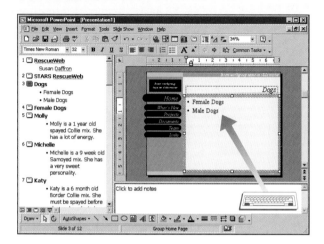

5 Change Web Options

You can change aspects of how the presentation appears and how files, pictures, and fonts are managed. (You should set these options before you save the file as a Web page as described in Task 2.) Choose **Tools**, **Options** to open the Options dialog box and click the **General** tab. Click **Web Options** and set options in the Web Options dialog box. Choose **OK** when you're done.

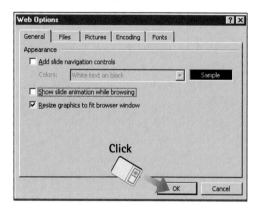

End

How-To Hints

Learn the Limits

When you design a presentation that will be viewed over the World Wide Web, you have no control over the audience (as opposed to an intranet, where you may have a better idea of who will see your site). Even though more and more Web browsers and computers support sound, animation, and video, many people still use old browsers and slow connections. Just because you *can* add lots of fancy stuff doesn't necessarily mean you should. If you add these effects, you may lose much of your audience. The best way to find out about the design limitations of the Internet is by searching the Internet itself. There are pages and pages of information on HTML, Web design, browser-safe colors, Web-friendly graphics, and much, much more.

How to Save as Web Pages

Although it's helpful to create a Web presentation with a wizard or template that's specifically designed for the task, *any* PowerPoint presentation can be saved as a Web presentation. Each slide in the presentation becomes a Web page. Saving the presentation as an HTML file doesn't necessarily mean it must be used on the Internet or an intranet, however. If you save the presentation in HTML format, anyone with a browser can view it. That person doesn't need to have a copy of PowerPoint or the PowerPoint Viewer to run your presentation. All they have to do is double-click the file in Windows Explorer and, if they have a browser on their system, your presentation appears in the window like any other Web page.

Begin

1 Open Presentation

Choose **File, Open**. In the Open dialog box, choose the folder where your file is located from the Look In drop-down box. Double-click the file to open it.

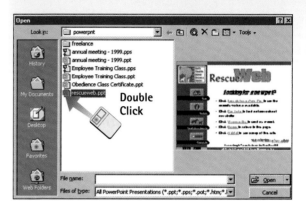

2 Save As

Choose **File, Save As** and change the **Save as type** drop-down box to **Web Page (*.htm, *.html)**.

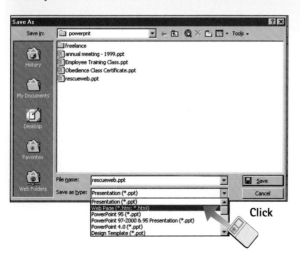

3 Choose Location

Click the **Save In** drop-down box to select a folder where the HTML file will be located. Type a filename in the File Name box.

4 Change Title

Click the **Change Title** button to open the Set Page Title dialog box and change the presentation title that appears in the title bar of the Web browser. Click **OK**, and then click **Save** to save the file. You or anyone else can still edit the HTML file in PowerPoint, just as you would a .PPT file.

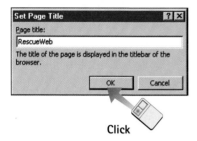

Click

5 Publish Web Page

In Microsoft parlance, the term *publish* means to save a copy of your HTML file to a Web server. You publish a Web page to a server when it's done and you don't want anyone else to edit it. In the Save As dialog box, click the **Publish** button to open the Publish as Web Page dialog box and set options. Click **Publish** when you're done.

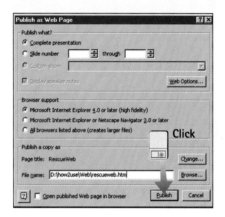

Click

6 Save As Web Page

Alternatively, you can choose **File**, **Save as Web Page**. You see the Save As dialog box with the Save as Type already changed to Web Page. Follow steps 3 through 5 as described.

Click

How-To Hints

Know Your Options

The Publish dialog box has a slew of options. You can choose to publish the entire presentation, part of it, or a custom show (custom shows are explained in Chapter 10, "How to Run Your PowerPoint Presentation," Task 1, "How to Set Up the Show"). You also can change Web Options as discussed in Task 1, step 5. Most importantly, you can indicate how PowerPoint should save the file to retain compatibility with various browser versions. Click the **Help** (? mark) button in the upper-right corner of the window and click the section buttons to find out what features are lost or changed when you select a browser option.

End

How to Add Hyperlinks

Hyperlinks are the "jumps" on Web pages you use to go to other Web pages. The hyperlink may take you to another page in the same Web site, or take you to a site on the other side of the globe. You can create hyperlinks so people can jump from place to place in your presentation just as they can on other Web pages. Although hyperlinks are most often used in the context of the Internet, you also can use them to jump from one presentation to another or to link to any file on your hard drive. Creating a hyperlink to a file can be useful during a training class for showing an example file to reinforce what you've just taught.

Begin

1 Insert Hyperlink

To insert a hyperlink, click the placeholder where you want the hyperlink to appear or highlight text that you want to be formatted as a hyperlink. Choose **Insert**, **Hyperlink**. The Insert Hyperlink dialog box appears.

2 Set Up Link

Under Link To, click **Existing File or Web page**, **Place in This Document**, **Create New Document**, or **E-mail Address**. Type any necessary hyperlink text to display. Then enter an Internet address, slide location, new document pathname, or email address to link to or select from the list. To help find the information, you can click one of the **Browse** buttons. Click **OK** to add the hyperlink.

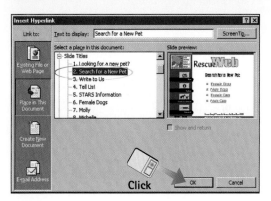

3 Change a Hyperlink Destination

You can go back and edit a hyperlink later if necessary. Click within the hyperlink and right-click it. Choose **Hyperlink**, **Edit Hyperlink** from the pop-up menu. The Edit Hyperlink dialog box appears.

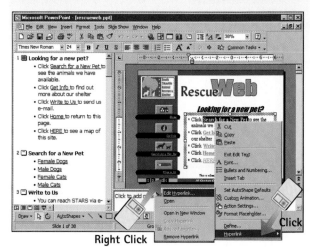

4 Remove Hyperlink

You use the Edit Hyperlinks dialog box to remove the hyperlink. Click **Remove Link** and your hyperlinked text is returned to normal text.

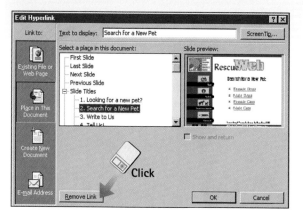

5 Add Action Buttons

Action buttons are navigation buttons that you can use in conjunction with hyperlinks to make it easier for viewers to move through your presentation. To add an action button, choose **Slide Show, Action Buttons** and click to select a button type. Click and drag to place it on the slide.

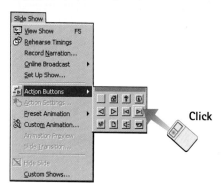

6 Add Action Settings and Sounds

After you draw the button, the Action Settings dialog box appears. Click either the **Mouse Click** or **Mouse Over** tab, depending on how you want the button to be activated. Click **Hyperlink to** and add a hyperlink destination, click **Run Program** to run an external program, or click **Play sound** and choose a sound. Choose **OK**.

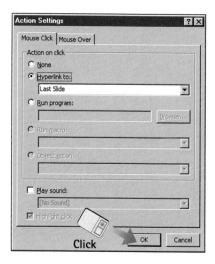

End

How-To Hints

Drag and Drop Hyperlinks

Another way to hyperlink to a file is to use drag and drop to create the link. Open Windows Explorer so you can see the file you want to link to in the window. Open your presentation and arrange the two windows on your desktop so you can see them both at the same time. In Explorer, click to select the file you want to link to, and then hold down the right mouse button and drag it into PowerPoint. On the pop-up menu that appears, choose **Create Hyperlink Here**.

Change Action Buttons

Action buttons are basically just AutoShapes, so you can change them as you would other AutoShapes. Click the button and choose **Format, AutoShape**. You can change attributes such as the color and add alternative text so people can tell what the graphic is as it's downloading.

How to Add Controls

If you've spent any time surfing the Internet, you've probably encountered Web pages that have more than just text on them. Sometimes a Web page may include buttons, scroll bars, or text boxes that look similar to the ones in your software programs. Any item you interact with is called a *control*. Behind the button or other graphic, however, a program exists that tells it how to react to user input. Any control can have properties assigned to it that tell it how to behave, as well as events attached to it that tell it what to do. Task 5, "How to Run Scripts," explains how to add the programming code to make your controls operate.

Begin

1 Show Control Toolbox

PowerPoint comes with standard controls such as command buttons and scrollbars. To add controls, the Control Toolbox must be visible. Click **View**, **Toolbars**, **Control Toolbox**.

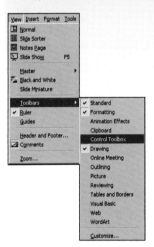

2 Click and Drag

Hover your mouse pointer over each icon in the Control toolbox to see a ScreenTip. Click a control on the Control Toolbox, then click and drag to draw a control onto the slide. You can size it like other PowerPoint objects.

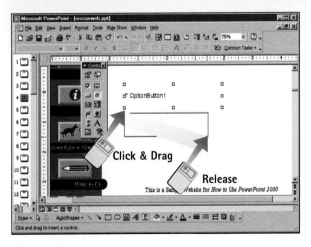

3 Edit Control Object

The first option button you create will say OptionButton1. To change the default text, right-click and choose the name of the control (such as **OptionButton Object**), **Edit**. Click and drag to highlight the text and type the new text.

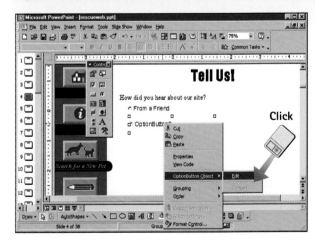

4 Change Properties

Right-click the control and choose **Properties**. The Properties window for the control appears with a list of the properties you can change on the left and their current values on the right. Click a value to change it. Depending on the property, you can either choose a new value from a drop-down box, type a new value, or load an item, such as a picture from a file.

5 View Code

To see the code behind the control, right-click and choose **View Code** or double-click the control. The code appears in its own development environment window, depending on the language you used to write the code (see How-to Hint).

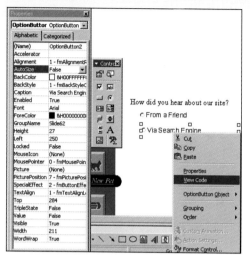

End

How-To Hints

Write Macros or Scripts

Controls don't do anything by themselves. You need to write code to make them work. You can write programming code in Visual Basic for Applications for controls you add to a presentation. (Macros are discussed in Chapter 12, "How to Make PowerPoint Work Your Way".) For controls in a Web presentation, you can write the code in either Microsoft Visual Basic Scripting Edition (VB Script) or Javascript. (Writing scripts is discussed in Task 5.)

Add More Controls

Other programs you install on your system add controls that you can access from the Control Toolbox. For example, Internet Explorer includes the Microsoft Active Movie control when it's installed, so you can play movies. You can access these other controls by clicking the **More Controls** button on the Control Toolbox.

How to Run Scripts

The controls you can add to your PowerPoint Web presentations are called ActiveX controls. However, there's nothing "active" about them until you add a macro or script to tell them what to do. In addition to writing scripts for controls, you can write scripts to do other things, as well. You can choose to write scripts in either Microsoft Visual Basic Scripting Edition (VB Script) or Javascript. For consistency, all of the examples in this task appear in VB Script.

Begin

1 Add Web Script Commands

To add scripts, add Web script commands to the Tools menu. Choose **Tools, Customize** to open the Customize dialog box. Click **Commands**. Under **Categories**, click **Tools**. Drag the **Insert Script, Remove All Scripts**, and **Show All Scripts** commands to the **Macro** submenu.

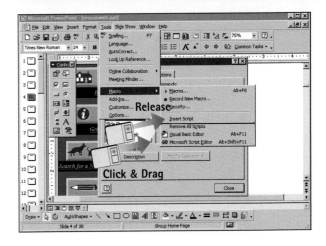

2 Insert Script

If you want to add a script, choose **Tools, Macro, Insert Script**. The Microsoft Script Editor appears. (If you have a large presentation, the Script Editor may take a while to appear.)

3 Write Script

In the Script Editor, you see the HTML code for your site. Click and type to add your new script code. For help using the Script Editor, choose any of the commands on the **Help** menu.

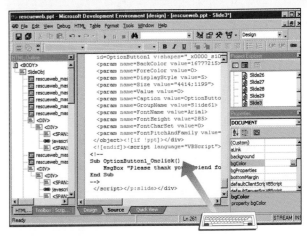

4 Refresh Page

When you add or modify the script code, you need to refresh the Web page to see the changes. Click the PowerPoint icon on the taskbar to return to PowerPoint. Click the **Refresh** button to show your changes.

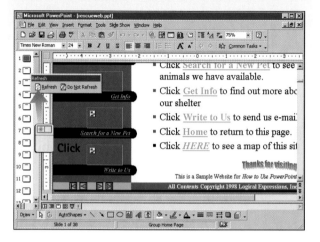

5 Remove Scripts

To remove scripts, choose **Tools**, **Macro**, **Remove All Scripts**. If you want to remove a single script and you don't see script anchors, display them by choosing **Tools**, **Macro**, **Show All Scripts**. Click the script anchor and press **Delete**.

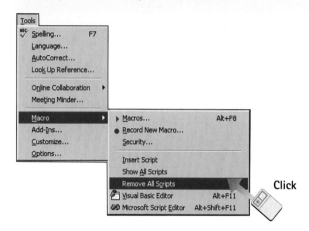

6 Change the Default Script

In the Microsoft Script Editor, click the **Source** tab. In the Properties Window, click in the value next to defaultClientScript. Change the drop-down box to the desired language (either **VBScript** or **Javascript**).

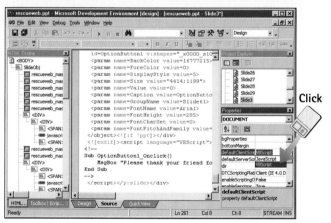

End

How-To Hints

Learn More

Hundreds of weighty tomes are written every year on Internet programming. It's an enormous and advanced topic. Because this book is about PowerPoint, it can only briefly touch on the outermost fringes of Internet programming. If you hate programming, don't worry about it! Find someone else to do it for you. However, programming is not rocket science and, if you are intrigued, you can easily learn the basics. Go to your favorite bookstore or library and look for books on Javascript, Visual Basic Script, or general books on Internet programming. The Internet itself is another outstanding resource. Just one of many examples is **www.developer.com**, where you'll find lots of links to tutorials created by experienced Javascript and VB Script programmers to help you get started.

How to Test in a Browser

After you've done a lot of work on a Web presentation, the final acid test is to find out what it looks like in a real Web browser. You can open any HTML file in Internet Explorer, so once your presentation is saved as an HTML file you can choose **File**, **Open** in Internet Explorer to view an individual *.htm file. However, this process can get tedious. There is an easier way. If you want to get a feel for how your presentation is going while you are working in PowerPoint, you can use the Web Page Preview to check it out and test all your links.

Begin

1 Open Presentation

Choose **File**, **Open**. The Open dialog box appears. Choose the folder where your file is located from the Look In drop-down box. Double-click the file to open it.

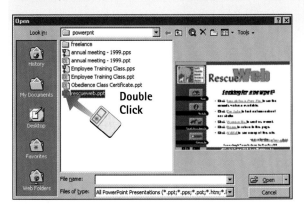

2 Web Page Preview

To quickly see how your presentation will look with the Web options you've selected, choose **File**, **Web Page Preview**. The presentation appears in your default browser.

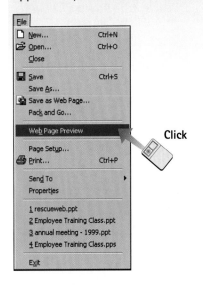

3 Test Presentation

Within the browser window, click all the hyperlinks you've set up to make sure they work. Also try out any scripts you've added to make sure they function correctly.

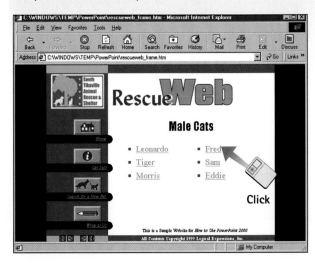

4 Open in Browser

If you have saved your presentation as a Web page (as described in Task 2), you can open it in a browser by using the standard PowerPoint Open dialog box. Choose **File**, **Open** and find your Web presentation (the files have an .htm extension). Click the down arrow on the **Open** button and choose **Open in Browser**.

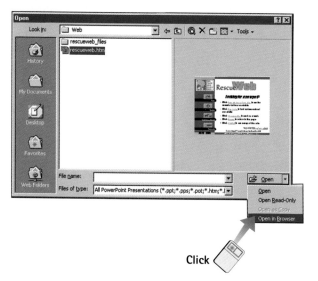

Click

5 Fit to Window

When you open a presentation, the slides automatically resize to fit the browser window. You don't have to manually adjust the slides to compensate for different screen resolutions.

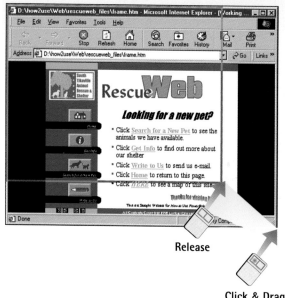

Release

Click & Drag

End

How-To Hints

Keep Track of Stuff

When you test your presentation, if something doesn't look right, it could be because the supporting file that the link points to has been moved. For example, if a bullet disappears or you see a big red X where a graphic should be, it usually means that the link to the file is "broken." When you save a presentation as a Web page, by default all these files are saved into a folder. When you move the presentation, you need to move the folder with the files as well. Similarly, if you test a hyperlink to an external file and it doesn't work, right-click it and choose **Edit**, **Hyperlink** to see where PowerPoint thinks it's supposed to be. Check in Windows Explorer to see if the file is really in that location. If not, either change the hyperlink or move the file.

Task

CHAPTER 12

How to Make PowerPoint Work Your Way

*W*hen you design software, you can please some of the people some of the time, and some of the people all of the time, but you can't please all of the people all of the time. When the folks at Microsoft were designing PowerPoint, they had to try to decide how most people would use it. But you aren't most people, and you probably create presentations just a little differently than the fellow in the next cubicle or some guy in Venezuela. Because no two people are alike, Microsoft has made it possible to customize PowerPoint so it works your way.

Apart from the thrill of controlling your PowerPoint universe, the customization features can save you a lot of time especially on the small stuff. It might seem minuscule, but those extra seconds you spend clicking through nested menus or buttons add up. All that mousing around turns into minutes and maybe even hours of time. If you spend just a half hour thinking about how you use the program and the work you do and rework PowerPoint to suit *your* needs, the result will be a serious productivity boost you'll realize almost immediately. Whether you put your most frequently used commands on a toolbar, write a macro to automate a repetitive task, or create a custom template, you'll end up spending less time wrestling with PowerPoint itself and more time getting your work done. ●

How to Customize Toolbars

Being able to transfigure your toolbars is incredibly powerful. It makes you look at PowerPoint's toolbars in a whole new way. Throughout this book, a number of hints explain why you never want to use the Print button. Now, you can delete it. Or, if you do a lot of grouping or arranging of objects, you may find the nested commands on the Draw toolbar inconvenient. You can give those commands the prominence they deserve with easy one-click access. And life is good.

Begin

1 Show Toolbars

An easy way to change your PowerPoint display is to show toolbars. Choose **View**, **Toolbars**. Toolbars that have a check mark next to them are the ones displayed on the screen. To remove a toolbar, remove the check mark.

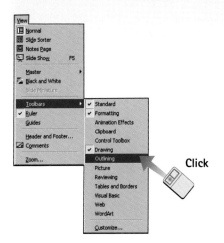

Click

2 Rearrange Toolbars

You can change where toolbars reside on your display. Toolbars can be either docked (attached to the side of the screen) or floating (a separate bar). Every docked toolbar has a vertical embossed line that you can click and drag to move the toolbar.

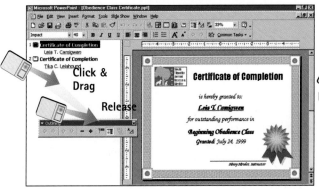

Click & Drag

Release

3 Dock Toolbars

When you move the toolbar away from the side, a thin bar appears at the top indicating that it is a floating toolbar. When you put it back at the side of the display, the bar disappears as it "docks" into place.

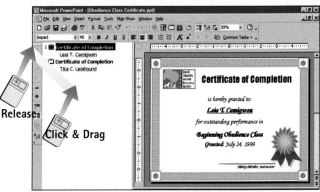

Release

Click & Drag

4 Add Buttons

You can add buttons to any toolbar or to a new toolbar (see step 6). All toolbars have an **Add or Remove Buttons** arrow (on the left of a floating toolbar and on the right of a docked one). Click the button and choose a button (checked buttons are already on the toolbar), or choose **Tools**, **Customize** and click the **Commands** tab. Click a category. Under Commands, click and drag a button to a toolbar.

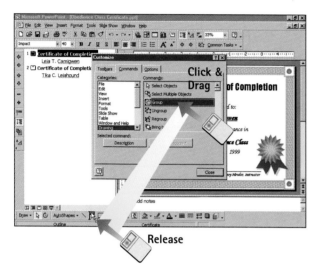

5 Change Buttons

Choose **Tools**, **Customize** and right-click a button on any visible toolbar (you might have to move the Customize dialog box out of the way). Choose an option from the list.

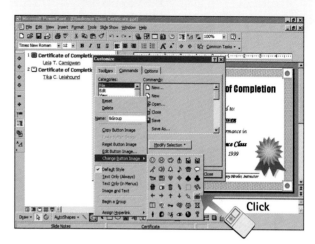

6 Create New Toolbars

If you want to seriously reorganize, you might want to create a whole new toolbar. Choose **Tools**, **Customize** and click the **Toolbars** tab. Click **New**, type a name, and click **OK**. A tiny undocked toolbar appears. Click the **Commands** tab and drag buttons to the toolbar as described in step 4.

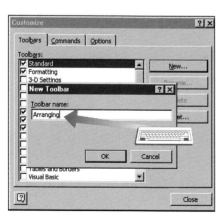

How-To Hints

Get Ideas

You could add a Close button to replace the Print button on the Standard toolbar. Or create a new toolbar with grouping alignment and order commands. You are limited only by your imagination.

Rearrange Buttons Quickly

If you don't like where your buttons are located, it's easy to move them around. Hold down the **Alt** key and click and drag the button to a new location on its current toolbar or any other toolbar that's currently displayed. To remove a button, hold down the **Alt** key and click and drag the button off the toolbar.

Customize Menus

Like toolbars, menus are customizable. Choose **Tools**, **Customize** and click **Commands**. Click a category to see its associated commands. Drag commands to a menu or submenu.

End

How to Change PowerPoint Defaults

Rebels lurk among computer users. If you would never put your stuff into a folder called "My *Documents*," you probably have been secretly yearning to change some of the PowerPoint default settings. If you look hard enough, there's usually a way to change most of the default settings in PowerPoint. You really have to look, though, because in some cases it's not obvious how to make the changes.

Begin

1 Change Default File Location

This folder is where PowerPoint looks first for your files. Choose, **Tools**, **Options** and click the **Save** tab. In the Default file location box, type the path for your folder, such as **D:\how2use**.

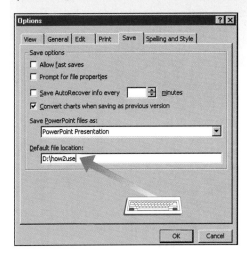

2 Set the Default Printer

Printer settings often can have an effect on formatting. If you have more than one printer that you use often, you may want to set it as the default. Click the **Start** button and choose **Settings**, **Printers**. You see your printers listed. Right-click on one and choose **Set as Default**.

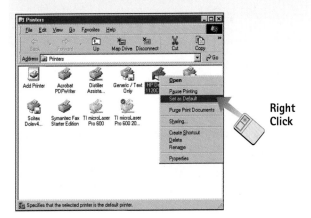

Right Click

3 Change Blank Presentation

Open a presentation that has the settings you like. Choose **File**, **Save As**. Change the **Save as type** drop-down box to **Design Template**. Type **Blank Presentation** in the File Name box and make sure you save it in the Templates folder. Click **Save** and if you see a message, click **Yes** to replace the existing Blank Presentation.

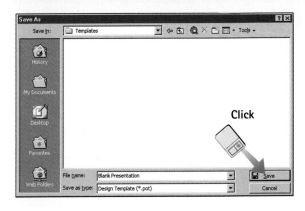

Click

4 Change AutoShape Defaults

Create an AutoShape or click to select an existing AutoShape that has the fill, line, and effects settings you want. On the Drawing toolbar, choose **Draw, Set AutoShape defaults**. The settings used in the AutoShape become the default settings for any new AutoShapes you create.

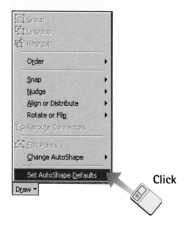

Click

5 Change Fill and Line Defaults

Changing the fill and line defaults is handy if you have to draw a lot of items that are colored the same. Select an object that has the line and fill attributes set the way you want. Choose **Format, Colors and Lines** and choose **Default for new objects**.

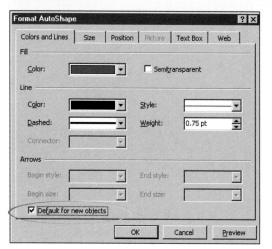

6 Change Text Defaults

If you have to create a lot of text objects, you may be tired of changing the font. Select the object that has formatted the way you like and choose **Format, Font**. Click **Default for new objects**.

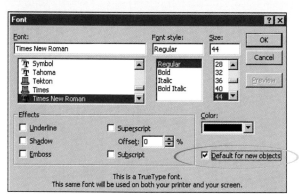

End

How-To Hints

Rename or Move My Documents

You can change the name of the My Documents folder. Or you can move the folder to a new location. First make sure you close all Office applications, including PowerPoint. In Windows Explorer, right-click the My Documents folder and choose **Rename**. Type the new name. To move the folder, click and drag it to a new location on your hard drive.

Get More Recently Used Files

By default, PowerPoint shows you the file-names of the four files you opened most recently when you click the File menu. However you can change the number of file-names that appear. Choose **Tools, Options** and click the **General** tab. Next to **Recently used file list**, use the spin arrows to decrease or increase the number (up to a maximum of nine).

How to Customize AutoCorrect

It's easy to get used to AutoCorrect. Having something fix every instance of "hte" back to "the" is great. But you can extend the functions of AutoCorrect to make it even more useful. For example, if you have a company name that's almost impossible to type, you can add it to the list of AutoCorrect entries to prevent future embarrassment. By adding, editing, and deleting AutoCorrect entries, you can make it work for you instead of against you.

Begin

1 Change Options

Choose **Tools**, **AutoCorrect**. To turn AutoCorrect on, you need to place a check mark next to **Replace text as you type**. The other options may or may not be helpful, depending on the type of text you type. Note that you can create exceptions for some options (see step 5), so if the corrections are useful most of the time, you might be able to leave the option on and add exceptions.

Click

2 Add an Entry

You add AutoCorrect entries by typing the incorrect spelling of a word into the Replace box and the correct spelling into the With box. Click **Add**. You also can add AutoCorrect entries when you do a spell check. During the spell check, click the **AutoCorrect** button in the Spelling dialog box to add the word.

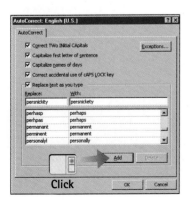

Click

3 Delete an Entry

If you want to delete some of the words from the list, use the scroll arrows to find the word in the list or start typing letters and the list goes to the closest matching entry. Click the entry to highlight it and click the **Delete** button.

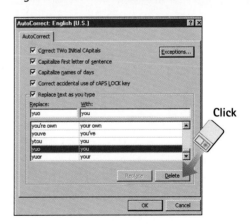

Click

4 Change an Entry

You can easily change an entry. For example, if you are a good speller, but a bad typist, some of the default entries may not be suitable for your particular mishaps. Click an item in the list and change either the **Replace** or **With** boxes. Click **Add**. You can delete the previous entry as described in step 3.

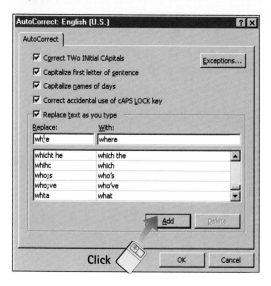

Click

5 Add Exceptions

There is an exception for every rule, and you can tell AutoCorrect when not to capitalize the first letter of a sentence or correct two initial capitals. Click **Exceptions** and click either the **First Letter** or **INitial CAps** tab. Add your exception and click **Add**. Choose **OK** when you are done.

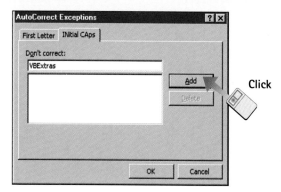

Click

End

How-To Hints

Use AutoCorrect "Shortcuts"

In addition to using AutoCorrect to fix typing and spelling mistakes, another less obvious way to use it is to expand long words or abbreviations. For example, if you work for a big company with an equally big name—such as Jones, Smith, Cogswell, and Elliot Enterprises—you might want to create an AutoCorrect entry called "jscee" that transforms this acronym into the full name.

However, if you try this tactic, make sure you don't add an entry that is a real word. For example, if your company name is Old Farm, and you create an AutoCorrect entry called "of," you'll see more of Old Farm than you probably want.

How to Create Your Own Template

After you've spent some time using PowerPoint, you'll probably come up with designs and even certain content you like that is uniquely your own. Because starting with a template can dramatically reduce the amount of time it takes to create a presentation, PowerPoint makes it possible for you to save your own templates. By saving repeating design and content elements into a template, you don't have to redo similar presentations from scratch every time. You can take the same approach if there's a PowerPoint template that's close to, but not quite, what you want.

Begin

1 Modify a Template

Choose **File**, **Open** and change the **Files of type** drop-down box to **Design Templates (*.pot)**. The PowerPoint templates are installed in a subfolder of the folder into which Office or PowerPoint was installed. Select a template from the list and choose **Open**.

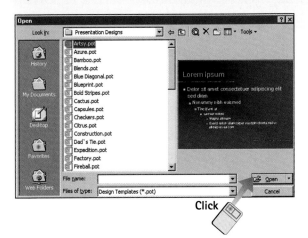

Click

2 Save As New Template

Make changes to the template, then choose **File**, **Save As** and change the **Save as type** drop-down box to **Design Template (*.pot)**. Type a new filename and click **Save**.

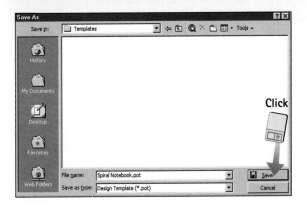

Click

3 Create a New Template

If you don't want to change an existing template, you can create your own from scratch. You can either start with a blank presentation by choosing **File**, **New** and double-clicking **Blank Presentation,** or you can start with an existing presentation and delete the presentation-specific text.

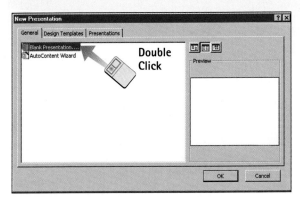

Double Click

4 Edit Master Slide

If you start with a blank presentation, switch to Slide Master view by choosing **View**, **Master**, **Slide Master**. Change the master slide as described in Chapter 6, "How to Work with Masters."

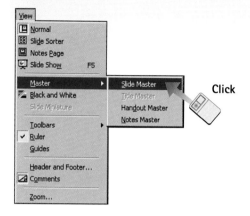

Click

5 Add Objects

You also may want to add your own company graphics or background objects, such as a logo, so you don't have to spend a lot of time working on design elements when you create a presentation later. Add graphics and other design elements as described in Chapter 4, "How to Work with Graphics," and Chapter 5, "How to Format Objects."

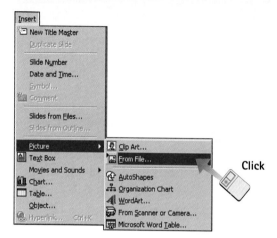

Click

6 Save in Template Folder

Choose **File**, **Save As**. Change the **Save as type** drop-down box to **Design Template (*.pot)**. The Save In box switches to the default template location. Type a filename and click **Save**. Your template is saved and will be available in the General tab of the New Presentation dialog box.

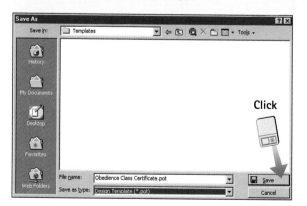

Click

End

How-To Hints

Change Presentation Templates

You can change Presentation templates the same way you change Design templates. Choose a template from the default folder, make your changes, and save it with a new name (with a ***.pot** extension).

Add Your Template to the AutoContent Wizard

You can add your own templates to the list of choices in the AutoContent Wizard. Choose **File**, **New** and click the **General** tab. Click **AutoContent Wizard** and choose **OK**. Click **Next** and click a type button (except All or Carnegie Coach—you can't add templates to these categories). Click **Add**. Find your template file, click to select it, and choose **OK**. Your template is added to the list.

How to Add Add-Ins

As the name suggests, add-ins are programs that you can add to PowerPoint to include new features. They insert themselves into the PowerPoint menus and work within PowerPoint as if they were an original piece of the program. PowerPoint's add-ins are the same concept as other similar add-on programs you may have used in other programs, such as Adobe's plug-ins or Quark's Xtensions. PowerPoint supports two types of add-ins. Most add-ins have a *.ppa extension and are written in Visual Basic for Applications. COM add-ins have a .EXE or .DLL extension and may be written in any programming language.

Begin

1 Find Available Add-Ins

Choose **Tools**, **Add-ins**. Unless PowerPoint has installed add-ins itself, the list of available add-ins will probably be empty. To find an add-in click **Add New**. Find the add-in and choose **OK**. When you load an add-in, you see a message about macros. Be sure to click **Enable Macros** or the add-in won't run. The add-in appears in the list with an × next to it, which means it's loaded.

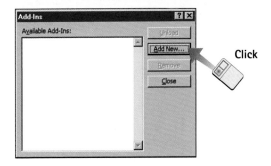

Click

2 Unload an Add-In

To unload an add-in, click an add-in name in the list that has an × next to it and click **Unload**.

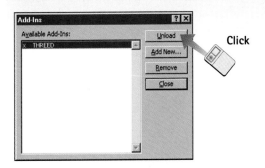

Click

3 Load an Add-In

To load an add-in that appears in the list, click any add-in without an × next to it to select it. Click **Load**.

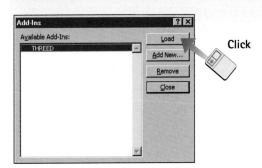

Click

4 Finding Other Add-Ins

Microsoft often has add-ins available for download from their Office on the Web site. Choose **Help**, **Office on the Web** or go to **http://officeupdate.microsoft.com/powerpoint/** and head for the download section.

Click

5 Use Advanced (COM) Add-Ins

Component Object Model (COM) add-ins are another type of program you can add to PowerPoint. To use one, you must add the command to the Tools menu. Choose **Tools**, **Customize** and click **Commands**. Click the **Tools** category and drag the **COM Add-ins** command to the Tools menu. The Tools menu opens. Release the mouse button when the command is in the correct location.

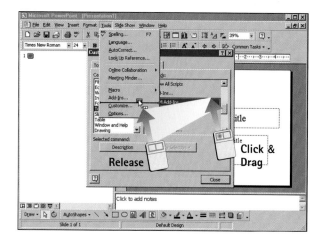

Release

Click & Drag

6 Load COM Add-In

Choose **Tools**, **COM Add-ins**. If you (or someone else) have already added add-ins, they appear in the list of available add-ins. Click **Add** to find an add-in. Select it and click **OK**.

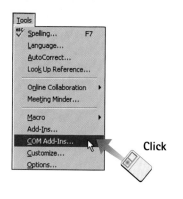

Click

End

How-To Hints

Write Your Own

Although Microsoft lets you download add-ins, you may not find the add-in you need to do what you want. Because add-ins are basically just programs that hook into and "talk" to PowerPoint, it's possible to write your own add-in by using PowerPoint's Visual Basic Editor in somewhat the same way you write macros (see Task 6, "How to Add Macros," for more on macros). If you don't have the time or programming skills yourself, you might talk a programmer friend who wants a new challenge into writing a custom add-in for you. You can find more information about writing your own add-ins in the *Microsoft Office 2000 Visual Basic Programmer's Guide*.

How to Add Macros

Everybody has routines they follow when creating presentations. A little bit of routine can be comforting, but a lot is boring. However, as in other Office products, you can create macros to automate repetitive tasks in PowerPoint. A macro is a small program made of all the commands you use to perform a given task. For example, suppose you need to scale all your pictures to 40 percent height and 40 percent width and give them a 1-point black border. Instead of choosing **Format**, **Picture** and making the changes to every picture in your presentation, you can record or write a macro to perform these steps for you when you click a toolbar button. Then with one click, you can magically make the changes.

Begin

1 Record a Macro

The easiest way to create a macro is to record it. Choose **Tools**, **Macro**, **Record New Macro**. Type a name for the macro. If you have more than one presentation open, click the drop-down box to select the presentation in which you want to store the macro. Click **OK** and a small toolbar appears with a Stop button.

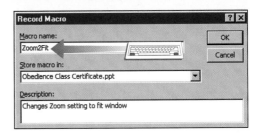

2 Stop Macro

Go through the sequence of commands you want to be recorded into the macro. (Think of it like a tape recorder for your PowerPoint actions.) Click the **Stop** button when you are done.

Click

3 Run the Macro

After you have recorded a macro, you can use it anytime you are working on the presentation. Choose **Tools**, **Macro**, **Macros**. Choose a macro from the list and click **Run** to play it. If you want to remove the macro, click **Delete** to delete the macro. (Editing a macro is described in Task 7, "How to Use VBA.")

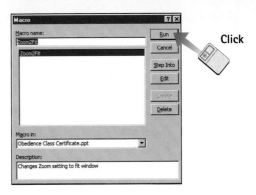

Click

4 Add a Toolbar Button

To make a macro run from a toolbar button, make sure that the toolbar you want to add the button to is displayed. Choose **Tools**, **Customize** and click the **Commands** tab. In the Categories box, click **Macros**.

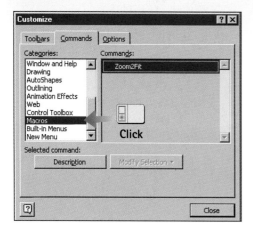

5 Drag to Toolbar

In the Customize dialog box, click and drag the macro name from the Commands box to a toolbar. A button appears with the macro name on it. Right-click the new button and choose **Change Button Image** if you want a picture to appear with the text. Right-click and choose **Default Style** if you want just the picture.

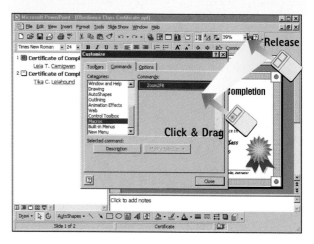

6 Change Security Level

Opening or downloading presentations or templates from unknown sources can be risky. Unfortunately, with macros comes the potential for macro viruses. To help prevent infection, you can change the security level, so you are warned before PowerPoint runs any macros. Choose **Tools**, **Macro**, **Security** and choose a setting that meets the needs of your situation.

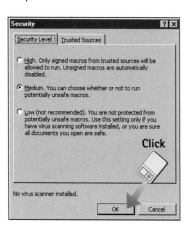

How-To Hints

Understand Macro Viruses

You may be wondering what all the fuss is about macro viruses. Unfortunately, it's not only possible to write useful macros, it's also possible to write macros that replicate themselves automatically and destroy data. To protect all your hard work from destructive viruses, you should install an anti-virus program that works with Office and read about PowerPoint's security settings. In the PowerPoint on-line help, do a search on "security" to find out more about what each of the security settings do (and don't do).

End

How to Use VBA

Recording macros is easy, but at some point you may need more macro power because it isn't always possible to record certain tasks. In these situations, you need to move into the world of Visual Basic for Applications (VBA). You use this programming language to write out the steps you want to perform. Once you learn how to use VBA and understand its syntax, you can create complex macros that let you access virtually every PowerPoint feature. When you write macros, you use the Visual Basic Editor, which includes many tools to make your programming experience easier and more productive.

Begin

1 Edit Recorded Macros

If you're just getting started with VBA, the easiest way to see how it works is to edit a macro you recorded. Choose **Tools**, **Macro**, **Macros** and select a macro in the list. Click **Edit** and you see your macro in the Visual Basic Editor.

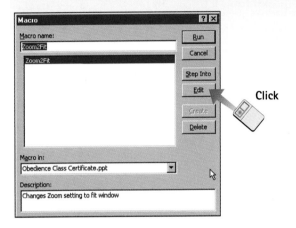

Click

2 Change Code

In the Visual Basic Editor, you can edit the code that appears in the window. You can delete or edit steps that you recorded incorrectly or add commands that you forgot or couldn't record from within PowerPoint. Choose **File**, **Close and Return to Microsoft PowerPoint** when you are done.

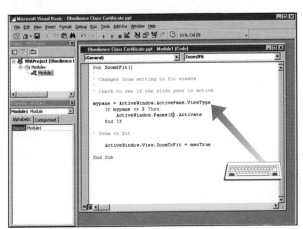

3 Create a New Macro

If your macro plans are big, you may want to write your macro from scratch. Choose **Tools**, **Macro**, **Macros**. Type a name for the new macro and click **Create**.

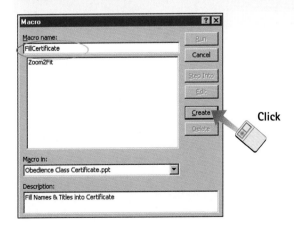

Click

4 Write Code

The Visual Basic Editor appears and you can begin typing your code. Macros can include their own dialog boxes with command buttons and other controls. You can see the project components in the Project window and you can use the Properties window to change the properties of the objects you add.

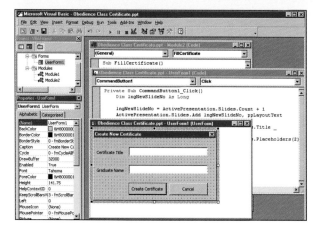

5 Use the Object Browser

Click the **Object Browser** button to view all the objects available to the project. (A PowerPoint object is a collection of related PowerPoint commands.) On the left you see the objects listed. On the right, you see the properties you can set, the methods you can call, and the events you can respond to for the currently selected object.

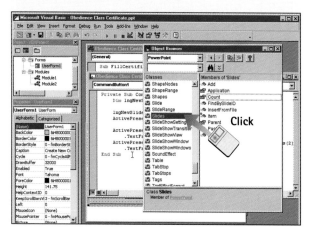

6 Debug Macros

Use the commands on the Debug menu to help you find out why a program doesn't work. You can use the step commands to go through the code one line at a time or use the breakpoint commands to tell VBA to suspend the execution of the program at a particular place.

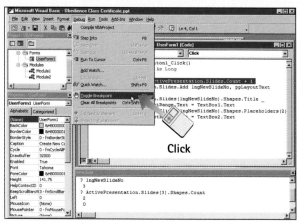

End

How-To Hints

Learn More

Programming VBA is a massive topic and is way beyond the scope of this book. If you don't know much about programming, learning how to use VBA to program PowerPoint is a good way to get started because it involves something you already *do* know: PowerPoint. Learning how to program isn't particularly difficult if you are reasonably logical and can break down processes into a series of steps. If you can conceptualize what you want to do, coding it is just a matter of learning the syntax of VBA itself. Many books have been written on how to use VBA. Microsoft also publishes a book called the *Microsoft Office 2000 Visual Basic Programmer's Guide*, which explains VBA in general and how you can use it with Office 2000 specifically.

Task

CHAPTER 13

How to Put it All Together

*I*f you're basically curious at heart, you may wonder how we authors create the samples for the software books you read. In most books, you might look at the pretty pictures and think, "Gee, I could never do that." Not in this book, because in this chapter I take you on a journey start-to-finish through the steps I went through to create the sample presentations you've seen throughout the book. By doing this, I hope you can better visualize how the information in this book works together. I've included cross-references to the appropriate chapters that include more detailed information.

This chapter shows you four projects for a fictitious animal shelter, affectionately dubbed STARS, an acronym for the South Tikaville Animal Rescue & Shelter. If you have Internet access, you can find links to all the presentations at **www.logicalexpressions.com**.

STARS is a non-profit corporation and, like every corporation, the board of directors must have an annual meeting. The first presentation is an onscreen presentation designed to be shown using a projector. The second presentation is a slide show for new employees that describes shelter policies. The third presentation is the STARS Web site. This site is designed to showcase the animals available for adoption. Because it must appeal to the most people, it doesn't use scripts, uses browser-safe colors, and has been published to remain compatible with the most browsers (you can see it at **www.rescueweb.org**). The last project is a certificate for graduates of STARS' dog obedience classes and is designed to be printed on a color printer.

Company Onscreen Presentation

The STARS annual meeting presentation is designed to be an onscreen presentation that is presented using a laptop connected to a projector. The president of the Board connects her laptop to a projector. Because it's an onscreen presentation, she can use transitions and other multimedia effects to keep the attention of those Board members who tend to nap during meetings.

The presentation is based on the "Soaring" Design Template. In the Slide Master, I changed the colors on the background and the graphic, so it wasn't quite as dark as the original. I also changed the fonts and color scheme used throughout the presentation and inserted the STARS logo at the bottom of the slides.

Begin

1 Create New Presentation

Choose **File**, **New** and click **Design Templates** (see Chapter 2, Task 2).

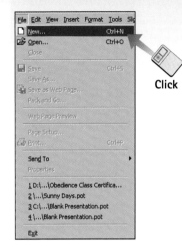

Click

2 Choose Template

Click **Soaring** and Choose **OK**. Choose an AutoLayout (I generally choose Bulleted List) and click **OK**.

Click

3 Switch to Slide Master View

Choose **View, Master, Slide Master** (see Chapter 1, Task 5).

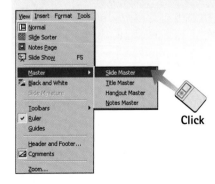

Click

4 Change Design Template

Choose **Format, Background**. Click the drop-down box and choose **Fill Effects**. In the Gradient tab choose new colors. I left the gradient the same, except I used two different deep blues. Click **OK**, and then **Apply to All** (see Chapter 6, Task 3).

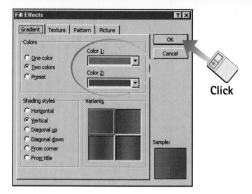

Click

5 Change Template Graphic

In the Slide Master, click the **Soaring** graphic to select it. In the Drawing toolbar, click the arrow on the **Fill Color** button to change the color (see Chapter 5, "How to Format Objects," Task 2). Click the arrow on the **Fill Color** button again and choose **Fill Effects** and change the gradient.

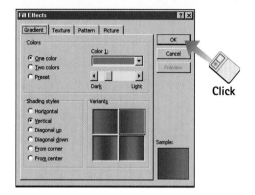

Click

6 Edit Slide Master Styles

Click in a placeholder and choose **Format, Font** (see Chapter 3). I used Impact for the Master title style and Verdana for the Master text styles. Both fonts are included with PowerPoint.

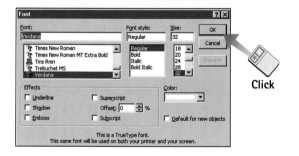

Click

7 Edit Bullets

In the Slide Master, click one of the bullets to select it. Choose **Format, Bullets and Numbering**. I chose to make the bullets yellow and I changed the bullet styles (see Chapter 3, Task 8).

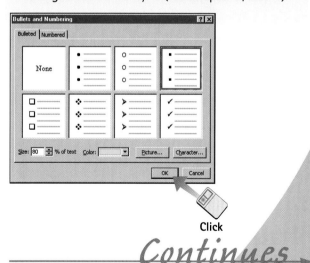

Click

Continues

8 Insert a Logo

Choose **Insert**, **Picture**, **From File** (see Chapter 4, Task 3). I drew the logo in a drawing program by modifying some clip art. I exported the logo as a .WMF file. After inserting the logo, I resized and positioned it.

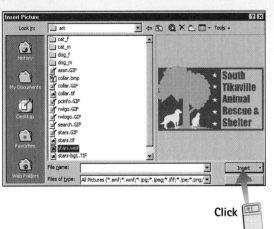

Click

9 Edit Title Master

Once I had the Slide Master set up, I made changes to the Title Master. Switch to Title Master view by choosing **View**, **Master**, **Title Master** (see Chapter 6, Task 4). In the Title Master, I resized the STARS logo to make it larger and placed it in the center of the slide.

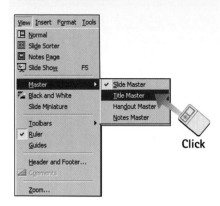

Click

10 Import Outline

Next I switched to Normal view (choose **View**, **Normal**). I prefer to write my outlines in Word and bring the text into PowerPoint. Choose **Insert**, **Slides from Outline** (see Chapter 9, Task 3).

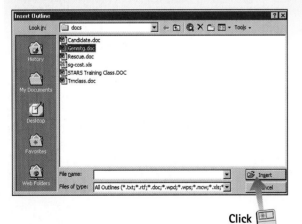

Click

11 Choose AutoLayout

The slides in the presentation use a number of different layouts. Click the slide with the layout you want to change. Choose **Format**, **Slide Layout** (see Chapter 2, Task 6).

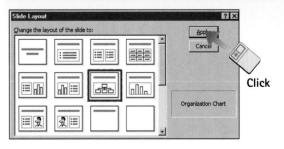

Click

12 Edit Text

After I imported the outline, I still had to do some text editing. In the Outline pane, click and drag to highlight the text you want to change (see Chapter 3, Task 1).

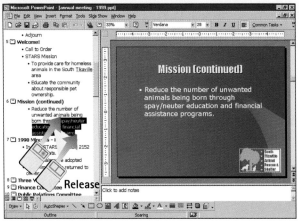

Click & Drag

13 Add Transitions

Because this is an onscreen presentation, I decided to include transitions. Switch to Slide Sorter view and choose **Slide Show**, **Slide Transition** (see Chapter 8, Task 1).

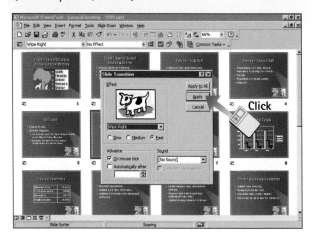

14 Show Presentation

As I worked on the presentation, I checked it out to see how it looked. Choose **Slide Show**, **View Show** (see Chapter 10, Task 3).

15 Rehearse Timings

The STARS presenters wanted to find out how long the presentation was, so they did a rehearsal. Choose **Slide Show**, **Rehearse Timings** (see Chapter 10, Task 3).

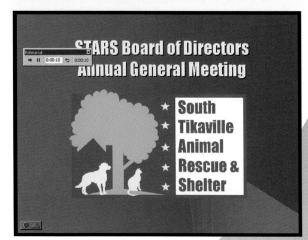

End

Training Class Slides

The STARS employee training class is a slide presentation. Because STARS doesn't have a lot of extra money, they don't have a computer available for presentations at the shelter, so they get slides made at the local service bureau.

I started with a Blank Presentation and built on it. I made most of the changes in the Slide Master. I changed the background, added AutoShapes, and changed the fonts and bullets. Certain topic heading slides also have a picture background that covers the entire slide. These graphics were inserted on the slides themselves, not on the Slide Master, because I wanted the topic headings to be visually different from the rest of the presentation.

Begin

1 Create a Blank Presentation

Choose **File**, **New** and double-click **Blank Presentation** (see Chapter 2, Task 3). Choose an AutoLayout (I generally choose Bulleted List) and click **OK**.

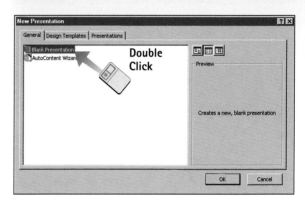

2 Add Background

Choose **Format**, **Background**. Click the drop-down box and click **Fill Effects**. In the **Gradient** tab, change the gradient settings. Click **OK** and then **Apply to All** (see Chapter 6, Task 3).

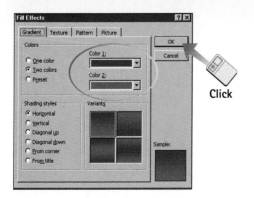

3 Switch to Slide Master

Choose **View**, **Master**, **Slide Master** (see Chapter 1, Task 5).

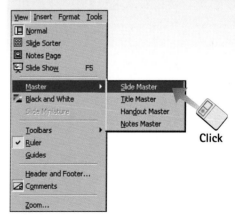

4 Add AutoShapes

The border on the left side of the slide is made up of five square AutoShapes and a long navy blue rectangle to the left of the boxes. Choose **Draw**, **AutoShape** and select an AutoShape (see Chapter 4, Task 5).

Click

5 Format Graphics

The five boxes are filled with a gradient that goes from the upper-left corner. Select the AutoShapes and choose **Format**, **AutoShape**. Click the **Color** drop-down box and choose **Fill Effects**. The rectangle is solid blue. None of the graphics have a line around them; the line color is set to **No Line**. (See Chapter 5.)

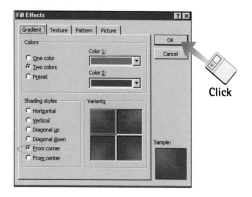

Click

6 Add Logo

Choose **Insert**, **Picture**, **From File** (see Chapter 4, Task 3). I drew the logo in a drawing program by modifying some clip art. I exported the logo as a .WMF file. After inserting the logo, I resized and positioned it.

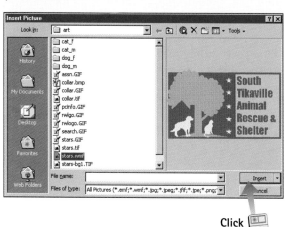

Click

7 Edit Slide Master

In the Slide Master, click in a placeholder and choose **Format**, **Font** (see Chapter 3). I used Impact for the Master title style and Verdana for the Master text styles. Both fonts are included with PowerPoint.

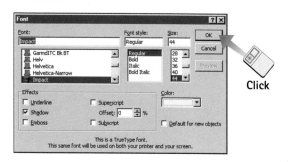

Click

Continues

8 Insert Title Slide

Once I had the Slide Master set up, I added a Title Master. In Slide Master view, choose **Insert, New Title Master** (see Chapter 6, Task 4). I added the same picture background to the Title Master as I did to the topic heading slides in step 10.

Click

9 Import Word Outline

Next I switched to Normal view (choose **View, Normal**). I prefer to do my writing in Word and bring the outline text into PowerPoint. Choose **Insert, Slides from Outline** (see Chapter 9, Task 3).

Click

10 Add Picture Backgrounds

The topic heading slides have a different background. Click in the slide and choose **Format, Background**. Click the drop-down box and choose **Fill Effects**. Click the **Picture** tab, choose **Select Picture**, and select the file. I created the background in a bitmap editing program and saved it as a .TIF file. Click **OK**, and then **Apply to All** (see Chapter 6, Task 3).

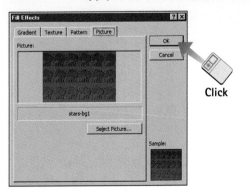

Click

11 Switch to Notes Master

The employees receive handouts they can refer to later, so I used the Notes Master to create notes pages. Choose **View, Master, Notes Master** (see Chapter 1, Task 5).

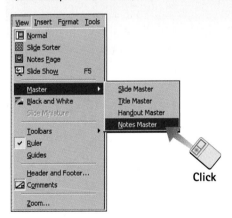

Click

12 Change Layout

In Notes view, I changed the layout so that the slide pane is smaller and the notes pane is larger (see Chapter 6, Task 6). Hold down the **Shift** key as you drag a corner handle to keep the slide proportional.

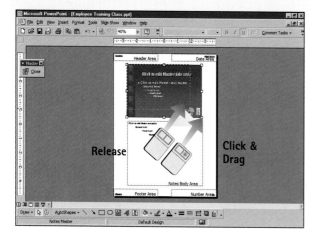

13 Add Graphic

The Notes pages also include the STARS logo. In Notes View, choose **Insert**, **Picture**, **From File** (see Chapter 6, Task 5). After inserting the logo, I resized and positioned it.

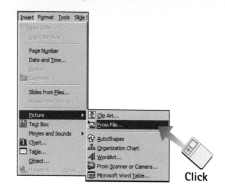

14 Print Notes

Choose **File**, **Print** and change the Print What drop-down box to **Notes Pages** (see Chapter 1, Task 2). Click **OK** to begin printing.

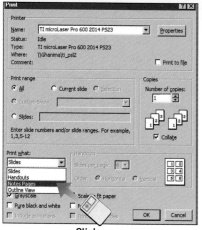

15 Send Slides to Service Bureau

I called my favorite service bureau and found out how they wanted the slides set up and sent to them from PowerPoint (see Chapter 10, Task 10). I chose **File**, **Page Setup** to verify that the **Slides sized for** option was set to **35mm Slides**.

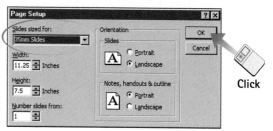

End

Corporate Web Site

RescueWeb is the STARS pet adoption Web site. The hope is that potential adopters will look at the pictures and descriptions of the animals available for adoption and be inspired to come into the shelter and adopt a new pet. Because it is being placed on the Internet, it uses simple navigational hyperlinks and the graphics are small to minimize download time. The colors are "browser-safe" so visitors using either PCs or Macintoshes can view the site. (You can see the site at **www.rescueweb.org**.)

To create the site, I started with the AutoContent Wizard and choose the Group Home Page. The default colors were unappealing to me, so I changed them. I also added graphics and lots of hyperlinks.

Begin

1 Run AutoContent Wizard

Choose **File**, **New** and double-click **AutoContent Wizard** (see Chapter 2, Task 1). In the opening panel, click **Next**.

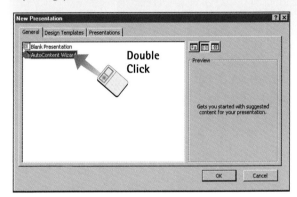

2 Choose Group Home Page

In the **Presentation Type** panel of the wizard, click **All** and choose **Group Home Page** in the list of presentations. Click **Next**.

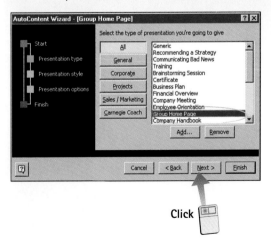

Click

3 Edit Information

In the Presentation Style panel, be sure to choose **Web presentation**. Click **Next** and in the Presentation Options panel, remove the check marks next to **Date last updated** and **Slide number**. I didn't include a title or a footer either. Click **Finish**.

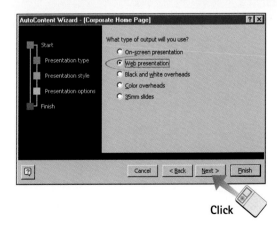

Click

4 Change Color Scheme

The default olive green and yellow color scheme wasn't what I was looking for, so the first thing I did was change the colors. Choose **Format**, **Slide Color Scheme** and click the **Custom** tab. Click items, change their colors, and click **OK**. Click **Apply to All** (see Chapter 2, Task 6).

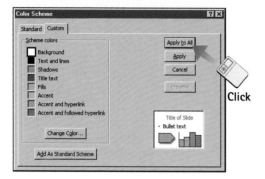

Click

5 Modify Slide Master Graphics

Choose **View**, **Master**, **Slide Master** (see Chapter 1, Task 5). The blue and green borders are AutoShapes. Choose **Format**, **AutoShape**. Click the **Color** drop-down box, choose **More Colors**, and click the **Custom** tab. I typed in the Red, Green, Blue (RGB) values to ensure I used "browser-safe" colors that are viewable on the Internet. The line color on the AutoShapes is set to **No Line**. Click **OK**. (See Chapter 5.)

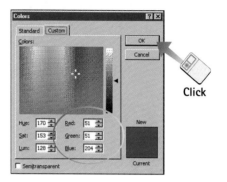

Click

6 Add Graphics

I imported the RescueWeb logo, the STARS logo, and the navigational graphics along the left side. I drew them in a drawing program and saved them all as .GIF files. Choose **Insert**, **Picture**, **From File** to import graphics (see Chapter 4, Task 3). After inserting graphics, I resized and positioned them.

Click

7 Format Graphic

On the inserted graphics, choose **Format**, **Picture** and click the **Web** tab. Click and type to insert alternative text for the Web (see Chapter 11). Click **OK** when you're done.

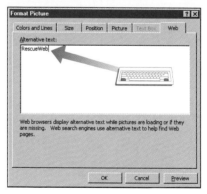

Continues

8 Format Photos

Each of the animal pages includes a photo. These graphics were saved as .JPG files and inserted into the slide. Choose **Insert**, **Picture**, **From File**, and then resize and position the picture. The photos have a 2-point black border around them. Right-click the photo and choose **Format Picture**. In the **Colors and Lines** tab, change the line settings (see Chapter 5, Task 1).

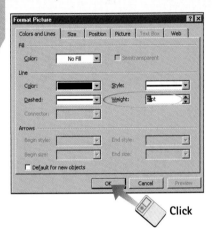

Click

9 Create Summary Slide

The slides listing a group of animals (such as female dogs) are summary slides. Switch to Slide Sorter view. Hold down the **Ctrl** key and click the slide titles to select them. Choose **Summary Slide** on the Slide Sorter Toolbar. Click and drag to move the new slide to the correct location.

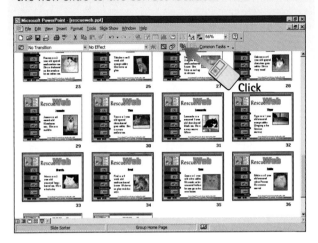

Click

10 Add Hyperlinks

I added hyperlinks throughout the presentation. Highlight text or click a graphic and choose **Insert**, **Hyperlink** (see Chapter 11, Task 3). Click **OK**.

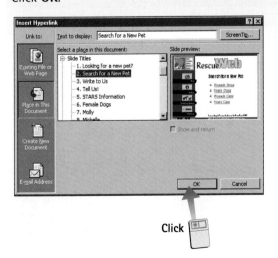

Click

11 Add Action Buttons

Choose **Slide Show**, **Action Buttons** and select a button. Click and drag to add it to the slide (see Chapter 11, Task 3). In the Action Settings dialog box that appears, choose an action for the button and click **OK**.

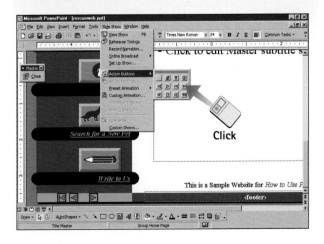

Click

12 Draw Site Map

I drew the Site Map with AutoShapes and connector lines. Click **Draw**, **AutoShape** and choose a shape or connector line. Click and drag to draw the AutoShape (see Chapter 4, Tasks 5 and 6).

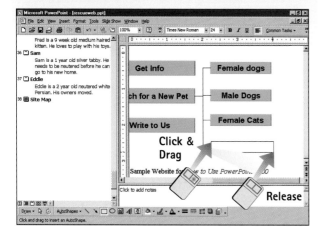

13 Test in Browser

As I was working, I tested the presentation a few times to see if it was working correctly. Choose **File**, **Web Page Preview** to see the presentation in your browser (see Chapter 11, Task 6).

14 Save As Web Page

I saved the presentation on my hard disk as an HTML presentation. Choose **File**, **Save As** and change the Save as type drop-down box to **Web Page (*.htm, *.html)**. (See Chapter 11, Task 2.)

15 Publish to Web

When I was finished with the presentation, I published the presentation and set the Web options (see Chapter 11, Task 2). Choose **File**, **Save as Web Page** and click the **Publish** button.

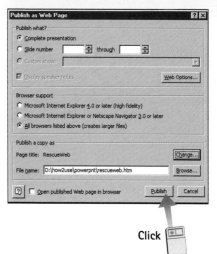

End

Certificate

The STARS certificate is given out to graduates of dog obedience classes. Much of the information is set up on the Slide Master, so creating a bunch of certificates only involves inserting slides, typing the graduate's name and the title on each slide, and printing the presentation. Draft copies are printed out on a laser printer and checked for accuracy. Final copies are printed on a color printer.

To create the certificate, I used the Certificate presentation template, moved much of the information onto the Slide Master, rearranged the placeholders, and added the STARS logo. I also ungrouped and recolored the AutoShapes that make up the border to make it more colorful.

Begin

1 Create New Presentation

Choose **File**, **New**. In the New Presentation dialog box, click the **Presentations** tab (see Chapter 2, Task 2).

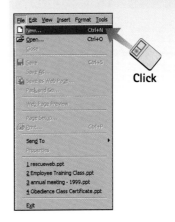

Click

2 Choose Certificate

In the list, choose **Certificate**. You see a preview on the right. Choose **OK**.

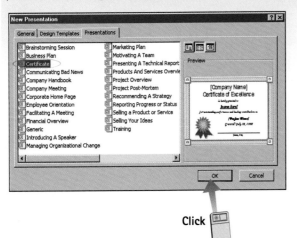

Click

3 Switch to Slide Master

Choose **View**, **Master**, **Slide Master** (see Chapter 1, Task 5).

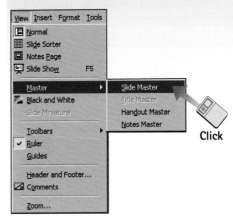

Click

4 Insert Logo

Choose **Insert**, **Picture**, **From File** (see Chapter 4, Task 3). The STARS logo was created in a drawing program by modifying clip art. I exported the logo as a .WMF file.

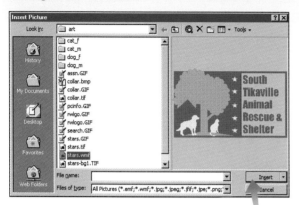

5 Format Logo

The logo was too big so I had to scale it. Click and drag to scale the logo so it fits in the corner (see Chapter 4, Task 3).

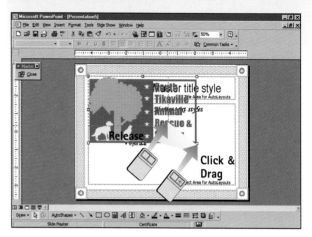

6 Modify Placeholders

I had to shorten the Title placeholder so it wouldn't overlap the logo. Click to select the placeholder and drag the left handle to the right (see Chapter 1, Task 6).

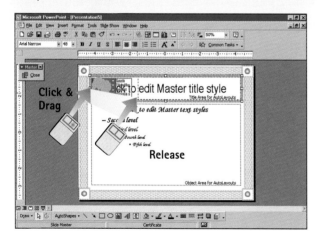

7 Add Text Boxes

I added text boxes on the Slide Master for much of the text that doesn't change from slide to slide. (I retained the Title placeholder so slides are easier to work with in the outline pane.) Click the **Text Box** button on the Drawing toolbar (see Chapter 3, Task 2) and type the new text.

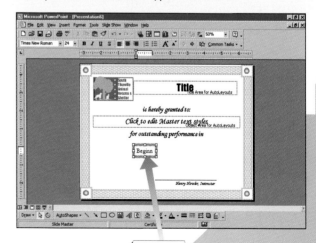

Continues

Certificate Continued

8 Cut and Paste Graphic

I cut and pasted the award graphic off the slide onto the Slide Master so it would appear on every slide. In Normal view, select the graphic and choose **Edit**, **Cut**. Choose **View**, **Master**, **Slide Master** and choose **Edit**, **Paste** (see Chapter 6). Click and drag to move it into the correct position.

Click

9 Ungroup Border

The borders are AutoShapes that have been grouped. Click the border to select it. On the Drawing toolbar, choose **Draw**, **Ungroup** (see Chapter 5, Task 4).

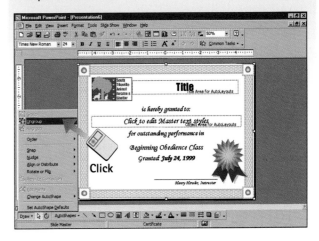

Click

10 Recolor Border

The bars are patterned rectangles. Click a rectangle to select it. On the Drawing toolbar, click the **Fill Color** drop-down arrow and click **Fill Effects**. Change the **Foreground** color to a teal green and choose **OK**. Then recolor the other AutoShapes to the same green (see Chapter 5, Task 2).

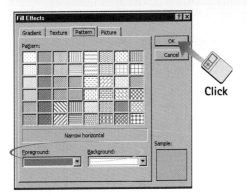

Click

11 Edit Styles

I changed the font sizes for the text on the certificate. Highlight text in a placeholder or text box and choose **Format**, **Font** (see Chapter 3, Task 3). Choose a new font and click **OK**.

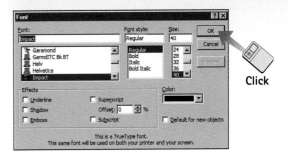

Click

12 Add Text

In Normal view, I typed the title text (Certificate of Completion) and the graduate's name for each slide (see Chapter 1, Task 6). I also created a macro to automate the task (see Chapter 12, Task 7).

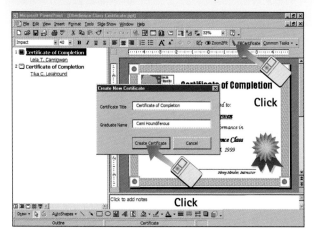

13 Preview in Black and White

Because color cartridges are expensive, I print out draft copies on my laser printer before I print anything with my color printer. To get an idea of what the certificate will look like on the laser printout, click the **Grayscale Preview** button to see what the slide looks like in black and white.

14 Print Draft in Black and White

Choose **File**, **Print**. Choose your laser printer and choose **Slides** from the Print What drop-down box. Be sure to click **Grayscale** (see Chapter 1, Task 2).

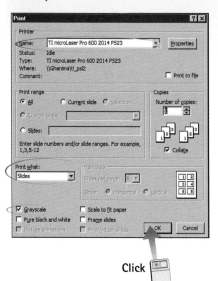

15 Print Final Print in Color

Once the draft copies have been proof-read for accuracy, choose **File**, **Print** to print the final certificates in color. Choose a color printer and choose **Slides** from the Print What drop-down box (see Chapter 1, Task 2).

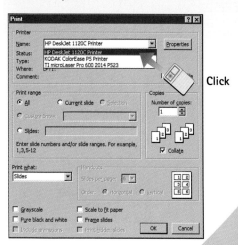

End

Task

CHAPTER 14

How to Improve Your Presentations

After you've learned all there is to know about PowerPoint, you may be wondering, "Okay, now what?" Learning the tool is only half the battle. Many people who are new to creating and giving presentations are not only unfamiliar with presentation graphics software, they also are unfamiliar with presentation design and public speaking as well. So now that you know how you can create your visuals in PowerPoint, it's time for a few general words on the rest of the process. If you want to create the best presentation possible, following some of these simple suggestions can help make your presentation the best it can be.

Task 1, "How to Improve Organization," discusses how to organize the ideas you want to talk about in your presentation and gives you a few tips for getting them out of your head and into your computer. An organized presentation makes it easier for your audience to follow what you are talking about. In Task 2, "How to Improve Writing," you find out how you can tighten up the writing in your presentations. You don't have much room on a slide, so you want to make the most of the space. Task 3, "How to Improve Design," is a quick lesson in graphic design. By following a few simple rules, you can improve your presentation's overall visual impression. Task 4, "How to Improve Presentation Skills," gives a few pointers on public speaking, and Task 5, "How to Improve Web Designs," explains some of the limitations you need to think about when you create presentations that will be viewed over the Internet.

How to Improve Organization

An organized presentation is easier for your audience to remember than a chaotic mishmash of ideas. Before you start working on your presentation, consider your audience. Are they familiar with the topic, or are you introducing them to something completely new? Once you've figured out who you are talking to, you should begin deciding what to say. First you need to generate ideas, and then you can begin rearranging them into an organized flow.

Begin

1 Brainstorm

Brainstorming is a tried-and-true way of generating ideas. Find a friend who knows something about your topic and start tossing ideas back and forth.

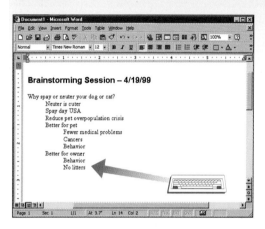

2 Try Mind Mapping

You can even brainstorm with yourself by using a technique called "mind mapping." Write down the main topic and circle it. Then write down words and concepts and circle them. Draw lines to join the circles and draw more circles based on the relationships you've generated. Concentrate on the flow of ideas, not the drawing itself.

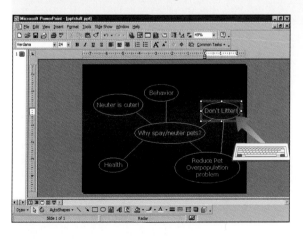

3 Research

Now start gathering information about the topics. Make sure you get all your facts straight and only trust reputable sources. (Although the Internet can be a useful research tool, remember you can't believe everything you read—*especially* on the Internet.)

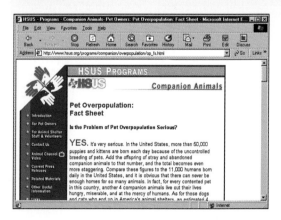

4 Outline

Once you have your ideas and research on paper, you are ready to begin organizing them. Often your brain is working on this process in the background as you come up with ideas, so organizing your ideas into an outline often goes quickly. You may want to use Word's Outline view or type your ideas into the Outline pane of PowerPoint's Normal view.

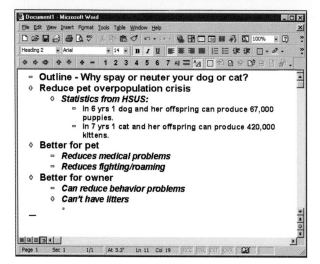

5 Reorganize

Once you think your outline is done, look at it again. You understand how items flow together, but make sure that someone who hasn't been thinking about the topic would understand as well. Make your changes. If you created the outline in a word processor, import it into PowerPoint. The outline doesn't have to be absolutely perfect, however. Remember that you can continue to rework it in PowerPoint as you go.

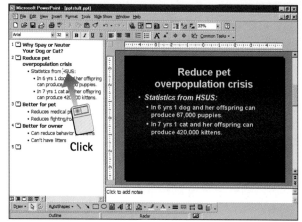

End

How-To Hints

Don't Worry

Many people get writer's block when they are working on generating ideas. If you get stuck during mind mapping or brainstorming, turn the document upside-down and start doodling or redrawing lines. Sometimes the act of looking at the document without being able to read the text allows the left brain to relinquish its logical hold on your thoughts, so your creative right brain can go wild. Another way to get unstuck is to check out the sample presentations provided in PowerPoint. Choose **File**, **New** and click the **Presentations** tab. Look for similar presentations and check to see if the template gives you ideas for organization or content.

How to Improve Writing

The words you choose in your presentation have a big effect on how it is perceived. A lugubrious, round-about writing style is difficult for your audience to follow and may very well put them to sleep. Use active words that excite and provoke action. Unlike a report that readers can leisurely read, in a presentation every word must count. Large amounts of text are difficult for an audience to read and comprehend, so keep your writing concise and to the point.

Begin

1 Be Concise

Slides are small, so you need to keep wordiness to a minimum. For example, instead of writing, "serve to make reductions in profit," write "reduce profit."

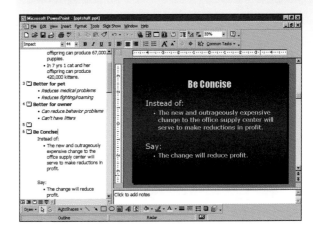

2 Use Active Voice

You want your slides to be as interesting as possible, so avoid the passive voice. In the active voice, a subject does something (as opposed to something being done to a subject). For example, write "I wrote the presentation" instead of "The presentation was written by me."

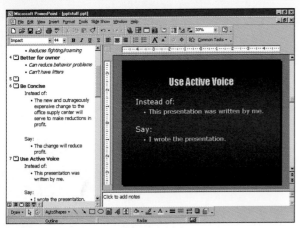

3 Use Parallel Construction

Presentations often include bullets and it's easy to confuse an audience if the points aren't parallel. If one bullet uses a particular grammatical construction, make the rest similar.

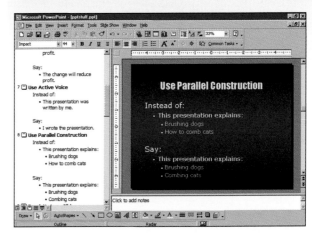

4 Break Up Long Slides

Slides crammed too full of text and graphics are hard to read. Remember that your slide will be viewed from far away. A slide should contain no more than five bullet points at the most, with each point no more than five or six words. Don't reduce font sizes to squish text on a slide. Crowding too much information on a slide makes the message less readable.

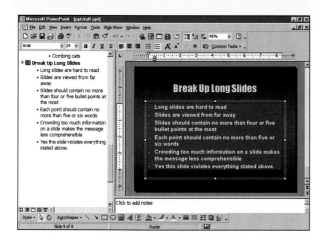

5 Proofread!

The most important thing you can do for your presentation is proofread it. A typo in a 20-page report is embarrassing; a typo projected 10-feet tall on a screen is completely mortifying. Running the spelling checker is no guarantee that the text is correct. Words may be spelled correctly but misplaced, so always proofread. Your audience will not forgive spelling mistakes easily.

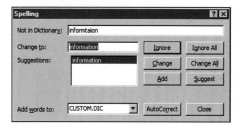

End

How-To Hints

Keep It Legible

You can set up PowerPoint to warn you if your slides get too long. Choose **Tools**, **Options**. In the **Spelling and Style** tab, click **Style Options**. You can set the number of bullets that may appear on a slide, the number of lines allowed in a title, and the number of lines allowed in a bullet. Select the appropriate legibility options and choose **OK**.

3

How to Improve Design

A good presentation design reflects well on the presenter, but, unfortunately, the converse is also true. If your design is amateurish or garish, your audience won't think much of the presentation as a whole. Good design should enhance rather than detract from your message. Make sure every design element you add has a logical reason for being on the slide. Adding random graphics just because you can often doesn't work out well.

Begin

1 Use White Space Effectively

In graphic design parlance, empty space is called "white space." Leave enough white space around objects to keep the slide from getting cluttered and difficult to read.

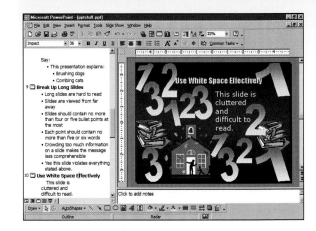

2 Be Consistent

Colors, graphics, backgrounds, and other slide elements should be used consistently. PowerPoint makes this easy to do using its masters (see Chapter 6, "How to Work with Masters"). Every title should look like every other title, and the slide background should be the same throughout, except for a Title slide or to indicate the introduction of a new topic.

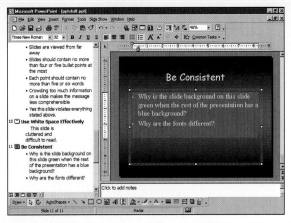

3 Exercise Restraint

PowerPoint has so many tools, it's easy to go a little crazy with fonts, graphics, animations, transitions, and sound. Resist the urge to throw in every possible effect or color in the PowerPoint palette.

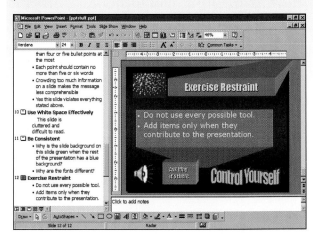

4 Choose Appropriate Visuals

The world is full of cheesy graphics and hard-to-read fonts. Think before you throw in that "kinda cool" free graphic you found on the Internet. You want to appear professional, and if the graphic or font doesn't strengthen your presentation, don't use it. Remember that the purpose of your presentation is to convey information, not to show off snazzy graphics.

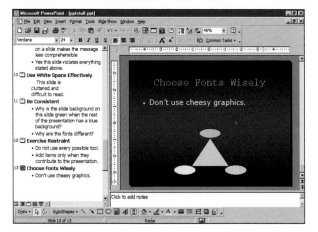

5 Choose Color Wisely

Color has an emotional impact, so be careful how you use it. For example, the color red is often used to convey danger (think Stop signs, for example), so exercise caution when you use it. In addition, certain colors, such as red and green, are difficult for color-blind people to distinguish, so be careful when using these colors. Be sure that you choose colors that are legible. For example, light colored text on a light background is difficult to read. Similarly dark text disappears into a dark background.

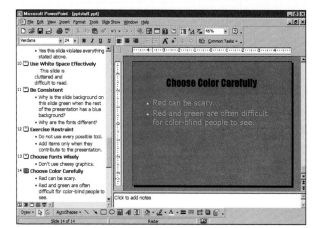

End

How-To Hints

Choose Appropriate Typefaces

There are two main types of fonts: serif and sans-serif. Serif fonts are typestyles such as Times New Roman that have little "tails." Sans-serif literally means without serif, and includes fonts such as Arial, which have no "tails." In printed documents, serif fonts are generally easier to read but, in a presentation, the cleaner lines of sans serif fonts are often easier to see, especially in a large room. If you are in doubt, create a quickie slide that uses the fonts you are considering and project it on a wall. Stand in the back of the room and see how well you can read it. Another thing to keep in mind: when you select typefaces, don't use more than two on a slide. If it's a formal presentation, also avoid flowery decorative typefaces. Try to stick with fonts that go well with your overall company image.

How to Improve Presentation Skills

Studies have shown that many people fear standing up in front of an audience and giving a presentation more than they fear death. You may wonder how anybody does it. Remember that in most presentation situations, the people are there because they *want* to be there. You have the information they need for one reason or another. Rest assured that if you give a good presentation, people will focus on the message and forget about the messenger.

Begin

1 Don't Fidget

One way to take the focus off you is to avoid fidgeting as it detracts from your presentation. If you have nervous habits, do what you can to control them while you're speaking.

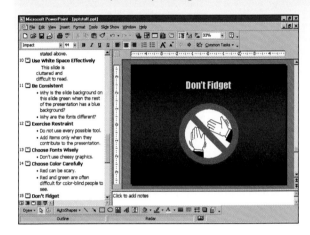

2 Don't Memorize or Read

Knowing your material is good; memorizing it is bad. Nobody likes to listen to a drone reciting text verbatim. Pay attention to your audience and actually talk to *them*. Also, reading from your notes is just as bad. You may feel more secure looking at your notes, but the audience will be wondering why you never look at them.

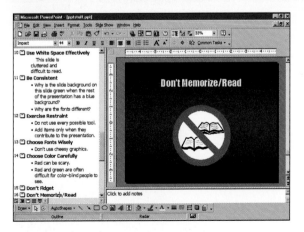

3 Pace Yourself

Slow down and pace yourself. Resist the urge to speak quickly and rush through every slide. Try to speak more slowly than normal and give yourself at least 10–20 seconds per slide (or more if it requires explanation).

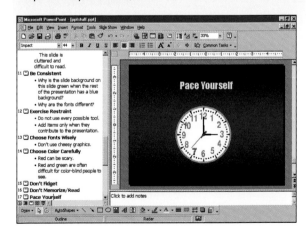

4 Be Prepared

The most important thing you can do is be prepared before a presentation. Try out all the equipment and do a dry run. Working the bugs out of the system beforehand takes some of the worry out of the presentation and gives you extra confidence you need to focus on the task at hand.

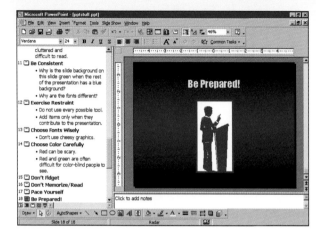

5 Rehearse, Rehearse, Rehearse

Part of being prepared is rehearsal. There's a reason why actors rehearse so much. Learning the presentation material is vitally important. Again, don't memorize word-for-word, but know the subject inside and out, so you can give the best presentation possible.

End

How-To Hints

Work the Audience

Experienced presenters monitor their audience. When you give your presentation, be sure to face your audience. Don't hide behind your computer and face away from them (they can't *hear* you if you aren't talking to them). Decide ahead of time how to answer questions. You can tell people that you'll answer questions on the spot or let them know that they should save their questions for a Q&A session afterward. If a question gets too complicated or diverges from the topic during the presentation, explain nicely that you'll discuss it with the person after the presentation. (And then do it—people remember these things!)

TASK

5

How to Improve Web Presentations

The Internet has opened up a whole new world for designers. It brings great new freedoms (no need for reprinting every time something changes) and great new limitations (you can't use every color in the rainbow). When you design for the Internet, you don't know your audience—you don't know what type of computer or software they have. If you want the most people to see your work, design for the lowest common denominator; curtail the colors, fonts, and effects you use.

Begin

1 Use "Browser-Safe" Colors

What you see on your computer screen isn't necessarily what someone else will see on a different computer. There are 216 common colors, composed of Red/Green/Blue (RGB) values, that you enter into the PowerPoint Color dialog box (see How-to Hint).

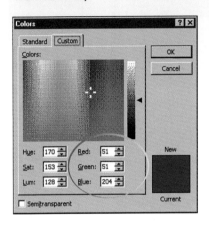

2 Keep Graphics Small

When you design for the Web, *everything* is downloaded. Keep graphics as small as possible. One rule of thumb is to not exceed 40KB worth of graphics on a page to keep downloading times reasonable.

3 Keep It Simple

We've all seen Web sites that were so laden with graphics that the actual content gets lost in the shuffle. Make sure you remove extraneous elements and focus on the message of your Web presentation.

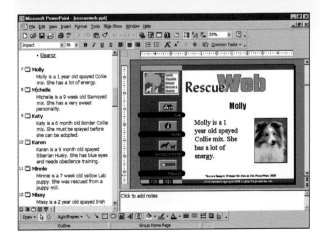

4 Design for the Masses

The Web is a worldwide medium, so you need to consider people with all types of backgrounds. Try to keep your graphics and text simple and easy to use, so that even people who aren't using the latest and greatest computer equipment or don't speak English as their first language can understand and appreciate your site.

5 Test Pages Thoroughly

Always test your Web pages. Just because it works in PowerPoint does not necessarily mean it will work on the Web. Try every hyperlink and make sure you don't get any nasty error messages. Once you've published it, get friends with different browsers and computers to try out your site, too.

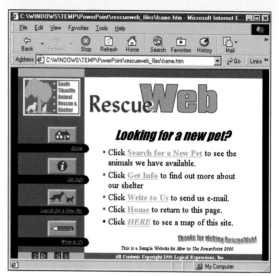

End

How-To Hints

Find Browser-Safe Color Palettes

By using browser-safe colors, you know (color-wise anyway) what your site will look like on virtually every browser. The 216 colors are all combinations of RGB values 0, 51, 102, 153, 205, and 255. Many people have put up color palettes on the Internet that give you the RGB values for the 216 browser safe colors. For example, Web color guru Lynda Wienman has included color palettes on her Web site at www.lynda.com.

Glossary

action buttons   Symbols you can insert into Web presentations to indicate navigational controls, such as Next and Back.

active voice   In a sentence, if the subject acts, the voice is the active voice, as in "I wrote the presentation." (See also **passive voice**)

active window   In Windows, the window that is currently affected by user input such as mouse movements and keyboard actions. The title bar of the active window is generally highlighted.

add-in   A separate program that can be loaded into PowerPoint to augment or include additional special features. (See also **COM add-in**)

adjustment handles   (See **handles**)

agenda slide   A special type of summary slide that lets you jump from one section of a presentation and automatically return to the agenda slide.

alignment   The positioning of text or an object along a vertical line (such as top, middle, or bottom) or a horizontal line (such as left, center, or right).

alternative text   Text you add to graphics or objects that appears while pictures are loading into a Web page.

animation   Visual or sound effects you can add to objects as they appear on a slide.

annotation   Comments you can write directly on slides during a presentation. The annotations are temporary and disappear when the slide show ends.

aspect ratio   The relationship between the height and width of an object. If you maintain an object's aspect ratio, the image is not distorted.

attachment   A file you include with an email message.

AutoContent Wizard   Wizard that walks you through the creation of a new presentation and lets you choose content and design elements.

AutoCorrect   PowerPoint feature that automatically corrects common typing and spelling mistakes.

AutoFit   PowerPoint feature that automatically decreases line spacing and font size to allow text to fit within a slide placeholder.

AutoFormat   PowerPoint feature that recognizes certain text such as two hyphens and automatically reformats it into a typographic equivalent such as an em dash.

AutoShape   Predrawn shapes you can include in a presentation.

axis   In a chart, the horizontal (x-axis) or vertical (y-axis) line that is used as a reference for plotting values in a coordinate system. A third axis (z-axis) can also be used to show depth.

B

background The underlying color, pattern, or texture that appears behind all of the objects on a slide.

bitmap An image made up of a collection of dots. Scanned images and certain image formats such as .BMP and .GIF are bitmap files. (See also **vector line art**)

bold A version of a typeface in which the letters appear with heavier or thicker lines.

borders The lines surrounding objects, graphics, or tables.

brainstorm A method of coming up with ideas that involves getting a group of people together, engaging in unfettered discussion, and writing down every idea (no matter how silly).

branch As a noun, in an organization chart, a manager and all of its subordinates. As a verb, to use a hyperlink to go to another presentation or place in a presentation.

brightness The lightness of an image. When you adjust brightness, you lighten or darken all colors equally. You can adjust the brightness of imported bitmap images in PowerPoint. (See also **contrast**)

broadcast (See **online broadcast**)

browser A software program used for viewing Web pages on the Internet. Internet Explorer and Netscape Navigator are two popular browsers.

browser-safe color One of the 216 common colors that are shared across browsers, operating systems, and computer platforms.

bullet A dot or other special character used to set off items in a list.

button An icon on a toolbar that you click to perform a certain action. Other buttons such as the OK button in a dialog box are clicked to cause certain actions to occur (the action depends on the button).

C

cascade In Windows, to arrange all the windows so that only their title bars show.

case In text, the type of capitalization used. For example, uppercase text is composed of all capital letters.

cell The box created where a row and column intersect. In PowerPoint, cells appear in chart datasheets and tables.

chart A graphical representation of data. In PowerPoint, charts are created in Microsoft Graph based on information you enter into a datasheet.

clip art Predrawn illustrations that can be used without paying an artist a royalty fee. PowerPoint comes with numerous clip art images.

Clip Gallery PowerPoint's repository for the clip art, pictures, photographs, sounds, and videos that can be inserted into a presentation.

clipboard A memory area used by Windows to store a copy of the last item cut or copied into it. (See also **Office Clipboard**)

close box The small button with an × on it at the upper-right corner of a window that you use to close a window, file, or program.

CMYK Stands for cyan, magenta, yellow, and black. The color model used in four-color process printing. Tiny dots of these colors when combined create the illusion of a full color spectrum.

collapse In Outline view or the Outline pane, to reduce the outline levels displayed. Collapsing is the opposite of expanding outline levels. (See also **expand**)

color scheme A set of eight coordinated colors that are used consistently throughout a presentation.

column A vertical row of cells in a table or a datasheet.

COM add-in   A Component Object Model add-in. Unlike other add-ins that have a .PPA extension, COM add-ins can be .EXE or .DLL files. (See also **add-in**)

comment   A virtual yellow "sticky note" that reviewers can add directly into a presentation.

connector   A type of line that connects two objects. If one of the objects is moved, the line changes position, so the objects remain connected.

contrast   The difference between the lightest and darkest parts of an image. You can adjust the contrast of imported bitmap images in PowerPoint. (See also **brightness**)

control   Any item a user interacts with while using a program, such as buttons, scrollbars, or text boxes. PowerPoint includes ActiveX controls you can add to Web presentations.

copy   To duplicate information. You can use the Copy command in conjunction with the Paste command to copy items from one place to another within a file or from one file or program to another. (See also **cut** and **paste**)

crop   To trim off the excess or unwanted portions of an image. PowerPoint includes a cropping tool you can use to crop images. Cropping does not affect the actual file, only its appearance within PowerPoint.

cursor   The arrow, vertical line, two-headed or four-headed arrow that indicates where your mouse is in relation to the screen.

custom show   A subset or arrangement of slides created from a given presentation.

cut   To remove information. You can use the Cut command in conjunction with the Paste command to move items from one place to another within a file or from one file or program to another. (See also **copy** and **paste**)

D

data point   A value plotted on a chart. The value originates from a cell in a datasheet.

data series   A group of related data points. The values originate from a row or column in a datasheet.

datasheet   The table of data that is associated with a given chart. In PowerPoint, charts are created in Microsoft Graph based on information you enter into a datasheet.

debug   In the Visual Basic Editor, the process of locating and fixing errors in programming code.

default   The original program preferences and settings within PowerPoint, until you specify an alternative. For example, the default working folder for Microsoft Office is called My Documents. PowerPoint attempts to save files in that location first, unless you give it a new location.

degree   A unit of rotation related to the fact that in geometry 360 degrees is a complete circle. In PowerPoint, you can specify rotation in degrees.

demote   In Outline view or the Outline pane, to increase the indention level. Demoting is the opposite of promoting. (See also **promote**)

Design Templates   Templates included in PowerPoint that include color schemes, slide and title masters, and formatting that works together to create a particular look.

desktop icon   (See **icon**)

dissolve   A transition effect or animation that causes one image to pixelate into another.

distribute   To spread objects equally across a given space.

docked toolbar   A toolbar that is attached to one side of the display and distinguished from a floating toolbar by its lack of a title bar. (See also **floating toolbar**)

download   To transfer a file from the Internet or other online service to your computer.

drag-and-drop   A type of editing where you use your mouse to select an object and move or copy it to a new location.

E

email   Short for electronic mail. A system allowing you to send messages from one computer to another over some kind of communications network, such as a local area network, online service, or the Internet.

embed   To bring an object into a presentation so it becomes part of the presentation without any link to the originating file. (See also **link**)

emboss   To make an object appear raised. Embossing is the opposite of engraving. (See also **engrave**)

Encapsulated PostScript file (.EPS)   A type of vector line art graphic format.

engrave   To make an object appear depressed or pushed in. Engraving is the opposite of embossing. (See also **emboss**)

EPS   (See **Encapsulated PostScript file**)

Excel   Microsoft's spreadsheet program, which is designed to work with numerical data. You use the program to perform mathematical calculations and other operations.

expand   In Outline view or the Outline pane, to increase the outline levels displayed. Expanding is the opposite of collapsing. (See also **collapse**)

export   To save or convert information so that it can be used in another program. Exporting is the opposite of importing. (See also **import**)

F

file   A named collection of information. PowerPoint presentations are saved as files with a *.ppt extension.

fill   The color added to a closed object, such as an AutoShape, text, or placeholder.

film recorder   An output device used by service bureaus to create high resolution 35 millimeter slides.

flip   Act of turning an object so it faces the opposite direction. (See also **rotate**)

floating toolbar   A toolbar that is not attached to any side of the display and appears with a title bar that allows it to be moved around the screen. (See also **docked toolbar**)

font   The characters of a given type size in a given typeface and style such as 10-point Times New Roman Italic. Often used interchangeably with typeface, typestyle, or type family. (See also **typeface**)

footer   Text that appears along the bottom of a page or slide and that is repeated on every page or slide. (See also **header**)

formatting   Attributes you apply to text or other objects to change their appearance. Formatting may include style attributes such as bold or italic or fill and line colors, for example.

G

Genigraphics   A service bureau that accepts files for output to 35mm slides, overhead transparencies, display prints, and posters. PowerPoint includes a wizard to facilitate file transfer to Genigraphics.

GIF   (See **Graphic Interchange Format file**)

gradient   A type of fill effect that gradually changes from one color to another color or from one shade of a color to another.

Graphic Interchange Format (.GIF) file   A type of graphic file format that is often used for files being placed on Web pages that will be viewed over the World Wide Web. GIF files are saved with a .GIF extension.

grayscale   A method of viewing and printing presentations in black and white, where the colors used are made up only of shades of gray ranging from black to white.

grid   Invisible horizontal and vertical lines designed to help aid in aligning and placing objects.

group   To combine a number of objects so they are treated as one. Grouping is the opposite of ungrouping. (See also **ungroup**)

guides   Non-printing lines you can display to aid in aligning and placing objects on a slide.

H

handles   Small boxes that surround an object when it is selected. Handles are used to change the size or scaling of an object. Adjustment handles are small yellow diamonds that let you change the appearance of an AutoShape in some way.

handout   Printed versions of slides that are given to the audience for reference. Handouts show only the slides and can be set up with up to nine slides on a page.

Handout Master   PowerPoint view where you set characteristics that will be common to all handout pages, such as the number of slides that appear on a page.

Handout view   (See **Handout Master**)

hanging indent   (See **outdent**)

header   Text that appears along the top of a page that is repeated on every page. (See also **footer**)

headline   (See **title**)

home page   (See **Web page**)

hotkey   (See **keyboard shortcut**)

HTML   (See **Hypertext Markup Language**)

hyperlink   A graphic or underlined text that you click to jump to another point in a presentation, another file, or a location on the World Wide Web.

Hypertext Markup Language (HTML)   The tagging language used to create pages that will be placed on a Web site that will be viewed over the World Wide Web.

I-J

icon   A small drawing that appears on the Windows desktop, Windows Explorer, or other software to delineate a file, program, or other object on the computer.

import   To bring information from another program into PowerPoint. Importing also can be referred to as inserting or opening a file in PowerPoint. Importing is the opposite of exporting. (See also **export**)

indent   As a verb, the act of moving a paragraph of text inward to set it off from other text. As a noun, the extra space at the beginning of a paragraph that results from indenting text. Indenting is the opposite of outdenting. (See also **outdent**)

insertion point   When entering text, the flashing line is the insertion point.

Internet   A communications network in which collections of computer networks and gateways are connected by using a protocol called TCP/IP. Sending and receiving email and accessing the World Wide Web are common uses of the Internet.

Internet Explorer   Microsoft's Web browser. (See also **browser**)

Internet service provider (ISP)   A business that, for a fee, gives its customers access to the Internet by letting them dial into a server that is connected to the Internet (sometimes called a local service provider).

intranet   A communications network set up within an organization that uses a similar setup and protocol as the Internet.

italic   A version of a typeface in which the letters appear slanted.

Javascript   A programming language used to write scripts that are inserted into Web pages that are to be viewed over the World Wide Web or an intranet.

Joint Photographic Experts Group (JPEG) file   A type of graphics file format that supports compression and that is often used for files being placed on Web pages that will be viewed over the World Wide Web. JPEG files are saved with a .JPG extension.

JPEG   (See **Joint Photographic Experts Group file**)

justify   To add extra space between words or letters to force a line of text to stretch to the width of the designated margins.

K-L

keyboard shortcut   Combination of keystrokes used to perform a certain action, such as Ctrl+C to copy an item.

keyword   Descriptive term entered to locate information in online help or to describe or find clip art in the PowerPoint Clip Gallery.

landscape   A horizontal page orientation. Landscape is the opposite of portrait orientation. (See also **portrait**)

leading   (See **line spacing**)

legend   A box placed near a chart to explain the meaning of colors or patterns used in the chart.

line art   (See **vector line art**)

line spacing   The vertical space between lines of type, measured in number of lines (1, 1.5, 2, and so on) or in points.

link   To bring an object into a presentation and retain a connection to the originating file. A linked file is a representation of the original file and can only be updated by changing the source file. (See also **embed**)

lobby page   Web page URL included in a reminder email for an online broadcast that contains information about the presentation.

logo   A symbol or nameplate used to identify a business.

M

macro   A series of commands that is either recorded or written to automate PowerPoint tasks. Macros are recorded using the macro recorder or written in the Visual Basic for Applications (VBA) programming language. (See also **Visual Basic for Applications** and **Visual Basic Editor**)

master slide   (See **Slide Master**)

maximize   To make a window fill the screen. You click the maximize button (a square) on any window to maximize it. You click the Restore button to return it to a window or minimize to reduce the window to a Taskbar button. (See also **minimize**)

media clip   A video, animation, or sound you can insert into a presentation. Media clips are located in the Clip Gallery.

meeting minder   PowerPoint feature that allows you to record minutes and generate action items during an online broadcast of a presentation.

merge cells   To turn two cells into one cell in a table. Merging cells is the opposite of splitting cells. (See also **split cells**)

Microsoft Visual Basic Scripting Edition   (See **VB Script**)

mind mapping   A one-person brainstorming technique in which you write down and free-associate topics by drawing and connecting circled topics.

minimize   To reduce the window to a taskbar button. You click the minimize button (–) on a window to minimize it. Click the taskbar button to return the window to the screen. (See also **maximize**)

monospaced font   Type in which the space occupied by each character is the same (in other words, a "w" takes up the same amount of space as an "i"). (See also **proportional font**)

movie   PowerPoint term for a multimedia video file, which may be some sort of animated or moving picture with or without sound. PowerPoint includes a number of movies in its Clip Gallery.

multimedia   A generic term for the combination of sound, graphics, animation, and video.

N

Normal view   PowerPoint view composed of three panes that contain the slide, outline, and notes, so you can see all three elements at the same time.

Notes Master   PowerPoint view where you set the layout and characteristics that will be common to all of the notes in a presentation, such as colors, repeating graphics, headers, footers, and text formatting.

notes pages   Presentation notes used by a presenter for reference during a presentation. May also be used as audience handouts. Also called speaker's notes.

Notes Page view   PowerPoint view that allows you to enter presentation notes.

nudge   To move an object slightly. In PowerPoint, you can nudge a selected object by using the arrow keys or the Nudge command on the Drawing toolbar. You also can nudge a shadow.

O

object   An object is any item on a PowerPoint slide such as a placeholder, graphic, or AutoShape. Object can also refer to an OLE object, which is an item that has been linked or embedded in the presentation. In VBA, an object also can refer to a group of related PowerPoint commands.

object browser   In the Visual Basic Editor, the object browser lets you view the PowerPoint objects available to the project in addition to the properties you can set, the methods you can call, and the events you can respond to for a given object.

object linking and embedding (OLE)   A feature that allows you to share information between programs using linked and embedded objects.

Office Assistant   (See **Presentation Assistant**)

Office Clipboard   A special type of clipboard used by programs in the Microsoft Office suite that lets you store copies of the last twelve items cut or copied into it. (See also **clipboard**)

OLE   (See **object linking and embedding**)

online broadcast   A meeting in which the presenter shows a presentation over some kind of network by using Microsoft NetShow.

online help   Information about how to use a program that is accessed from within the program itself.

organization chart   Graphic depiction of a company structure that shows people and their relationships to one another.

outdent   As a verb, to make the first line of text extend farther to the left than the rest of a paragraph. As a noun, the space resulting from outdenting text. Also called a hanging indent. Outdenting is the opposite of indenting. (See also **indent**)

Outline view   PowerPoint view that shows the presentation outline in a large pane. Outline view is used to write and organize the presentation content.

overhead transparencies   Clear plastic film on which presentation visuals are printed either in color or black and white. The transparencies are shown using an overhead projector.

P–Q

Pack and Go   A wizard that collects all the components of a presentation together into a specific location and compresses them so it can be moved to a different computer. To run a packed presentation it must first be unpacked.

Palette   (See **color scheme**)

pane In certain PowerPoint views, adjustable area that shows a component of the current presentation (such as the slide pane).

parallel construction A principle of grammar stating that words doing the same work within a sentence should be written by using a similar grammatical construction.

passive voice In a sentence, if the subject is acted on, the voice is the passive voice, as in "The presentation was written by me." (See also **active voice**)

paste To place information from the clipboard into a given location. You use the Cut or Copy command in conjunction with the Paste command to move or copy items from one place to another within a file or from one file or program to another. (See also **cut** and **copy**)

paste link To paste a link to a file or a part of a file, instead of the information itself.

paste special PowerPoint command that lets you link or embed objects in a presentation. (See also **Object Linking and Embedding**)

pattern A type of fill effect that is composed of two colors in a particular arrangement.

pica A typographic measurement. Twelve points equal one pica.

picture In PowerPoint, any graphic that can be inserted, such as a illustration, clip art, photograph, or bitmap.

pixel The smallest dot in an image or on a screen. Pixels are related to resolution. The more pixels in an image of a given size, the higher the resolution. (See also **resolution**)

placeholder Boxes on a slide that appear with a border made up of dots or slashes. Slide objects such as text, charts, tables, and graphics can be inserted in placeholders.

plot area In a chart, the area where data is plotted. It is the space within the axes and may include gridlines and tickmarks.

points Units of measure used to specify type sizes, line width, and line spacing. One point is approximately 1/72 of an inch.

pop-up menu A menu that appears when you right-click an item.

portrait A vertical page orientation. Portrait is the opposite of landscape orientation. (See also **landscape**)

PostScript A page description language developed by Adobe Systems. It is a programming language designed to instruct a device, such as a printer, how to print a file.

PowerPoint Viewer A program that allows people without PowerPoint installed on their systems to view presentations created in PowerPoint.

Presentation Assistant Animated character that provides tips and hints on how to use PowerPoint. You also can use the Presentation Assistant to access the PowerPoint online help. Also called the Office Assistant.

projector A device that is attached to a computer that projects a presentation onscreen.

promote In Outline view or the Outline pane, to decrease the indention level. Promoting is the opposite of demoting. (See also **demote**)

proportional font Type in which the space occupied by each character varies according to the width of the character (in other words, a "w" takes up more space than an "i"). (See also **monospaced font**)

publish PowerPoint term for placing a copy of an HTML version of a presentation in a specific location so it can be viewed over the World Wide Web.

R

ratio (See **aspect ratio**)

recolor To globally change a color or colors in an image, such as a clip art image.

resize handles (See **handles**)

resolution   The number of pixels in an image, generally indicated in dots per inch. The more pixels (dots) in an image of a given size, the higher the resolution. Higher resolution images are better quality but result in larger file sizes. (See also **pixel**)

RGB   Stands for Red, Green, Blue. The color model in which colors are made up of different values of the component colors red, green, and blue. Because RGB is used by computer monitors, it is used to specify colors that will be viewed over the Internet.

Rich Text Format (RTF) file   RTF is a type of text file format that can be imported into PowerPoint. Files are saved with an .RTF extension.

rotate   Act of turning an object so it is facing a different direction. (See also **flip**)

routing slip   A list of recipients who are to review a presentation often in a designated order, so that each recipient on the list reviews the presentation and passes it on to the next person.

row   A horizontal row of cells in a table or a datasheet.

RTF   (See **Rich Text Format file**)

ruler   Calibrated guide designed to aid in aligning and moving objects. Also used to set tabs or indents.

S

sans serif   Typefaces without serifs, the little strokes or "tails" on the end of characters. Arial and Helvetica are sans serif typefaces.

scale   To change the size of an image while maintaining its aspect ratio.

ScreenTips   The small yellow descriptive text that appears if you hold your mouse over a toolbar button.

script   Programming code inserted into a Web page to add special features. In PowerPoint, Web scripts may be added in VB Script or Javascript.

scroll   To move around the page so you can see different areas.

scrollbar   Narrow bars on the side of a window or pane you use to scroll different parts of an area into view.

selection handles   (See **handles**)

serif   Small ornamental strokes or "tails" on the ends of characters in certain typefaces. Also refers to typefaces containing serifs. Times New Roman and Garamond are two serif typefaces.

service bureau   A business that offers output services to high resolution image setters or film recorders. You give them files and for a fee they give you the slides or film output generated from the files.

shadow   An effect you can add to an object to make it appear as if the object were casting a shadow.

shortcut key   (See **keyboard shortcut**)

skew   To distort an object so it is slanted.

slide   Generically within PowerPoint, a slide is a single rectangular image that is shown during a presentation. In PowerPoint, a slide is the equivalent of a page in a document. A slide can also refer to the output from a film recorder.

Slide Master   PowerPoint view where you set characteristics that will be common to all slides in a presentation, such as colors, repeating graphics, footers, and text formatting.

slide navigator   Feature used during a show that lets you go to a given slide by choosing its title from a list.

Slide Show view   PowerPoint view that lets you see how the presentation will appear when you present it.

Slide Sorter view   PowerPoint view that shows you all the slides in a presentation in a miniature format. This view is generally used for reorganizing slides and adding transition effects.

Slide view   PowerPoint view that shows you the slide in a large pane. It is most useful for working on the design elements of a presentation.

smart quote   Typographic or "curly" quotation mark (as opposed to straight quote).

snap   Act of dragging an object so it aligns with the underlying grid, a guide, or other object.

speaker notes   (See **notes pages**)

split cells   To turn one cell into two cells in a table. Splitting cells is the opposite of merging cells. (See also **merge cells**)

spreadsheet   (See **worksheet**)

Start menu   Menu on the Windows 95/98 desktop that is accessed by clicking the Start button. The Start menu is used to access programs, documents, and system settings.

status bar   Informational area at the bottom of the PowerPoint window that shows you the current slide number and the Presentation Design that has been applied.

subscript   Character or characters printed slightly below the surrounding text. Often used in mathematical or chemical formulas.

summary slide   Slide created by compiling titles of other selected slides in a presentation.

superscript   Character or characters printed slightly above the surrounding text in smaller type. Often used in mathematical or technical notation or to indicate footnotes or endnotes.

symbol   Special characters often accessed from special symbol typefaces that can be inserted into a presentation.

T

tab   As a verb, to move text to the left of a specified amount to align columns or lines of text. As a noun, the character used to add a certain amount of space. Setting tabs is the act of indicating the amount of space a tab character occupies.

table   Numerical data that is set up in rows and columns.

Tagged Image File Format (TIFF) file   A type of bitmap graphic file format that can be read on both Macintoshes and PCs. TIFF files are saved with a .TIF extension.

Taskbar   The horizontal bar at the bottom of the Windows 95/98 desktop that includes the Start button and buttons indicating which programs or documents are currently open. By clicking the program buttons, you can switch from one to another.

template   A previously designed set of slide masters and/or slides that includes design elements and placeholders. PowerPoint templates are saved with a .POT extension.

text box   A graphic that contains text. PowerPoint treats text boxes as graphic objects, so the text in a text box is not included in the outline or spelling checks.

texture   A type of fill effect that looks like a textured object such as marble, paper, or stone.

three dimensional (3D)   An effect you can add to objects to make them appear as if they are being depicted in three dimensions (height, width, and depth).

thumbnail   A miniature view that shows a rough layout of a design. In PowerPoint, Slide Sorter view shows slide thumbnails.

TIFF   (See **Tagged Image File Format file**)

timings   The times you set to indicate the length of time a slide should remain onscreen during a show. You can set timings manually or have PowerPoint record them during a rehearsal.

title   Placeholder used to hold the heading text that appears at the top of a slide.

title bar   The long colored bar that extends across the width of the window. It includes the program name and name of the file on which you are working.

Title Master   PowerPoint view where you set characteristics that will be appear on all slides using the Title Slide Layout, such as colors, repeating graphics, footers, and text formatting.

toolbar Bars on the screen filled with buttons you can press to run PowerPoint commands. Toolbars can be movable (floating) or fixed (docked).

toolbar button (See **button**)

ToolTips (See **ScreenTips**)

transition A special effect you can add to change how slides move from one to another. Dissolves and wipes are two of many transitions you can add.

transparencies (See **overhead transparencies**)

typeface One design of type, such as Times New Roman. A type family includes all the variations of a particular typeface, such as Times New Roman, Times New Roman Bold, and Times New Roman Italic.

U–V

ungroup To break apart a group of objects into its component parts so the individual objects can be edited separately. Ungrouping is the opposite of grouping. (See also **group**)

URL Stands for Uniform Resource Locator. On the World Wide Web, a URL is the address of a Web page or other destination on the Internet.

VBA (See **Visual Basic for Applications**)

VB Script A programming language similar to Visual Basic and VBA that is used to write scripts that are inserted into Web pages that are to be viewed over the World Wide Web or an intranet.

vector line art Graphic generated by a mathematical expression and stored as lines and curves instead of as a series of dots as in a bitmap. Windows metafiles (.WMF) and Encapsulated PostScript (.EPS) are two vector line art formats. (See also **bitmap**)

video (See **movie**)

views Ways of looking at presentation components. Views include: Normal, Outline, Slide, Slide Sorter, Slide Show, Handout, Notes Page, and the Master views.

Visual Basic Editor Development environment you use to create programs and macros in Visual Basic for Applications.

Visual Basic for Applications (VBA) The programming language used in Office applications to create macros.

W–Z

Web page A page that is written in HTML and designed to be viewed over the World Wide Web.

Web script (See **script**)

white space The empty space in a layout. Leaving sufficient white space generally makes a layout easier to read.

Windows clipboard (See **clipboard**)

Windows Metafile A vector line art graphic format used in Microsoft Windows. The files have a .WMF extension.

wizard An automated program composed of dialog boxes that ask questions and receive input to take you step by step through a task, such as creating a new presentation.

WMF (See **Windows Metafile**)

Word Microsoft's word processing program, which is used to create text-intensive documents.

WordArt A program that runs within PowerPoint that you use to create special text effects.

worksheet Term used in Microsoft Excel to indicate a set of rows and columns on a page that is used to store and work with data. An Excel workbook is made up of multiple worksheets.

World Wide Web (WWW) One part of the Internet that is made up of Web pages written in HTML and that is viewed using a browser. (See also **browser**, **HTML**, **Internet**, and **URL**)

wrap To force text to conform to a particular shape. In PowerPoint, you can force text to wrap within a placeholder.

x-axis   In a chart, the horizontal line that is used as a reference for plotting values in a coordinate system. (See also **axis**)

x height   The height of a lowercase letter x in a given font.

y-axis   In a chart, the vertical line that is used as a reference for plotting values in a coordinate system. (See also **axis**)

z-axis   In a chart, the third axis that is often used to show depth when plotting values in a coordinate system. (See also **axis**)

Zoom   To change the magnification level of a view or pane.

Index

Site Maps, Corporate
   Web site sample, 231
   tables, 130
Drawing toolbar, 40, 72
duplicating
   AutoShapes, 69
   slides, 30
**Duplicating Slide
   command (Insert
   menu), 30**

E

**Edit Hyperlink dialog
   box, 194**
Edit menu
   Copy command, 30, 39
   Copy Setup command,
      129
   Cut command, 39, 148
   Deleting Slide
      command, 29
   Find command, 50
   Links command, 151
   Paste command, 30,
      39, 148
   Paste Special
      command, 149
   Replace command, 51
   Select command, 126
   Sound Object
      command, 143
   Undo command, 17,
      29
edit points, 71
**Edit Points command
   (Draw menu), 71**

**Edit WordArt Text dialog
   box, 72, 74**
editing
   AutoShapes, 71
   bullets, 221
   connectors, 71
   controls, 196
   data, 118
   information, 228
   links, 151
   macros, 216
   Microsoft
      Excel, 155-157
      Word tables, 159
   objects, 151
   Slide Master, 211, 221
   tables, 133
   text, 38, 223
      in Slide view, 38
      WordArt, 74
   Title Master, onscreen
      sample, 222
effects
   animation, 138
   copying, 83
   fills, 81
   multimedia, 135
   transition, 136
email, 252
   sending
      presentations, 164
      *slides as attachments,
         164*
embedding, 252
   files, 150
   pasted data, 149
embossed text, 44, 252

**Encapsulated PostScript
   file (.EPS), 252**
engrave, 252
entering
   organization charts
      information, 124
   tables, information, 131
   text, 38
      in Outline view, 38
      *in presentation
         templates, 25*
      in Slide view, 38
**EPS (Encapsulated
   PostScript), 252**
erasing annotations, 174
Excel, 252
**Exit command (File
   menu), 7**
**exiting PowerPoint 2000,
   7**
Expand All button, 14
Export button, 183
**exporting Meeting
   Minder information,
   183**

F

File menu
   Close and Return to
      Microsoft PowerPoint
      commands, 216
   Close command, 9, 152
   Exit command, 7
   Open command, 9, 153
   Pack and Go command,
      184